GOTŌ SHINPEI
STATESMAN OF VISION

JAPAN LIBRARY

GOTŌ SHINPEI
STATESMAN OF VISION
Research, Public Health, and Development

KITAOKA Shinichi
Translated by Iain Arthy

Japan Publishing Industry Foundation for Culture

Note to the reader:
This book follows the Hepburn system of romanization, with long vowels indicated by macrons. The tradition of placing the family name first has been followed for Japanese, Chinese, and Korean names.

Gotō Shinpei, Statesman of Vision: Research, Public Health, and Development
Kitaoka Shinichi. Translated by Iain Arthy.

Published by
Japan Publishing Industry Foundation for Culture (JPIC)
2-2-30 Kanda-Jinbocho, Chiyoda-ku, Tokyo 101-0051, Japan

First English edition: March 2021

This book is a translation of *Gotō Shinpei: Gaikō to vijon*.
Originally published in the Japanese language by CHUOKORON-SHINSHA, INC. in 1988.
English publishing rights arranged with the author.

Book design: Miki Kazuhiko, Ampersand Works
Jacket and cover photographs: MeijiShowa/Aflo, KINGENDAI.. PL/Aflo, Kyodo News
Photographs in the text: Gotō Shinpei Memorial Hall

Printed in Japan
ISBN 978-4-86658-183-5
https://japanlibrary.jpic.or.jp/

CONTENTS

PREFACE TO THE ENGLISH TRANSLATION   7

PREFACE: Why Remember Gotō as a Foreign Policy Leader?   13

CHAPTER 1 ————————————————————————————

MEDICAL STUDENT AND PUBLIC HEALTH ADMINISTRATOR   21

  1. Boyhood and Youth   21

  2. At the Public Health Bureau   31

CHAPTER 2 ————————————————————————————

CIVILIAN GOVERNOR OF TAIWAN   45

  1. Consolidating Japanese Rule   45

  2. "Civilizing" Taiwan   55

  3. Relations with China and the United States   66

CHAPTER 3 ————————————————————————————

PRESIDENT OF THE SOUTH MANCHURIA RAILWAY   75

  1. Assumption of the Presidency   75

  2. The SMR's Initial Policies: "Dairen-centrism" and Military Preparations in
     Civilian Garb   87

  3. International Relations and the South Manchuria Railway   97

CHAPTER 4 ————————————————————————————

BUREAUCRATIC GOVERNMENT AND PARTY POLITICS   111

  1. The Second Katsura Cabinet   111

  2. Out of Office   122

  3. The Taishō Political Crisis and Katsura's New Political Party   128

CHAPTER 5 ————————————————————————
WORLD WAR I AND JAPAN 137
 1. Critic of the Ōkuma Cabinet   137
 2. The Terauchi Cabinet Assumes Power   143
 3. China and Russia   150

CHAPTER 6 ————————————————————————
LOST OPPORTUNITIES 165
 1. The Postwar World and Japan   165
 2. Negotiations with Joffe and the Rebuilding of Tokyo   174
 3. Twilight Years   184

EPILOGUE   197

Timeline of Gotō Shinpei's Life   202
References   210
About the Author   215

PREFACE
TO THE ENGLISH TRANSLATION

This is an English translation of a biography of Gotō Shinpei, which I first published in 1988.

To begin with, as Gotō Shinpei is a name presumably unfamiliar to many in the English-speaking world, I would like to tell you a little about him.

Gotō was born in 1857 to a *bushi* (samurai) family in northeastern Japan. His father was a retainer of a small feudal domain, that was under the suzerain authority of the Sendai, or Date, domain, the dominant feudal power in northeastern Japan.

Gotō, however, lost his *bushi* status in 1869—the second year of the Meiji era—and was degraded to the farmer class as a consequence of the pro-Tokugawa Sendai domain's defeat in the Boshin War, a civil war between domains loyal to the former Tokugawa shogunate and the newly established government under the emperor in Kyoto at the time. Now that Gotō was on the losing side in the Meiji Restoration, and would have to live as a member of an impoverished hinterland farming family, he realized that he had no choice but to acquire certain skills if he wanted to go out into the world on his own. As a self-supporting student, he studied assiduously to become a physician. At the age of twenty-four, as a licensed doctor, he was quickly promoted to head of both the Aichi Prefectural Hospital and Aichi Prefectural Medical School in Nagoya in central Japan. Gotō resigned from these posts only a few years later to work at the Ministry of Home Affairs' Public Health Bureau to pursue his strong interest in providing preventive medicine to as many people as possible. His distinctive approach to public health administration was to first conduct exhaustive on-site research on local lifestyle, customs, and habits, and then implement up-to-date, relevant policies. In 1890, Gotō left Japan to study in Germany and earned a medical doctorate there two years later, aged thirty-five. Upon his return, the home ministry appointed him head of the Public Health Bureau. However, he had to relinquish this post in 1893 as he was implicated in a political scandal.

A great opportunity came around for him in 1895. At the time, Japan, though elated with its victory in the Sino-Japanese War, was faced with the unprecedented task of quarantining 230,000 troops returning from the war front on the Chinese continent and the Korean Peninsula. In the war with the Qing dynasty of China, the number of Japanese soldiers killed in action stood at around 1,000, but the number of war-front deaths from disease was ten times higher. Therefore, an extensive quarantine operation for returnee soldiers was critical. Gotō, assigned by the army, poured all his energy into the pressing mission and led the quarantine operation to a success, something quite rare at the time anywhere in the world. He was consequently reappointed head of the Public Health Bureau.

Another result of the Sino-Japanese War was that Taiwan was ceded to Japan by the Qing dynasty. Gotō, in his capacity as the Japanese government's Public Health Bureau chief, examined the sanitary-hygiene situation in the new colony and presented his views to the government. In 1898, Kodama Gentarō, a powerful figure in the army, with whom Gotō became acquainted when he undertook the above-mentioned quarantine operation, was appointed governor-general of Taiwan. Kodama asked Gotō to become director of civil affairs, a post soon afterward renamed civilian governor. At the time, the supreme authority in Taiwan under Japanese rule was the governor-general, a post assumed by members of the top military brass. In his role, Gotō was responsible for the whole of civil administration in Taiwan. Moreover, Kodama had so much confidence in Gotō that the chief civil administrator was able to exercise his administrative expertise at his own discretion. When Kodama had to spend much of his time in Tokyo, as he concurrently held ministerial portfolios within the Japanese government, he let Gotō effectively govern Taiwan on his behalf.

In Taiwan, too, Gotō implemented his region-tailored policies based on meticulous surveys of local customs. Applying such an approach, he succeeded in eradicating opium addiction among residents of Taiwan, while improving the island's water supply and sewerage systems and transforming Taipei into a modern city with a set of urban development projects. He received much applause from the Taiwanese populace as he built schools and hospitals for their use. He also led infrastructure construction, such as roads and railways. He was credited further with improving the land ownership system and pressing ahead with agricultural reforms, contributing to the remarkable development of Taiwan's agricultural sector. Many people in Taiwan feel indebted to Gotō for laying the foundation of their prosperity today. (Two translated versions of this book were published in Taiwan a long time ago).

The year 1906 brought another turning point for Gotō. A year earlier, in 1905, the Russo-Japanese War ended in a victory for Japan, securing the transfer of Russian interests in South Manchuria with their linchpin being the rail link from the area of Lüshun (also known as Port Arthur) and Dairen to Changchun. Recognized for his achievements in Taiwan, Gotō was appointed the inaugural president of the South Manchuria Railway Company established by the Japanese government. It was initially thought he would face an uphill challenge in Manchuria, but he led the company to become a successful railway operator by carrying out a large-scale rail track renovation project to enhance rail connectivity with the port of Dairen. Gotō enjoyed public support as he actively advanced massive urban development plans, including school and hospital construction, in Dairen, Changchun and other areas. In Manchuria, too, Gotō thoroughly researched—and respected—local customs and adopted large-scale innovative initiatives.

In 1908, Gotō left Manchuria for Tokyo to assume the post of communications minister in the Japanese government and that of president of the Railway Agency within the cabinet as well. While in those posts, he made outstanding achievements. In contrast, his involvement in political party activities ended up with no significant success. He was appointed home minister in 1916 and foreign minister in 1918. While serving as foreign minister, he endorsed Japan's dispatch of troops to Russia to participate in the Siberian Expedition by World War I Allies, or Entente Powers, which included Japan. The expedition eventually ended in failure. Despite such a setback, Gotō, who did not harbor anti-Soviet sentiments, took the initiative in the first half of 1923, in his capacity as a person cooperating with the government from outside the cabinet, in helping Japan and the Soviet Union embark on negotiations for the restoration of diplomatic relations. In late 1927, he left for Moscow to have a meeting with Joseph Stalin—which took place in January 1928—with a view to improving Japan-USSR relations.

Among all of Gotō's achievements, the one that deserves particular attention was a large-scale urban remodeling initiative for the then city of Tokyo, which he unveiled in 1920 after being appointed its mayor. He invited Professor Charles A. Beard from Columbia University, a renowned historian, political scientist, and an authority in urban planning, to come to Tokyo and make recommendations to reshape the city. To inspect Gotō's past achievements, Beard toured Taiwan and Manchuria as well and highly praised the mayor as a "statesman of research" for implementing scientific, research-based initiatives. In the end, however, Gotō's plans for Tokyo were not supported by politicians and bureaucrats because of their scale and price.

In April 1923, Gotō resigned as mayor. On September 1 of that year, the Great Kantō Earthquake devastated Yokohama and Tokyo, killing more than 91,000 people. One day later, Gotō was appointed home minister for the second time. He invited Beard to come to Japan again in the hope of fundamentally reconstructing Tokyo. His ambitious initiative included massive plans to construct road networks, expand road width, upgrade plazas located in front of railway stations, and lay green belts and parks. Again, however, Gotō's initiative fell through as it faced opposition from landowners as well as politicians and bureaucrats colluding with them. Emperor Shōwa (1901–1989), who was the prince regent at the time, noted later in life that Tokyo would have suffered far less from US air raids during the Pacific War if Gotō's plans had materialized in full.

Although Gotō had no opportunity to become prime minister, he was a truly extraordinary statesman, leaving behind a series of outstanding legacies in the history of modern Japan.

Tsurumi Yūsuke (1885–1973), a Railway Agency official turned author turned politician and Gotō's son-in-law, compiled a four-volume biography titled *Gotō Shinpei* in 1937 and 1938. However, almost no scholarly publications or ordinary biographies about Gotō—except for one novel depicting his life—were produced for fifty years from that time until 1988, when I published this biography in Japanese. In that sense, my book featuring Gotō contributed to the revival of the Japanese public's interest in him. In 1995, the Great Hanshin Awaji Earthquake, also known as the Kobe Earthquake, occurred, stimulating the public's interest in sharing Gotō's disaster management expertise. In fact, several books focusing on his approaches were subsequently published. The calamity in and around Kobe was followed by the Great East Japan Earthquake in March 2011. Since then, the Japanese people have been repeatedly warned of the possibility of further destructive earthquakes in the not-too distant future. In that context, I believe we have every reason to reappraise Gotō's visions.

In addition, particularly from today's perspective, there are two reasons to focus anew on Gotō's achievements. The first is COVID-19. Given the still-raging worldwide coronavirus pandemic, Gotō's approach to public health administration provides an important perspective.

The other reason is our commitment to developing countries. Incidentally, I am currently serving as president of the Japan International Cooperation Agency (JICA), overseeing its wide-ranging efforts to assist developing countries.

I, of course, oppose colonialism anywhere. That said, I want to point out that there were good and bad aspects of colonial management, with some of the good ones able to teach us about furthering progress in developing countries.

Gotō was just four years junior to Cecil Rhodes (1853–1902). He was undoubtedly conscious of what the British mining magnate was doing in the Cape Colony, a British colony in present-day South Africa. Gotō was completely different from Rhodes, who was exclusively devoted to expanding the glory of the British Empire and adding to his personal wealth as well. Gotō made every effort to carry out more civilized colonial rule by undertaking urban development, infrastructure improvements, and school and hospital construction, among others, all of which were beneficial to the people in each colony. One day, Gotō was asked what would happen when a colony became developed. He answered: "Fruit falls off the trees when it is ripe." With this metaphor, Gotō implied that it was desirable for each colony to become independent someday.

It goes without saying that there were cases of oppression, bloodshed and exploitation while Gotō was responsible for colonial administration. He might have utilized plans to build schools and hospitals in the territories under Japanese rule as a means to appease the local population, yet there is no question that his methods differed from the way Western countries ruled their colonies, with their primary purpose to pillage and exploit them. Gotō aimed to show what a new civilization should look like by applying to Taiwan and Manchuria what he selectively learned from the West but refined on his own.

Today, Cecil Rhodes and other past colonial rulers are subject to bitter attacks. On the other hand, assisting in the advance of developing countries is still an important task. It is therefore worth giving fresh consideration to Gotō's civil-administration approaches. This is the main reason why I have now decided to publish an English translation of my 1988 book.

Kitaoka Shinichi
December 2020
(amidst the COVID-19 pandemic)

PREFACE:
Why Remember Gotō as a Foreign Policy Leader?

Gotō Shinpei died in 1929 at the age of seventy-one. Although he never formed a government as prime minister, he had a truly illustrious career. He proved himself a colonial administrator of unrivalled ability as civilian governor of Taiwan and first president of the South Manchuria Railway. His achievements in laying the foundations for the Japanese national railway system during his three terms as director-general of the Railway Board were unquestioned. The grandeur of his vision as an urban planner when he served as mayor of Tokyo, and later home minister in the aftermath of the 1923 Great Kantō Earthquake, was still fresh in memory at the time of his death. The exhaustive research and ambitious planning that characterized all his undertakings drew high praise from the eminent American scholar Charles A. Beard.

Gotō's accomplishments in these fields are still more or less acknowledged today. But almost forgotten is the high regard in which he was held by many of his contemporaries as a foreign policy leader.

Shinobu Junpei, a distinguished scholar of international law and historian of diplomacy, wrote a short tribute for the journal *Gaikō jihō* (Revue Diplomatique) entitled "Count Gotō as a Diplomatist," which saluted Gotō's diplomatic achievements over the decades and lamented his passing. Even if Shinobu's assessment is to be taken with a grain of salt, as he was a personal friend of Gotō's, the words of one of the era's foremost commentators on diplomatic affairs cannot be ignored. Gotō was even more lionized by the public. Many called him "the one and only people's diplomatist."

In what regards was Gotō admired as a "diplomatist"? To begin with, Shinobu credited him with bringing a breath of fresh air to the stifling corridors of Japanese diplomacy when he became foreign minister in 1918, breaking the precedent that had restricted the post to career diplomats and former career diplomats. Except during the first few years of the Meiji era, only two foreign ministers before Gotō—Inoue Kaoru and Ōkuma Shigenobu—had come from non-diplomatic backgrounds, and both possessed a wealth of diplomatic experience, having played important roles in early Meiji period. They had been involved in making foreign policy since before Japan even had a foreign ministry. Gotō was, therefore, in effect the first foreign minister without a diplomatic background.

Gotō, moreover, had a decidedly undiplomatic personality. Notorious for being inconsistent and impulsive in his words and actions, he seemed quite unsuited to the task of leading the foreign ministry with its penchant for order, stability, and trust. Katō Takaaki, leader of the Kenseikai (Constitutional Association) party, was scathing when he learned of Gotō's appointment. "Absolutely bizarre," he remarked. "Geniuses, hotheads, and madmen are by nature almost indistinguishable. I don't know which Baron Gotō is, but at any rate he appears to be an odd fellow . . . Most knowledgeable observers will doubtless have certain misgivings." A political rival of Gotō's and a proud former diplomat himself, Katō was hardly likely to welcome Gotō's installation as foreign minister. But even so, his comment reveals genuine surprise and perplexity at the unexpected appointment.

After Gotō, only four other non-diplomats would serve as foreign minister in prewar Japan: Tanaka Giichi (when prime minister), Ugaki Kazushige, Nomura Kichisaburō, and Toyoda Teijirō. Tanaka and Ugaki assumed the post in order to take China policy in a new direction, having had long experience dealing with Chinese issues during their army days. Nomura and Toyoda were both appointed from the navy in a bid to break the impasse in relations with the United States. By contrast, neither domestic politics nor international relations made Gotō the obvious choice for the job. What then enabled him to become in effect the first foreign minister without a diplomatic background?

In his article, Shinobu praises Gotō for having been an effective foreign minister. He mockingly calls Tanaka, whose foreign policy was already unravelling at the time, the "Generalissimo of Foreign Affairs" and bitingly describes his conduct of foreign policy as "like a divisional commander piloting a battleship," contrasting it with Gotō's, who was "the right man in the right place" at the diplomatic helm.

Yet Gotō left the post of foreign minister after just five months, with no significant achievements to his name save the disastrous Siberian Expedition. Between June 1917 and September 1922, he was a member of the Provisional Research Council on Foreign Relations (with the status of a minister of state), but he kept a low profile, except during his stint as foreign minister. Even taking into account his actions on the Provisional Research Council on Foreign Relations, Gotō's actual tenure as foreign minister can only be described as a failure. Why was such a figure described as "the right man in the right place" and considered "the one and only people's diplomatist"?

This question arises because the word diplomacy has several meanings; hence "diplomatist" (*gaikōka*), what we might now call a "foreign policy leader," is an ambiguous term. Let us set aside Gotō for a moment to consider this issue further.

Diplomacy may first be defined, with the emphasis on negotiating with other countries, as the management of international relations by negotiation. This is what British diplomat and writer Harold Nicolson means when he states that diplomacy is the execution of the foreign policy decided by the government, and the art of diplomacy is the art of negotiating agreements between sovereign states.[1] By this definition, diplomacy is carried out by diplomats and other representatives of government.

Second, the term diplomacy is sometimes used synonymously with foreign policy, with one qualification: whereas war is part of foreign policy, it is not part of diplomacy. Diplomacy therefore means foreign policy minus war. Diplomacy in this case is defined as the formulation of a basic foreign policy strategy—which countries to befriend, which to be wary of, what course to steer between them—and its implementation by a variety of means excluding war. This is probably what diplomacy conjures up in most people's minds.

In the Meiji era, diplomacy (together with war) was regarded as an effective means of guaranteeing a nation's survival and prosperity amid the power politics of international relations. An outstanding diplomatist had a good

---

[1] Harold Nicolson, *Diplomacy* (London: Oxford University Press, 1950), 7ff.

understanding of what the world's great powers were up to and safeguarded the security and growth of his nation by shrewdly forming alliances of convenience as the situation demanded. This perception matched what the Japanese of the day knew about diplomacy from history, whether the classic age of diplomacy in Europe, the Spring and Autumn and Warring States periods in ancient China, or that of the Warring States period of sixteenth-century Japan. A diplomatist was thought of as a Bismarck as opposed to a Moltke, or to cite an example from ancient China (with which many at that time would have been familiar), a Lin Xiangru as opposed to a Lian Po.

There is a third, broader meaning in which the term "diplomacy" may be used. It can refer to all dealings with other nations. Some diplomatic issues arise from contact between countries or peoples that differ in their cultural practices, political institutions, ethnicity, and race (what may collectively be termed "culture"), and those issues do not sit well with the concept of diplomacy as primarily a matter of power politics. The most serious diplomatic issues facing contemporary Japan, for example, concern external economic relations, particularly trade disputes. Many of these are inexplicable in terms of power politics, since they stem from cultural differences at various levels: work ethic, business practices, corporate-government relations, and so forth. Such issues were in the past seldom viewed as diplomatic in nature because traditional diplomacy was conducted mainly within a single culture. Europe in the classic age of diplomacy and China in the Spring and Autumn and Warring States periods, not to mention Japan in the sixteenth century, were relatively unaffected by contact with other cultures.

Viewing the question in this light reveals the complexity and difficulty of the problems confronting Japan in its foreign relations after it joined the community of nations in the second half of the nineteenth century. It was not merely a matter of power politics. To begin with, the adoption of Western culture was in and of itself a foreign-relations issue that Japan needed to handle carefully in its determination to reform. Further, Japan's eventual acquisition of colonies led to another set of problems with intercultural relations.

No matter how Japan strove to catch up to the Western powers, it was never treated as a complete equal. The obstacles were too great. And by the time it barely gained admission to the ranks of the world's great powers by becoming a colonial empire, the techniques of imperial diplomacy that it had mastered proved largely ineffectual, for it found itself hemmed in by China, Russia, and the United States, each of which espoused its own version of anti-imperialism.

Assessing the career of a Japanese foreign policy leader, therefore, is not simply a matter of tallying up his tangible achievements, such as treaties concluded or interests secured. It requires delving further and considering what place he envisioned for Japan in a world dominated by the West. One must also consider how he sought to overcome problems arising from cultural differences, even if one focuses primarily on the diplomacy of power. These questions are, above all, what fascinate me about Gotō Shinpei as a foreign policy leader.

First, Gotō offered unique views on Japan's basic diplomatic strategy. He advocated neither the pro-Anglo-American stance that dominated Japanese foreign policy, nor pan-Asianism, nor going it alone, but rather collaboration with China and Russia (and later the USSR). He also did much to overcome cultural barriers. Having studied Western medicine, he established a Western-style system of public health in Japan as a home ministry bureaucrat, and he implemented government programs among foreign peoples as a colonial administrator. Thus, when the term diplomacy is understood in its broadest sense, it is hardly surprising that Gotō should have been considered a foreign policy leader by his contemporaries.

This book will attempt to elucidate the intellectual underpinnings of Gotō Shinpei's foreign policy and determine his place in the evolution of Japanese diplomatic thinking. By so doing it should serve as a sketch of Japanese foreign policy and domestic politics from the 1880s to the later 1920s, while identifying several hallmarks of Japanese diplomacy.

Let me briefly comment on the methodology followed in this book. I believe that when analyzing the policies and ideas of a politician, it is wrong to concentrate exclusively on his writings and policy memoranda. When out of power and not in a position to carry out his ideas, a politician, and indeed almost anyone, will say virtually anything. What he advocates will invariably take account of his political self-interest. His true policies, therefore, are only those that he seeks to carry out when he is in a position of influence, even at a heavy cost, even if he has to abandon other available options. Those policies alone genuinely reflect his ideas. If one does turn to his writings and memoranda as a source of his ideas, they must be corroborated by his political deeds. Such caution is especially imperative in the case of Gotō. His memoranda are full of leaps of logic and contradictions, and it would be the easiest thing in the world to portray him as either a liberal or a totalitarian, an advocate of Westernization or an ardent nationalist, simply by stringing together passages from his writings. I have sometimes described the political milieu in which he operated in greater detail than may seem warranted, because it was essential to identifying the ideas behind his actions.

This book may be somewhat too polemical for an ordinary biography. But focusing specifically on Gotō's qualities as a foreign policy leader is one means of depicting a figure with such a multifaceted career. I have also touched on the main biographical details of Gotō's life, since this book is intended for the general reader. You are welcome to read it as a conventional account of a fascinating man. I would be delighted if, as you follow Gotō's career, you develop a greater interest in the dynamics of Japanese politics and diplomacy in his day and their relevance to contemporary Japan. I am convinced that, as long as Japan must deal with the United States, China, and Russia as neighbors, each of which is unique in its own way, and remains one of the few developed non-Western nations, Gotō Shinpei will deserve a place in history as a foreign policy leader.

Notable Places in Gotō Shinpei's Life

Mizusawa, Japan, where Gotō was born; Taipei, Taiwan, where he administered the island of Taiwan as civilian governor, and Dairen, Manchuria, where he served as president of the South Manchuria Railway.

CHAPTER 1

MEDICAL STUDENT AND PUBLIC HEALTH ADMINISTRATOR

1. Boyhood and Youth

Origins and Early Years

Gotō Shinpei was born on July 24, 1857, in the village of Shiogama, Isawa county, in the old province of Rikuchū[1]. He was the son of Gotō Sanetaka, a retainer of the Rusu clan, a distinguished local family. The history of the Rusu clan goes back to fourteenth century, but they had lost their independence by the end of the Sengoku period in the sixteenth century and became vassals of the powerful warlord Date Masamune (nephew of Rusu Masakage, then head of the clan). He granted them a fief with an annual yield of 20,000 *koku*[2] of rice. The Rusu moved to Mizusawa Castle in 1629 and ruled the surrounding area for more than two centuries. Owing to their long history, they were one of the highest-ranking families in the Date domain of Sendai. Although not an independent clan of daimyo (feudal lords), they organized their household like one and displayed commensurate pride.

The Rusu clan had lost most of their lands and income—they originally ruled over a territory with an annual yield of some 180,000 *koku* (somewhat over 900,000 bushels)—but they still had a large retainer corps to support on their now modest means. Accordingly, the Rusu territory had an

---

1 Rikuchū, in northern Honshu, was later renamed Mizusawa, which was incorporated in 2006 into present-day Ōshu City, Iwate Prefecture.

2 The size of a fief during the Edo period was measured by its nominal income in *koku* of rice. One *koku* was equivalent to approximately five bushels, considered enough to support one person a year.

abundance of people at its disposal, but it was exceedingly poor. Past glory and present decline, a location far from the center of power, and poverty are often cited as favorable conditions for nurturing high achievers. Native sons of the tiny Rusu fief, with its minuscule income of 20,000 *koku*, included scholar of Western learning Takano Chōei and geographer Mitsukuri Shōgo in the mid-nineteenth century, and admiral, governor-general of Korea, and prime minister Saitō Makoto in the late nineteenth to the first half of the twentieth century, not to mention Gotō Shinpei himself.

The Gotō family was certainly not affluent. It was paid an annual cash stipend of somewhat more than three copper *kan*, equivalent to 10–15 *koku* (approximately 50–75 bushels) of rice, about a quarter of the way down the list of stipends paid by the Rusu clan to its vassals—which incidentally gives an idea of how poor the entire clan was. Shinpei's father served as *koshōgashira* (chief page) and his grandfather served as *metsuke* (inspector). The family therefore appears to have ranked somewhere between fifth and twentieth in the Rusu clan hierarchy. They occupied a low position in the upper echelon or a high position in the middle echelon of the retainer corps. Shinpei's father, Sanetaka, a man of strong moral fiber and considerable learning, relinquished samurai status to become a common farmer after the Meiji Restoration. He died in 1883 at the age of sixty-three (by the traditional Japanese reckoning, whereby you are one year old at birth and become a year older on each New Year's Day). His mother, Rie, the eldest daughter of the Sakano family, hereditary physicians to the Rusu clan, was a lively and practical woman who lived with Shinpei for most of his career. She died in 1923 at the age of ninety-nine (again by the Japanese reckoning). Shinpei also had an older sister and a younger brother.

One other relative must not be omitted: Takano Chōei (1804–1850), a scion of the main branch of Gotō's family and his grandfather's second cousin. Takano, a famous medical doctor and scholar of Dutch learning, was imprisoned and eventually driven to suicide for his criticism of the seclusionist policy of the central government (*bakufu*). However, after the Meiji Restoration and long after his death, he came to be regarded as one of Japan's most influential visionaries of the time. Takano died seven years before Gotō was born, but was still vividly remembered in Mizusawa. Gotō's paternal grandfather, who doted on him as an infant, had resigned from the post of inspector owing to the Takano Affair.

Gotō reportedly first learned of his relationship to Takano when as a boy he was mockingly called "son of a rebel!" In the last years of the Edo period, Takano's name was certainly inauspicious. Gotō's grandfather repeatedly warned him not to follow in his footsteps. But soon that name became a source of pride as Takano came to be seen as a harbinger of the Meiji Restoration. Gotō later wrote that his grandfather's counsel made good sense in "the feudal age," but today he believed that he "must diligently strive to be like Chōei."[3] For a provincial lad in straitened circumstances from a domain on the losing side in the civil war following the Meiji Restoration, being related to a harbinger of the Meiji Restoration was a bright ray of hope. Gotō's kinship with Takano further kindled his interest in national affairs and his fascination with Western civilization.

Gotō appears to have been a remarkably clever boy but also an incorrigible mischief-maker. In March 1867, at age nine, he was appointed *okugoshō* (personal page) to the Rusu clan, but he was evidently quite a prankster. As he later recalled, "I could not stop myself from being unruly, despite being in the presence of my liege lord. I was frequently reprimanded by my lord."

It was not long, however, before his fortunes took a dramatic turn for the worse. In 1868, the Sendai domain joined the alliance of domains in northeastern Japan opposed to the Meiji Restoration and was defeated in the Boshin War. Much of the domain's territory was then confiscated, so that its official annual income fell from more than 620,000 *koku* (approximately 3,100,000 bushels) to 280,000 *koku* (approximately 1,400,000 bushels). Meanwhile the Rusu clan's retainers were given a choice. Either they could emigrate to Hokkaido, the northern island of Japan, and retain their samurai status, or they could remain on their native soil and become farmers. The Gotō family chose to stay and farm the land. That was in the second lunar month (March/April) of 1869, when Gotō was eleven. He later recalled that

---

3   "Letter to Nagayo Sensai, March 7, 1882" in *Ketteiban: Seiden Gotō Shinpei* [Official Biography of Gotō Shinpei: The Definitive Edition], vol. 1, ed. Tsurumi Yūsuke (Tokyo: Fujiwara Shoten, 2004), 397.

this was the most distressing experience of his boyhood, but it may actually have been a stroke of good fortune for him.

In September 1869, Isawa was organized into a prefecture under the direct control of the new Meiji government. As a result, Gotō's talents came to the notice of the government officials who arrived to administer it. Most of them were from the southwest of Japan, and the Japanese spoken in the northeast particularly among the farmers and other commoners was so different that it was almost incomprehensible to them. They therefore recruited the most capable boys from local families to run errands for them so that they could better govern the area. Gotō was one of those selected.

His abilities particularly caught the eye of the *daisanji* (senior counselor) Yasuba Yasukazu, a samurai from the Kumamoto domain in Kyushu, the southern island of Japan, who was a disciple of the well-known scholar and reformer Yokoi Shōnan. Later he was appointed to the House of Peers by the emperor, created a baron, and served as head of the Hokkaido government. He had a close relationship with Gotō, as we shall later see. In 1883, Gotō married his second daughter Kazuko.

Yasuba took Gotō into his home as a student boarder. Toward the end of 1869, he entrusted him to the care of a subordinate, Okada Shunzaburō, deciding the boy would benefit from quieter surroundings with fewer visitors. Okada, who later took the name Agawa Mitsuhiro, was a native of Ise who had studied under the Confucian scholar Yasui Sokken. He too was to have a considerable influence on Gotō, although in a different way from Yasuba.

In October 1870, Yasuba was transferred to Kumamoto to take up a senior post in the Kumamoto prefectural government. This further stimulated Gotō's desire to learn and improve himself, and he began to dream of going to Tokyo. It so happened that Yasuba's successor as senior counselor of Isawa, Kaetsu Ujifusa, was to travel to the capital on official business in the second lunar month (March/April) of 1871. Gotō persuaded his father and Agawa to let him accompany Kaetsu. In Tokyo, Kaetsu arranged for him to stay with Sōmura Shōzō, then a junior official at the Dajōkan (Council of State), as a student boarder and houseboy.

Gotō's sojourn in Tokyo proved completely unproductive owing to Sōmura's busy schedule and unsympathetic attitude, as well as Gotō's own indigence. Stories survive about his conduct during his stay. Once he was so infuriated at being told to boil the rice that he deliberately half cooked it in protest. On another occasion, indignant at being called the "son of an enemy of the imperial court" (because he was from a domain that had fought against the imperial government after the Restoration), he laid into Sōmura, asking how he dared talk of enemies of the court now that imperial power had been restored and respected by everyone. Such episodes, however, merely testify to how poor Gotō was at expressing himself. Until his dying day he had a fairly heavy northeastern accent, and he was not good at logically presenting his thoughts when he spoke. Moreover, when he first came to Tokyo he was only thirteen, and he had studied little except the Chinese classics. No wonder he was incapable of calmly conveying his thoughts and wishes. Ridiculed as a country boy and the son of an enemy of the court, and unable to defend himself coherently, Gotō returned home despondent in early 1872, after less than a year in Tokyo, with nothing to show for it. Before his trip to the capital he had been known as one of the three prodigies of Mizusawa. He was, to his considerable pride, the first of the three to go to Tokyo, but when he arrived home, the other two were gone. He was the only one left behind.

Studying Medicine

In May 1873, Gotō had a second opportunity to leave home to study. Agawa, who in November of the previous year had been transferred to Sukagawa in Fukushima Prefecture, encouraged him to become a doctor and promised some help with tuition if he would enroll in the medical school there. Gotō was reluctant to pursue a medical career because, as he wrote in his autobiography, he considered medicine to be "the petty art of those in long sleeves" (as opposed to samurai, who tied their sleeves back). Physicians, he thought, were "toadies of the court and nobility."[4] It was true that in the Edo period medicine had been regarded as an unmanly profession. Agawa, concerned about his overexcitable temperament, urged Gotō to pursue it nonetheless out of a desire to set him on the path to a stable career. It was

---

4   "Letter to Nagayo Sensai of March 7, 1882"

also his father's wish. At any rate, since no other educational opportunities were available, Gotō accepted Agawa's offer and made his way to Sukagawa.

Sukagawa Medical School was a rather rudimentary institution at the time. The curriculum relied mainly on reading Japanese translations of European medical textbooks, which was considered a poor second best to reading them in the original. Gotō, convinced that he needed to study medicine in the original languages, decided to develop his language skills by enrolling in a special program at Fukushima School of Western Studies instead. That was in late May 1873. If possible, he hoped eventually to enter the Tōkō University (later Tokyo Imperial University Medical College).

Gotō, however, did not fit in at Fukushima School of Western Studies. The teaching staff appears to have been of poor quality, as was often the case in those days due to a lack of capable people. In addition, Gotō may have failed to apply himself because he had been reluctant to begin studying medicine in the first place. He was evidently not good at forms of study like language learning that required perseverance. He threw himself into mathematics and land surveying and devoted his free time to reading the Japanese translation of Samuel Smiles' *Self-Help*, abandoning the all-important study of English. He ended up withdrawing from the school after just half a year and returning home in January 1874.

Agawa and his father scolded him severely and prevailed on him to transfer to Sukagawa Medical School, where, in February 1874, he started studying medicine in Japanese. Gotō thus entered medical school by sheer coincidence and against his will. Once there, though, he was fascinated by his first encounter with modern sciences, such as physics, chemistry, anatomy, and physiology, and began studying furiously. He received almost no money from home, only a pittance from Agawa, but being dirt-poor did not bother him in the least.

Gotō, it turned out, was quick to distinguish himself once his interest was roused. In July 1875, he became deputy head of the dormitory and student prefect, and in March 1876 he was appointed head of the dormitory. Many of the students were already doctors with their own practices attending the school to acquire new knowledge. That Gotō succeeded in keeping them in line testifies to his rare academic prowess and ability to command respect.

Thus, while determined "to be like Chōei" and fascinated by Western civilization, Gotō stumbled repeatedly on his circuitous route to learning about it. Moreover, since he ended up studying medicine in Japanese rather than in the original European languages, he ultimately failed to acquire a thorough grounding in Western civilization. Some of his later behavior appears to relate to the conflicted nature of this first encounter with Western civilization.

For example, he often displayed an antipathy for the young elite who had pursued their studies in the formal education system. He famously called Tokyo Imperial University "a training school for cripples" and scornfully dismissed the law faculty curriculum in particular as "a shallow survey of jurisprudence." When his nephew Shiina Etsusaburō (later vice president of the Liberal Democratic Party) graduated from Tokyo Imperial University's faculty of law in 1923 and was about to join the Ministry of Agriculture and Commerce, Gotō told him to keep the ministry waiting a couple of years and spend the time studying the natural sciences, since his education so far had been useless.

On the other hand, Gotō was well known for boldly recruiting able individuals to work under him, most of whom were imperial university and particularly law faculty graduates. Similarly, when he endowed a chair in colonial policy in honor of Kodama Gentarō, the recipient was none other than the faculty of law of Tokyo Imperial University. This seemingly self-contradictory attitude was a product of a sense of inferiority engendered by the conflicted mindset referred to above.

That mindset manifested itself in another way as well. Gotō approved of how the Western powers conducted their colonial and foreign policies, and argued that Japan should basically model their own policies on them, yet he also emphasized the distinctive character of Japan and Asia. In that regard he differed from the young bureaucrats (typically in the foreign ministry) who went seamlessly from accepting Western civilization to asserting that Japan should cooperate with the Western powers. But he differed equally from most pan-Asianists, who rejected the Western powers' modus operandi as "hegemonism" and contrasted it with the "righteousness" of the Asian way.

The Nagoya Years

In August 1876, at age nineteen, Gotō moved to Nagoya, where he became a physician, third class, at Aichi Prefectural Hospital with a monthly salary of ten yen. Financially, this position was not particularly attractive. He had been offered other work on better terms, but one of his old benefactors, Yasuba, had been in Nagoya as governor of Aichi Prefecture since the previous December, and another, Agawa, had been posted there in January 1876 after being transferred to Tokyo in July 1875.

Gotō around the age of 20

More importantly, Nagoya, being a major urban center in Japan at that time, was a good place to pursue his studies. "Not for a moment did I forget my desire to study in a large city," he wrote in his autobiography, "for I did not believe in being content with minor accomplishments." Aichi Prefectural Hospital had its own medical school, where the Austrian physician Albrecht von Roretz taught and the well-known doctor and translator Shiba Ryōkai also worked. Roretz, with the position of "instructor," was paid 300 yen a month. Shiba, "hospital deputy instructor and medical school instructor and interpreter," was paid 250 yen a month. In comparison, the "medical school deputy instructor and director of medicine" was paid eighty yen, while the rest of the hospital staff each made no more than twenty yen. This goes to show how dominant the figures of Roretz and Shiba were.

In a letter to his father immediately after his arrival, on August 30, Gotō wrote, "I should be able to study a great deal here. The instructor is a Germanist, so I intend to begin studying German from the rudiments." In October, with that goal in mind, he became a boarder at Shiba's private school and commuted to the hospital from there. Shiba, an outstanding linguist, was a prolific translator, and Gotō would often take down his dictation as he worked. Many of Shiba's translations, done at the request of the Tokyo police department, related to the sanitary police or forensic medicine, and that is said to have stimulated Gotō's interest in public health administration. His stay at Shiba's home, though, lasted less than a year, until Shiba left Nagoya in April 1877. What with working at the hospital and preparing for his exams (see below), Gotō's study of German could have made little progress.

That year, 1877, witnessed the outbreak of the Satsuma Rebellion. A large temporary army hospital was set up in Osaka for sick and wounded soldiers, and many well-known doctors gathered there to treat them. Gotō was eager to join the effort and gain experience, and after taking his medical licensing exam in June, he traveled to Osaka in July to visit the hospital's director, Ishiguro Tadanori. With Roretz's approval, he temporarily resigned from the Nagoya hospital and started working as a staff doctor at the Osaka hospital in September. There, working primarily in the surgery ward, he built up valuable experience. Now that he was treating large numbers of patients alongside many renowned physicians, he finally began to develop confidence in his own abilities as a doctor. Previously he had been an apprentice; now he was a full-fledged physician.

This was also a significant experience for Gotō in that he was taken under the wing of Ishiguro, one of the main architects of the Japanese army medical corps. As is typical of the founder of a new institution, Ishiguro was constantly on the lookout for men of ability from all over the country, and he had heard about Gotō from the director of the hospital in Sukagawa, a former student, and the head of the army garrison hospital in Nagoya. He had also met Gotō once over a meal in Nagoya. These developments led to Gotō's visit to Ishiguro and his tour of duty in Osaka. Having observed Gotō's abilities firsthand there, Ishiguro was to become his constant backer. Impressed with Gotō's abilities, Ishiguro helped him obtain a position at the home ministry. Later he recommended him to oversee the quarantine of personnel after the Sino-Japanese War. It was largely thanks to Ishiguro that Gotō went from being a provincial doctor to a central government bureaucrat and then a colonial administrator with ties to the army.

By November of 1877, Gotō's duties in Osaka were winding down, and he was hired as a staff doctor at the army garrison hospital in Nagoya. He returned to Aichi Prefectural Hospital in March 1878, and his subsequent career advancement was meteoric. He was appointed acting head of Aichi Prefectural Hospital and Medical School in December 1879 and provisional head in May 1880, before becoming official head of both institutions in October 1881. He was only twenty-four. He was so young that he was often mistaken for a locum, which was reportedly what prompted him to grow a bushy beard.

The most celebrated episode from Gotō's years as hospital director followed the attempted assassination of Jiyūtō (Liberal Party) leader Itagaki Taisuke. In April 1882, Itagaki was stabbed by a would-be assassin while in Gifu on a speaking tour. No doctor was willing to examine his wounds owing to fears of being associated with the Liberal Party that was regarded as a rebellious group. When Gotō was asked, however, he immediately rushed to tend to the injured statesman. After Gotō had finished treating him and left, Itagaki turned to his aides and said, "That doctor is a rather unusual fellow. What a shame not to make him a politician."[5]

Gotō proved an effective administrator during his time as head of the hospital and school. It was then that the managerial skills he was later to display in abundance first manifested themselves. When Roretz's term of service expired in May 1880 and he left Nagoya, Gotō replaced him with several Japanese physicians instead of hiring another highly paid foreign doctor. He also completely reorganized Aichi Prefectural Hospital and Medical School, making both familiar names throughout Japan. In May 1882, regional medical schools all over the country were classified into Grades A and B, with graduates of Grade A schools immediately being granted a license to practice. Thanks to Gotō's improvements, Aichi Prefectural Medical School was granted Grade A status.

Gotō's success as a manager was due in no small part to the backing of two influential men, Roretz and Yasuba (who remained governor of Aichi until March 1880). In later years he continued to exercise his considerable abilities with powerful support from men of influence. And throughout his career, the constant pillars of his managerial strategy remained recruiting capable people and tearing down old organizational structures to build new ones. These traits go all the way back to his Nagoya years.

---

5 Itagaki Taisuke, ed., *Jiyūtōshi* [History of the Liberal Party], vol. 2 (Tokyo: Iwanami Bunko, 1958), 143.

Having achieved success at Aichi Prefectural Hospital and Medical School, Gotō did not rest on the laurels. His interests broadened from the treatment of disease to its prevention in the form of public health policy. On the advice of Roretz, in October 1878 he submitted a recommendation to Governor Yasuba proposing the creation of "health police medical officers" with the goal of "eliminating the risk that medical treatment will be needed." Elaborating on this recommendation, in December he wrote a "Blueprint for the Establishment of Sanitary Police in Aichi Prefecture" and later conferred about it with Nagayo Sensai, head of the home ministry's Public Health Bureau. He also set up an independent organization, the Aishūsha, dedicated to raising health standards, and proposed merging the medical schools of the three prefectures of Aichi, Gifu, and Mie. He was steadily expanding into new areas of activity.

Nagayo had closely followed Gotō's career and invited him to join the bureau on the recommendation of Ishiguro, who said the man was too good to leave to languish in the provinces. Gotō accepted. In a letter of March 7, 1882 to Nagayo stating his ambitions, Gotō asked rhetorically, "Are a good statesman and a good doctor any different?" His desire was to bring the benefits of his own medical knowledge to as many people as possible. That was for Gotō the proper goal of civilization; it was why he strove "to be like Chōei."

2. At the Public Health Bureau

Early Days as a Public Health Official

In January 1883, Gotō was appointed to a junior position at the Ministry of Home Affairs and began working in its Public Health Bureau. It had taken him almost a year to sort out his personal affairs after he was offered a position at the ministry.

Nagayo, the head of the bureau, can justly be called the founder of public health administration in Japan. He headed the bureau for sixteen years, from its establishment in 1875 (when it was called Bureau VII) until 1891. The very concept of public health or hygiene was new to Japan. Indeed, Nagayo

Gotō with his newlywed wife, Kazuko (photographed September 1883)

is said to have coined the Japanese word for it (*eisei*). But neither Nagayo nor Gotō had any intention of imposing modern public health institutions and policies at a stroke.

The first major task that Gotō undertook at the Public Health Bureau was an inspection of health conditions in the three prefectures of Niigata, Nagano, and Gunma, between April and June 1883. He made meticulous preparations and drew up a detailed list of questions encompassing not only medical care and hygiene, but also a wide range of other issues including geography, living standards, and local products and customs.

In his report on the survey, Gotō noted that "the way of hygiene (*eisei*)" invariably existed wherever humankind dwelt, even if the concept of hygiene was lacking. He considered it an "instinctive function" of man. He went on to observe that when countries differed in geography and climate, so too did their "rules" of hygiene. Foreign institutions could not therefore simply be transplanted to Japan. Gotō affirmed that "the first priority in enhancing hygiene today" was to investigate conditions of hygiene in all parts of the country and to "assess their advantages and disadvantages in light of the ideal." This was the motivation behind his in-depth survey.

Gotō reiterated these ideas in his 1890 book *Eisei seido ron* (On Public Health Systems), stating, "What a public health administrator must pay attention to the most are physiographical factors and the history of customary methods of hygiene among the people." He further asserted, "When implementing a public health system, one must not forget to take account of changes in social conditions, popular sentiment, mores, and occupations. This is indeed, I believe, an essential requirement for anyone engaged in vital affairs of state." This investigation of health conditions undertaken by Gotō soon after he joined the Public Health Bureau was the first of the extensive surveys for which he later became famous. One must not rush to impose civilization, he argued; one must investigate local conditions and devise a methodology suited to them.

Principles of National Hygiene

In 1889, Gotō published his first book, *Kokka eisei genri* (Principles of National Hygiene), a work of the greatest importance to understanding his political thinking. In it he defines humans as, first and foremost, a species engaged in a desperate struggle for survival in a world where the fittest survive and the law of the jungle prevails. Driven by their "physiological urge" (or "innate character")—meaning "the power to express the nature with which the body is endowed"—they constantly vie to attain "physiological integrity," meaning "living conditions sufficient for healthy mental and physical development."

Gotō then goes on to assert that humans are unable to create order independently, by themselves. The struggle for survival arising from the instinct for self-preservation ends up threatening to undermine self-preservation. An entity is therefore needed to create order by mediating that struggle, and to direct communal efforts to produce an abundance of "necessities" by harnessing nature, thereby ensuring the "physiological integrity" of each individual. From this need arise "sovereigns" or "rulers," and the state comes into being.

According to Gotō, the state, having emerged in this fashion, possesses a "life" of its own. Naturally, then, it also has its own "physiological urge" by virtue of being a living entity, and it seeks to achieve "physiological integrity." Moreover, the state is, in view of its origins, "the highest organism," while people are merely accorded the status of "molecules in the aggregate called the corporeal state."

This theory of the state, which Gotō asserted was rooted in "biology," was not particularly original. It was an amalgam of the social contract, organic theories of the state, and social Darwinism. Still, it faithfully reflected his experiences studying and practicing medicine and his stance as a public health official. Those seeking physiological integrity without knowing how to achieve it were patients, or the benighted populace ignorant of what civilization was. The "sovereigns" or "rulers" who reigned over them as the absolute embodiment of reasons of state, conversely, were the doctors, or the bureaucrats of the Meiji state with their civilizing mission.

While Gotō recognized the universality of the "physiological urge" ("the power to express the nature with which the body is endowed") among individuals and states, he also accepted that there were differences: individuals and states each had their own "customs" adapted to their environment, and these were "second nature." This respect for "custom" and rejection of the hasty imposition of "theory" were of a piece with the emphasis he placed on the patient's symptoms and physical condition during treatment. It also related to the great importance that he attached to survey work as a public health official.

What place, incidentally, did "civilization" occupy in this theory of the state? Above all, it was seen to underpin "statecraft" in its role of maintaining social order and increasing productivity, and accordingly to have the function of building a wealthy, powerful nation. Since Gotō saw the world as a battleground for survival and the state as a living organism, he naturally took competition among states for granted. Their relative levels of civilization would determine the victor. This aspect of his thinking, too, faithfully reflected the course being charted by the Meiji state.

The "biological" view of the state articulated in *Principles of National Hygiene* was clearly stamped with Gotō's experiences as a student of medicine and a public health administrator. It already contained many of the elements of the political thinking that he was later to espouse, but it did not extend to international relations, and it was largely abstract. The question of how Gotō's views developed and matured through his exposure to the real world remains to be considered.

Studying in Germany

In April 1890, at age thirty-two, Gotō left Japan to study in Germany while retaining his position at the home ministry. His stay was far from luxurious. Only his research costs were defrayed by the government; otherwise he paid his expenses himself.

This trip was the fulfillment of a decade-old dream. Gotō had been planning to study abroad at least since the end of 1880. The best and indeed virtually the only way to cure his inferiority complex that came from having only been able to study Western medicine in Japanese translation in a remote corner of northeast Japan was to study it at the fountainhead. There he was to have his second encounter with Western civilization, one more direct than his initial encounter when he trained as a doctor.

This second encounter with Western civilization in Germany, however, left him even more conflicted. On the positive side, he was deeply struck by the efficacy, sophistication, and universality of Western civilization and became even more convinced of its validity as a model. He was particularly impressed with the progress of Germany's public health policies and its social policies in general, and devoted himself to assimilating them. He also attended three international conferences during his stay: the Tenth International Medical Congress in Berlin (1890), the International Congress of Hygiene and Demography in London (1891), and the Fifth International Conference of the Red Cross in Rome (1892). He was deeply moved by the warm welcome he received at each, and could not help but feel indignant at the Japanese government for failing to participate more actively. He became keenly aware both that the comity of nations sharing the universal values of Western civilization was open to Japan, and that Japan had so far failed to become a full member.

Gotō was to an extent successful in acquiring a knowledge of Western civilization, as demonstrated by the medical doctorate he earned in Germany. But in the end, he proved unable to acculturate himself to the West. One of his fellow students in Germany, Kanasugi Eigorō, recalled that Gotō "had no talent for languages" and "so disliked dealing with foreigners that he did his very best not to go near them." Although Gotō could read German, everyone, including himself, knew that he spoke it poorly. He became homesick and on quite a few occasions exasperated his compatriots by talking about how he craved a bowl of rice or some pickled plums, or exclaiming that he was quitting government service and going home to Japan.

Kanasugi also told the following story. When at a certain party Gotō was asked to dance by the daughter of the host, he replied, "Sie sind barbarisch" (You're barbaric). The young lady was outraged, and there was a huge commotion. Kanasugi, shocked, attempted to gloss over the matter by explaining that Gotō did not speak German well. He had meant, Kanasugi explained, that *his* own upbringing was barbaric, so he was unworthy to dance with such a lady, but had misspoken. He then promptly took his leave. But Gotō's German was not so bad that he would have confused "I" and "you." He was furious at Kanasugi for interfering. He was adamant that he had firmly refused the young lady's request because of his conviction that dancing was barbaric. The two men did not speak for several days afterwards. According to another fellow student, Okada Kunitarō, when a German once said to Gotō that he presumed Japan must be a protectorate of China, Gotō abruptly struck him with his walking stick and fled without bothering to disabuse or enlighten him.

Kanasugi and Okada attributed such behavior to Gotō's lack of conversational ability and his eccentricity and combativeness, but that was surely not all. It was also a manifestation of the sense of inferiority that he inevitably developed due to his inability to fully identify with the West even as he acknowledged its merits, as well as his frustration at himself because at the emotional level he had an antipathy to the West yet lacked the means to express it.

In short, the conflicted, ambivalent relationship with Western civilization that Gotō had developed as a student of medicine was not remedied by his studies in Germany. On the contrary, it became even more conflicted and evolved into an ambivalent relationship with the West itself.

A word must also be said about the effect of Gotō's studies in Germany on his political thinking. Gotō was primarily interested in Germany's social policies, as has already been mentioned. He had been interested in Bismarck's social policies, especially sickness, disability, and old-age insurance, since before his departure for Germany and worked on legislation modeled on those programs. Meanwhile, in *Principles of National Hygiene*, Gotō had characterized the state as a living organism and concluded that state governance was for that organism the equivalent of "hygiene" ("affairs of state are in a broad sense a form of hygiene"). Observing Germany's social policies firsthand, he must have felt that they seamlessly unified both these interests of his. His "biological" view of the state, as he termed it, now assumed a decidedly practical bent.

Also significant was Germany's international position at the time. Gotō arrived in Germany immediately after Bismarck was dismissed as chancellor. The country had, shedding the purely European character it possessed under Bismarck, commenced its evolution into a global power. For Gotō it epitomized the organic state bursting with vitality.

Gotō remained, however, more impressed with Bismarck than the Kaiser. Many years later he wrote as follows in the preface he contributed to a Japanese edition of Bismarck's speeches published in December 1918. For Bismarck, the state was "not a product of theory but the crystallization of real power." It was "an organism with a continuous life spanning past, present, and future and possessing its own identity." He therefore endeavored to conduct government "on the basis of the state's inherited character" and to "gain the advantage at the global level by taking account of current trends." To the superficial observer, Bismarck appeared to have "attempted to govern the state according to his own judgment and wishes," but in fact he well understood the power of "a force far greater than the individual will," namely "the natural factors attendant on conditions such as the state's origins, evolution, and historical relations with its neighbors." Hence, "while pursuing an independent policy of militarism," Bismarck did not "abandon the diplomacy of cooperation." Therein, Gotō declared, lay his true genius.

It is not easy to pinpoint when Gotō came to interpret Bismarck's view of the state and diplomacy thus. Still, given that he became fascinated with the chancellor during his studies in Germany, it would be safe to say that he began to form this impression, at least vaguely, at that time. This idea of managing international relations on the basis of history (or convention) rather than theory clearly indicates that he viewed Bismarck, and international relations, not in the usual balance-of-power terms but rather through the prism of his own "biological principle."

Gotō's stay in Germany thus solidified his "biological" view of the state and extended it to embrace foreign policy and international relations as well.

Head of the Public Health Bureau

Gotō returned to Japan in June 1892 and was appointed head of the home ministry's Public Health Bureau in November. Nagayo had resigned as head in August 1891 and named Gotō his successor, although someone else stood in for him until he got back from Germany.

After becoming head of the Public Health Bureau, Gotō was in such high spirits that he seemed a different man from the one he had been during his stay in Germany. Kanasugi, who had observed him then, snidely remarked on his metamorphosis. "Having become head of the Public Health Bureau upon his return to Japan, the Count [Gotō] was so full of himself that he swept all before him . . . The taciturn, silent fellow he had been in Germany was instantly transformed into a voluble talker. His words suddenly acquired a keener edge."

On taking up his new post, Gotō applied his considerable abilities to transplanting to Japan, in his own inimitable way, the new knowledge of "civilized" medicine and hygiene that he had acquired in Germany. One case in point was his opposition to and suppression of a campaign to reinstate traditional Japanese medicine, which arose immediately after he became head of the bureau. During the fifth session of the Diet in 1892–93, a bill revising medical licensing regulations, aimed at restoring traditional Japanese medicine to equal status with Western medicine, was tabled by several Diet members representing the interests of traditional medical practitioners. Gotō, with the cooperation of physicians in the Diet opposed to traditional medicine, as well as Ishiguro Tadanori, then head of the army's medical bureau, and Deputy Justice Minister Kiyoura Keigo, killed the bill by relentlessly arguing, on the grounds of public health, military hygiene, and forensic science, that practitioners of traditional medicine served no purpose. Gotō was absolutely ruthless. There was surely a more amicable way to resolve the issue, but for Gotō, convinced as he was of the need to "civilize" Japan, there could be no compromise.

Another well-known example was the establishment of the Institute for Infectious Diseases under Kitasato Shibasaburō (also known as Kitazato). One of the obstacles Gotō encountered was the opposition of the Ministry of Education and Tokyo Imperial University, which wanted to keep all research bodies under their own control. Gotō had no patience whatsoever for bureaucratic turf wars. This issue was, with the help of Fukuzawa Yukichi (the most influential intellectual in Meiji Japan, founder of Keio

University and *Jiji shinpō* newspaper), resolved by agreeing that the institute would start out under private management and later be transferred to government control. Another obstacle was the opposition of local residents to the establishment of the infectious diseases institute in their neighborhood. Gotō had little tolerance for such opposition rooted in ignorance. One day, he instructed a subordinate to surreptitiously paint over the institute's signboard with black ink. He wanted to give the locals the impression that the opposition movement had done the terrible deed and thus convince them to abandon the cause. He had no qualms about resorting to a little subterfuge to thwart some ignorant, benighted locals who stood in the way of his civilizing mission. In this case it was the task of developing tuberculin under the direction of the gifted Kitasato. Gotō believed strongly in his civilizing mission, and when he saw the chance to further it, he stopped at nothing.

Generally speaking, however, Gotō adhered to his belief in respecting custom, true to the "biological" principle. Indeed, he devoted his first year or so as head of the Public Health Bureau to investigative work. Just when he was ready to start getting things done, however, he suffered a serious setback—his arrest and imprisonment in the Sōma Affair.

The Sōma Affair

The Sōma Affair revolved around Sōma Tomotane, the former daimyo of Sōma domain in what was now Fukushima Prefecture. Tomotane had been confined to his residence since 1879 on the grounds of mental illness. But certain individuals claimed that he was in fact perfectly sane, and that he was being forcibly confined as part of a plot to replace him with his half-brother as head of the Sōma family. Nishigori Takekiyo was the chief of these proponents. Nishigori was a former retainer of Sōma domain who remained loyal to the clan even after the feudal domains were abolished in 1871. The affair generated considerable interest because it was reminiscent of the succession disputes that occasionally tore apart daimyo families in the Edo period. Nishigori was lionized as a paragon of samurai honor for remaining loyal to Tomotane.

Having studied in Sukagawa, Fukushima Prefecture, Gotō was familiar with the Sōma family name. Moreover, the head of administration at Aichi

Prefectural Hospital, Imamura Shūei, was a native of the Sōma domain and sympathized with Tomotane's predicament. Gotō met Nishigori through Imamura at the end of 1883 and agreed to assist him. He called for Tomotane to be thoroughly reexamined and pointed out deficiencies in the Tokyo police department's regulations on the handling of the mentally ill. He thus secured remedial action on both counts. In 1887, he gave his tacit support when Nishigori abducted Tomotane from the hospital in Sugamo, Tokyo, to which he had been committed. Gotō even hid Tomotane in his own home for a while. This was clearly a crime, but the government turned a blind eye to his actions. Negotiations on revising the unequal treaties with the Western powers were about to resume, and it would not do to draw international attention to the issue of human rights in Japan by letting the matter escalate any further.

Thanks in part to Gotō's efforts, Tomotane's circumstances improved. In April 1887, he was moved to his own home to convalesce in relative comfort. The affair appeared to have been resolved.

It erupted again, however, when Tomotane suddenly died five years later, in February 1892. Nishigori claimed that he had been poisoned and he made plans to sue the Sōma family and its head butler. Gotō, when asked for advice upon his return from Germany, tried to dissuade him. Even if Tomotane had indeed been poisoned, he argued, it would be difficult to find evidence of it now. Nishigori, however, refused to listen and instituted legal proceedings in July 1893. The Sōma family countersued Nishigori for slander. Tomotane's remains were disinterred and autopsied in September. Sure enough, no evidence of poisoning was found. Now the tables were turned, and Nishigori and his supporters found themselves on the defensive. Gotō, who had guaranteed a loan for Nishigori, was arrested and jailed in November on suspicion of being an accomplice. He was suspended from his duties as head of the Public Health Bureau in December.

In May 1894, the Tokyo district court found Gotō not guilty on the grounds of insufficient evidence. The prosecution appealed, but in December the Tokyo court of appeals upheld the original decision. The ruling was final. Gotō was officially innocent.

Gotō became entangled in the Sōma Affair not so much out of a traditional sense of samurai honor as because of his indignation at the uncivilized treatment of the mentally ill. They were cursorily examined, confined on inadequate grounds, and treated inhumanely under the guise of hospitalization. He wanted to ameliorate such abuses. In that regard the Sōma Affair was part of the fight for civilization that Gotō had been pursuing as a public health official, but his actions were reckless in the extreme. Nishigori, as it turned out, appears to have been an adventurer after fame and the Sōma family fortune. Gotō had been unwise to overcommit to his cause. The six months Gotō spent in jail (he was conditionally released on May 25) was the price he paid for his folly.

The Temporary Army Quarantine Department

Once he was found not guilty, Gotō was reluctant to resume his bureaucratic career. He was downright disgusted that all those who had been attracted to his side by the power he wielded as bureau head, and even his colleagues in the bureau had promptly abandoned him when he was thrown in jail.

In January 1895, however, he became a member of the Central Sanitation Committee on the recommendation of Ishiguro, who persuaded him to accept the position by emphasizing that it was not a bureaucratic one. Ishiguro was reluctant to see Gotō's talent go to waste, but he was also alarmed by Gotō's fiery, prickly temperament and believed he must not be allowed to leave the government and become a threat. Quite a few other friends and acquaintances evidently felt likewise.

The Sino-Japanese War was drawing to a close and the problem of quarantining the returning troops had become a pressing issue. The number of Japanese soldiers killed in action was about 1,000, while the number of those who died from disease was ten times higher. Therefore, those returning from overseas had to be strictly quarantined before coming home. Soldiers needed to be examined for infection with non-native diseases, bathed, and their belongings disinfected. All returnees were subject to quarantine and needed to be admitted to a designated quarantine station. Ishiguro, who as head of the army medical corps bore chief responsibility for the matter, recommended Gotō to Army Vice Minister Kodama Gentarō as the best man for the job. The setup of the Temporary Army Quarantine Department was officially announced in March. It was to be established in April and headed by Kodama, with Gotō serving as administrative director.

Quarantining the troops was a massive undertaking. Quarantine stations were established in three locations near the port of Ujina in Hiroshima, including the island of Ninoshima. Between five thousand and six thousand men were inspected per day on that island, and between twenty-five hundred and three thousand at each of the other two stations. The three stations covered a total area of approximately 218,200 square meters and were occupied by buildings with a floor space of 69,400 square meters. Moreover, they needed to be equipped with the latest facilities. Gotō ordered this massive construction job to be performed in two months, and got it done on schedule. The quarantine process commenced on June 1, and the inspection of 687 vessels (with a total tonnage of 1,135,000 tons) and 232,000 men was completed in two months, an achievement for which Japan could be proud.

This was the busiest period in Gotō's busy life. Stories are told, doubtless largely true, about how he only got three hours' sleep a night and did not go to bed for forty-three days straight. When Gotō returned to Tokyo on August 21 after shutting down the quarantine department's facilities in Hiroshima, he was so haggard that he was almost unrecognizable. He could barely speak from exhaustion.

Gotō had had his back to the wall. Recovering from the Sōma debacle depended on his success at this assignment. Ishiguro sent him a letter of encouragement on June 13. "Everybody knows that you are highly capable, but since the Sōma Affair you give people the impression of being something of a charlatan," he wrote. "My hope is that you will now show them that you veritably overflow with sincerity."

Gotō more than lived up to Ishiguro's expectations. Meanwhile Kodama took him under his wing and gave him a free hand by shielding him from critics inside and outside the army. The two would later team up in Taiwan as governor-general and civilian governor respectively.

Head of the Public Health Bureau Again

In September 1895, Gotō was again appointed head of the Public Health Bureau on the recommendation of Ishiguro and Nagayo. He devoted his second tenure in that post primarily to advancing the social policies that he had learned in Germany. Just as he had once gone from treating disease to preventing it, and thus came to join the Public Health Bureau, so now did his interest shift from the health of the body to the health of society.

The specific policies that Gotō attempted to implement covered a wide range. His highest priorities were establishing large hospitals for the poor, and setting up a workers' sickness insurance program (equivalent to today's health insurance system), with the goals of poverty relief and prevention.

Of particular interest is how he planned to fund those policies. When he first drew up a proposal on the subject in 1895 for submission to Prime Minister Itō Hirobumi, he suggested financing them with the war indemnity paid by China. Despite the need to build up the military, develop industry, and improve transportation facilities, implementing such "constructive social programs" was, he argued, the best way to "strengthen the foundations of the state." Moreover, as a result of the Tripartite Intervention by Russia, Germany, and France over the terms of the Treaty of Shimonoseki, which ended the first Sino-Japanese War and paved the way for Japanese expansion in China, Japan agreed to restore the Liaodong Peninsula to China in return for a further indemnity from the Qing government. According to Gotō, certainly one of the few people in Japan who welcomed the loss, this made conditions even more favorable, since it freed up the funds that would have had to be spent on administering the territory. This plan for funding social programs, however, fell through. Next Gotō advocated raising taxes to pay for them. Among several concrete proposals he presented, one was, interestingly, for a kind of earmarked tax.

In the end, none of Gotō's proposed social policies came anywhere close to realization. Given the state of Japan's finances and the political situation, there were many more pressing needs. It was not until the last years of the Meiji era, after the Russo-Japanese War, that such policies were to start being implemented to any extent, as the government became alarmed at the spread of socialism. Far ahead of his time, Gotō was trying to go too far, too fast.

Generally speaking, Gotō was most successful when he led a specific project, that is, when the task at hand was obvious to all. When, by contrast, he headed a regular organization—that is, when it was not yet self-evident what needed to be done—his achievements were often mediocre. By this time the heroic early days of public health administration in Japan were already over, and now the job was becoming routine. Gotō was beginning to look beyond the ordinary responsibilities of the home ministry's Public Health Bureau, as evidenced by how he advocated fusing public health programs with poverty relief. He would not, however, be at the Public Health Bureau for much longer.

Japan found itself facing a clear conundrum in the area of public health: the problem of Taiwan, which it had recently acquired as a result of the Sino-Japanese War. This obviously concerned Gotō, given the nature of his job. On the particularly troublesome issue of opium, he had advocated a gradual ban on the drug since returning to the Public Health Bureau in 1895. That led to his resignation as head of the bureau in 1898 to become Director of Civil Affairs in the government of Taiwan.

CHAPTER 2

CIVILIAN GOVERNOR OF TAIWAN

1. Consolidating Japanese Rule

Appointment as Civilian Governor

In March 1898, Gotō was appointed director of civil affairs in the Government-General of Taiwan, a post renamed civilian governor when the bureaucracy was reorganized that June. As such he was the second-highest-ranking official on the island after the governor-general. He was to hold that position for eight years and eight months—until he became president of the South Manchuria Railway in November 1906—during which time he did much to consolidate Japanese rule over Taiwan.

Gotō was appointed by Kodama Gentarō, who had just been installed as the fourth governor-general of Taiwan. Kodama, who had been deeply impressed with Gotō's abilities during the quarantine of personnel following the Sino-Japanese War, trusted him implicitly and gave him a free hand for more than eight years, until his own appointment as chief of the Army General Staff in April 1906. While governor-general of Taiwan (1898–1906), Kodama concurrently held a number of other posts in the Japanese government. He was appointed to a member of cabinet as minister of the army, minister of home affairs, and minister of education (December 1900–March 1902 and July–October 1903), and then served in several senior staff positions in the army, including deputy army chief of staff, in which capacity he was effectively supreme commander of the land campaign in the Russo-Japanese War. While Kodama was thus occupied with other pressing duties, especially after he became deputy army chief of staff, Gotō was the de facto governor-general of Taiwan.

After Kodama resigned as the governor-general in April 1906 and returned to Japan, Gotō stayed on as civilian governor at the request of General Sakuma Samata, Kodama's successor and like Kodama, a native of the old feudal domain of Chōshū (present-day Yamaguchi Prefecture). When Gotō left Taiwan half a year later to become president of the South Manchuria Railway, he continued to serve as adviser to the Government-General of Taiwan, a post created especially for him, which demonstrated how indispensable he had become. Indeed, no one was more influential than Gotō during the fifty years Japan ruled Taiwan.

The decision to appoint Gotō director of civil affairs was not Kodama's alone. Prime Minister Itō Hirobumi urged him to take the post immediately after forming his third cabinet in January 1898. He had had his eye on Gotō ever since Gotō advocated initiating a set of social programs funded by the war indemnity from China. Itō's army minister, Katsura Tarō, was likewise of the opinion that Gotō should be given the job. When Katsura had served as second governor-general of Taiwan (June–October 1896), he had planned to establish a public health agency on the island and put Gotō in charge of it. At any rate, by early 1898 it was obvious to all that the current governor-general, Nogi Maresuke, had been a failure, and Itō, Katsura, and probably Kodama reached a consensus that making Gotō director of civil affairs was the best way to retrieve the situation. The Kodama-Gotō combination emerged once Nogi's resignation was decided, although the decision to appoint Gotō appears in fact to have predated Kodama's own appointment as governor-general.

A Rocky Start to Colonial Rule

What was the state of Japanese rule in Taiwan at the time? Taiwan, which was ceded to Japan in the Treaty of Shimonoseki ending the Sino-Japanese War, legally became Japanese territory when the treaty was ratified and took effect in May 1895. The annexation, however, was far from peaceful. The inhabitants, unhappy at the prospect of becoming part of Japan, initially fought back by declaring Asia's first democracy, the Republic of Formosa.[1] Japanese

---

1   See Ng Yuzin Chiautong, *Taiwan minshukoku no kenkyū* [Study on the Republic of Taiwan] (Tokyo: Tōkyō Daigaku Shuppankai, 1970).

forces, having landed on the island at the end of May, entered Taipei in June and held a ceremony there to mark the official start of Japanese rule. They encountered fierce resistance in central and southern Taiwan, however, and only in November was Imperial General Headquarters in Japan notified that the entire island had been subjugated. An extensive insurgency broke out again immediately afterward, and the Imperial General Headquarters was unable to disband until May 1896. Under the first governor-general, Kabayama Sukenori (May 1895–June 1896), therefore, the

Gotō as civilian governor of Taiwan

colonial government had to devote all its efforts to pacifying the island. The second governor-general, Katsura Tarō (June–October 1896), resigned after only four months due to political developments in Japan. He spent only ten days in total in Taiwan. The third governor-general, Nogi Maresuke (October 1896–February 1898), likewise proved unable to suppress the anti-Japanese guerrillas—the *dohi* or "bandits" as they were called. Nogi was himself of questionable ability, and so too was his director of civil affairs. In short, before Kodama and Gotō arrived, the Japanese authorities had been unable to establish even a modicum of peace and order, let alone make any real progress developing Taiwan. There was reportedly a basic consensus that Japanese rule in Taiwan should be modeled on the French policy of assimilation in Algeria, but it was not clear what that meant. The difficulties that Japan encountered governing Taiwan led some pessimists to advocate selling it off to another country.

Respect for Local Autonomy and Conventions: The "Biological Principle"

To what, then, did Gotō attribute the initial failure of Japanese rule in Taiwan? In short, he believed that the Japanese had fundamentally erred in disregarding and disdaining local practices. In "An Emergency Proposal on the Governance of Taiwan" (January 25, 1898), drawn up before he assumed the post of civilian governor, Gotō wrote, "Where does the administration of Taiwan most require improvement? The most urgent task of all, surely, is to revive the conventions of self-government that have long existed on the island."

Taiwan, long considered "beyond the pale" of Chinese civilization, had been left to its own devices by the Qing government, but for that very reason, Gotō argued, it had developed a remarkably high degree of autonomy. In such areas as policing, justice, and taxation it had established robust institutions, although unlike the modern ones of today. These "conventions of self-government" were for Taiwan a kind of civil law. Yet the Japanese authorities had recklessly destroyed such autonomous institutions and issued a battery of new laws and regulations in a bid to impose at a stroke the outward trappings of civilized government. There lay the source of the failure. Future policy, Gotō asserted, should focus on reviving the old ways, with the colonial government playing a supervisory role and gradually implementing reforms only where shortcomings existed. Such an approach would simplify the task of administration and be far more effective.

Gotō explained this policy to Kodama and won him over, persuading the new Government-General to cancel announcement of his own policy for governing the island. Gotō believed that government should be conducted in accordance with the "biological principle," namely respect for local practices; and there was no point in laying out a purely notional administrative policy without fully investigating those practices first.

This biological principle, a phrase Gotō coined when he was with the Public Health Bureau, was deeply entrenched in his thinking. In later years he would often stress that it had been the secret to successfully governing Taiwan.

> You know, you can't make a flatfish's eyes like a sea bream's. A sea bream has its eyes on both sides of its head. A flatfish has its eyes on one side of its head. Just because that's strange, you can't reposition them to be like a sea bream's. A flatfish has both eyes on one side out of biological necessity. It's futile to insist that eyes are invariably supposed to be positioned on both sides of the head. That holds true in government as well.

Social conventions and institutions all arise for good reasons, out of longstanding necessity. Blindly attempting to impose the institutions of a civilized nation on a backward one, without understanding those reasons, is an act of tyranny by civilization. It mustn't be done. Therefore, when I was administering Taiwan, first I did a thorough scientific investigation of the island's old customs and institutions, and I then ran the government in accordance with the circumstances of her people. Those who would instantly transplant the legal institutions of Japan's home islands to Taiwan without understanding any of this are instantly trying to replace a flatfish's eyes with a sea bream's; they are ignorant of the true art of government.[2]

Goto's respect for local conventions may not seem unusual to modern eyes. But in those days, when there was a deep-seated prejudice against the "barbaric" as the antithesis of civilization, it showed remarkable insight.

Survey of the Old Customs of Taiwan

Gotō inaugurated a massive survey to ensure that local conventions were indeed respected. To assist him in this effort, in 1900 he invited Professor Okamatsu Santarō of Kyoto Imperial University to Taiwan, and in 1901, organized the Provisional Research Council on the Old Customs of Taiwan, chaired by himself. Another professor from Kyoto Imperial University, Oda Yorozu, joined the council in 1903. The council's output included the three-volume *First Report on the First Survey of the Provisional Research Council on the Old Customs of Taiwan* (1903) and the four-volume *Second Report* on the same (1906–07); the two-volume *Second Survey of the Provisional Research Council on the Old Customs of Taiwan: Report on Economic Materials* (1905); the thirteen-volume *Private Law in Taiwan* (1910); and the seven-volume *Administrative Law in Qing China* (1910–1914). The last, written by Oda Yorozu, has been described by one leading authority on modern Chinese political and diplomatic history as "a comprehensive, systematic study of

---

2   Tsurumi Yūsuke, ed., *Gotō Shinpei*, vol. 2 (Tokyo: Keisō Shobō, 1965), 399.

Qing institutions unlikely ever to be surpassed."[3] Much the same holds true of the rest of the council's output.

Although originally undertaken for political purposes, Gotō's survey adopted a thoroughly scholarly approach, and it proved to be a cultural enterprise of enduring value thanks to the powerful backing he gave it. When Oda seemed daunted by the magnitude and complexity of the subject matter, Gotō won him over by stressing that the project was a grand enterprise of cultural benefit to the world, one that only the Japanese were capable of carrying out.[4] For Gotō, this was more than merely a political undertaking. Being able to contribute to world civilization was itself a source of joy to him.

Establishing Peace and Order: The "Surrender Inducement" Policy

Anti-Japanese resistance was the greatest challenge Gotō and Kodama faced in applying the biological principle to governing Taiwan. Under Nogi, a so-called three-tier security system had been adopted to fight the guerrillas. Areas of guerrilla activity fell under the jurisdiction of the army and the military police, lowland and built-up areas fell under the jurisdiction of the civilian police, and intermediate areas were the joint responsibility of the civilian and military police.

The three-tier security system seemed at first to make sense, but in fact made no sense at all. To begin with, the army and the civilian police typically did not get on well. They had different chains of command and a fundamentally different mindset. Regular forces were of no use against guerrillas who faded into the population. By the time the army arrived, the guerrillas had disappeared; the troops then became unduly suspicious of the ordinary inhabitants and resorted to gratuitous violence. Having lost comrades in fighting against the guerrillas, they were out for blood and became unnecessarily confrontational. Such incidents were common in Taiwan.

Perceiving these defects in the security system, Gotō and Kodama

---

3 Banno Masataka, "Oda Yorozu no *Shinkoku gyōsei-hō* o megutte" [On Oda Yorozu's *Administrative Law in Qing China*], *Shisō* (February and June 1962).

4 Ibid.

decided to abolish it. On May 25, upon arriving in Taiwan to take office, Kodama in a speech to local officials made clear his intention of placing the civilian police on the front lines. Then, on June 3, in a speech to senior army officers, he declared, "My job is to rule Taiwan, not to subjugate it." The three-tier system had been rooted in the idea of defending against and fighting an enemy. Instead, in a major policy shift, the guerrillas were now to be isolated by establishing a police presence among the populace and, at the same time, called on to surrender.

This policy shift was underpinned by a new way of looking at the guerrillas. Kodama, in his speech of June, stated that Taiwan had always had "bandits" (*dohi*), as the guerillas were referred to, who refused to obey the government. The bandits the Japanese authorities now had to deal with, however, typically differed in that they owned property and were trusted by the local inhabitants. In many ways, Kodama surmised, it was understandable that such previously law-abiding people should have decided to operate outside the law. Some had done so, say, to avenge a father or brother wrongfully killed by the Japanese army, others because they had lost their longstanding rights with the imposition of new institutions under Japanese rule. For these reasons, Kodama explicitly denied any intention of crushing the guerrillas immediately.

It is not known whether this view of the guerrillas was originally Kodama's or Gotō's, but both undoubtedly agreed on the new direction. The colonial government initiated a policy of actively encouraging guerrillas to surrender. It adopted several means to that end, including granting amnesty for past crimes and providing jobs and money. Although this "surrender inducement" policy had been in place since Nogi was governor-general, it had failed to produce adequate results owing to the three-tier security system and other factors. Only under Kodama and Gotō did it at last begin to have an effect. Gotō in particular made a point of attending surrender ceremonies all over the island in an effort to further the policy.

Misunderstandings were rife because of cultural differences. Some so-called bandits attending the surrender ceremonies were under the mistaken impression that the colonial authorities, bringing as they did money and other incentives, were the ones who were surrendering. Minor misunderstandings and disputes at these proceedings occasionally resulted in violence.

It should not be forgotten that the successes of the Kodama-Gotō years were not achieved without bloodshed. According to Gotō himself, a total of 11,950 "bandits" were killed between 1898 and 1902.[5] In 1902 alone, when the last major counter-insurgency campaign was mounted, the number reached 4,676, some of whom were criminals, pure and simple. Nonetheless, combat deaths fell dramatically, replaced by judicial executions, which itself was progress of sorts. Still, it is a fact that there was brutal repression. While isolating the guerrillas and persuading them to surrender through a policy of conciliation, Kodama and Gotō also went on the offensive against hold-outs throughout Taiwan. By 1902, their strategy had eliminated guerrilla resistance.[6]

The Gradual Prohibition of Opium

Alongside guerrilla resistance, opium was another difficult problem facing Taiwan's Japanese rulers. In November 1895, Gotō, then head of the Public Health Bureau, had submitted a memorandum to the home minister stating his views on the opium issue. It met with the government's approval and marked the start of Gotō's involvement in Taiwanese affairs.

There were at the time many different opinions in Japan on what approach to take to the control or prohibition of opium in Taiwan. The colonial authorities on the island intended to institute a gradual prohibition over time, but that idea was strongly opposed in Japan, where the view that opium should be strictly outlawed on humanitarian grounds prevailed. In his memorandum, Gotō dissented. He argued that a gradual prohibition was the most sensible policy and set out a wide range of ideas for implementing it.

His proposal was as follows. First, create a government monopoly on opium and establish licensed retailers in various locations selling only

---

5   Gotō Shinpei, "Nihon shokumin seisaku ippan" [Aspects of Japanese Colonial Policy], *Nihon shokumin seisaku ippan: Nihon bōchō ron* [Aspects of Japanese Colonial Policy: Japanese Expansionism], with an introduction by Nakamura Akira (Tokyo: Nihon Hyōronsha, 1944), 64.

6   Kō Seikai, *Nihon tōchika no Taiwan* [Taiwan under Japanese rule] (Tokyo: Tōkyō Daigaku Shuppankai, 1972).

medicinal opium. Second, identify all opium addicts through a physician's diagnosis and issue each with a passbook, permitting only passbook holders to purchase opium. Third, tax opium at a prohibitive rate and use the revenues to improve public health conditions in Taiwan, especially with respect to opium addiction. This proposal was adopted in its essentials by the Itō cabinet in February 1896 and implemented by means of the Taiwan opium ordinance of January 1897. These developments led to Gotō's appointment as public health adviser to the Government-General of Taiwan in April 1896.

Because of Governor-General Nogi's coolness to the idea of a gradual ban, however, Gotō's plan made little progress. It was not until Gotō became civilian governor and took personal charge of implementing the gradual prohibition that an all-out effort was made to identify all opium addicts, a task finally completed in September 1900. The total stood at 169,000, a figure that almost perfectly matched the addicted population as estimated from opium imports. That number fell to 62,000 seventeen years later in 1917 and 26,000 by 1928. The colonial government did not halt opium production until 1944, however, and only disbanded its monopoly in 1945. The prohibition of opium thus took decades to implement fully.

On the whole, Gotō's policy of gradually prohibiting opium was a success, considering the Herculean nature of the task. Still, it could be faulted for having failed to meet its goal somewhat sooner. The authorities were rather lax in treating addicts and catching and punishing illegal users, because income from the opium monopoly was an important revenue source for the colonial government, which therefore had little incentive to reduce it.

This was an almost unavoidable drawback of a government monopoly. When Gotō first recommended creating one, Nagayo Sensai was reportedly concerned that a revenue-generating monopoly would inevitably create an incentive to sell more opium. Gotō intended to eliminate that risk by limiting the use of earnings to public health spending, but profits went instead into general revenues. As a result, everyone including Gotō appears to have been bedazzled by the earnings from opium.[7]

---

7 See Ryū Meishū, *Taiwan tōchi to ahen mondai* [The Rule of Taiwan and the Opium Problem] (Tokyo: Yamakawa Shuppansha, 1983).

Land Survey of Taiwan

While grappling with this pair of difficult challenges—guerrilla resistance and the opium problem—Gotō also embarked on an ambitious set of administrative policies. The first was a land survey of the island. The Taiwanese landholding system was extremely complex. First there were large landholders (*dazuhu*, literally "large-rent householders") or "reclamation masters" (*kenshou*), who acquired land by clearing it for cultivation. Then there were small landholders (*xiazuhu*, literally "small-rent householders") or "reclaimer householders" (*kenhu*), who acquired the right to cultivate land from large landholders. Further, small landholders would often rent out their land to tenant households (*dianhu*). Tenant households paid small landholders a rent called *xiaozu* or "small rent," while small landholders paid large landholders a tax called *dazu* or "large rent." The small landholder was in effect the actual owner of the farmland, and large landholders did not have the right to dispose of it. The ratio of "large" to "small" rent was between 1:9 and 3:7. There was thus a complex and varied web of rights and obligations not easily reconcilable with Japanese or Western law.

To complicate things further, many land plots in Taiwan were unregistered, and even under Qing rule their extent was completely unknown. When Taiwan was made a separate province in 1885, the new governor, Liu Mingchuan, promptly embarked on a survey of the entire island, but everywhere the surveyors encountered resistance from local inhabitants, and there was even the occasional uprising. The attempt thus ended in dismal failure. That was how difficult it was merely to survey the land. When the Japanese authorities took over, they further needed to disentangle a mesh of rights and obligations and replace it with a modern arrangement. One of the main objectives of Gotō's survey of the old customs of Taiwan described above was to facilitate that task.

The land survey, which was effectively under the direction of Nakamura Yoshikoto, later vice president and then president of the South Manchuria Railway, commenced when the Temporary Taiwanese Land Survey Office was established in July 1898, with Gotō assuming the post of director. Gotō delivered a speech at the project's commencement in which he urged respect for local sensibilities. He told his listeners they would often find themselves surveying areas where there were tombs, but that they must not think "they're only native graves, so they don't matter." He encouraged them to go out of their way to consider the feelings of the people, his concern for which was the natural consequence of the importance he attached to respecting local customs.

In 1904, when the land survey was largely complete, the colonial government bought out all the large landholders with public bonds and granted the small landholders complete ownership of the land. The large rent was accordingly abolished, and small landholders were thereafter obligated to pay a tax equivalent to their existing small rent plus the large rent. The survey also brought to light a large number of unregistered plots, so that 1.7 times more land was uncovered than had been expected. Determining land ownership and ensuring its exclusivity in this fashion was, needless to say, an essential precondition for modernization and modern capitalism. When, in 1904, historian and politician Takekoshi Yosaburō witnessed what this project had achieved, he wrote that land tax reforms carried out by the Meiji government in Japan in 1874 were "child's play" by comparison.[8] Gotō considered this land survey one of his three greatest achievements in Taiwan, along with building the railway and constructing the harbor at Keelung.

2. "Civilizing" Taiwan

Developing a Transport Network

Having thus laid the foundations for Japanese rule in Taiwan, Gotō proceeded to implement a wide range of ambitious projects for developing the colony. He concentrated particularly on building a transport network of roads, railways, and harbors. This was indispensable for both more efficient governance of the island and industrial growth.

First, there was the problem of roads. When Japan took control of Taiwan, the island had almost no roads to speak of. There were pathways some thirty centimeters wide connecting villages and linking them to the towns, but

---

8   Takekoshi Yosaburō, *Taiwan tōchishi* [Japanese Rule in Taiwan] (Tokyo: Hakubunkan, 1905).

there were no modern roads connecting one town to another. That state of affairs made political unity impossible, besides of course presenting a serious obstacle to economic development.

The Japanese therefore put a great deal of effort into road building in Taiwan, about which Gotō was especially enthusiastic. He was later to become famous for the broad avenues he constructed, a predilection first displayed in the island colony. The length of road built during his term as civilian governor was as follows: 5,500 kilometers with a width of one *ken* (1.8 meters), 2,900 kilometers with a width of over one *ken*, 800 kilometers with a width of over three *ken* (5.4 meters), and 80 kilometers with a width of over four *ken* (7.2 meters). Most of these roads were built by surrendered guerrillas and local inhabitants conscripted as laborers.

The next issue was railways. Under Qing rule, about one hundred kilometers of track had been laid between Keelung and Hsinchu, a task that took seven years, starting in 1887. But it was a rickety railway indeed. The bridges were of timber, and whenever the train approached a slightly steep gradient, the passengers—who paid fares that varied from day to day—had to get out and push from behind.

After Japan annexed Taiwan, the Taiwan Railway Company, a private concern, was established with plans to build a railway traversing the island. The government, which welcomed this, granted the company a railway concession, let it have the existing track between Keelung and Hsinchu for free, and gave it many other privileges besides. Owing to the economic slump following the Sino-Japanese War, however, the company failed to raise the expected funds, and the start of construction was repeatedly delayed.

When Gotō arrived in Taiwan, the project was still stalled. Advocating government ownership, Gotō scrapped Taiwan Railway's 10-million-yen plan and drew up a 30-million-yen plan in its place. Once the necessary funding had been obtained with the passage of the Taiwan Public Works Bonds Act in 1899, he established the Taiwan Railway Department, which he headed himself, and pushed forward with the project while giving a free hand to Hasegawa Kinsuke, whom he had recruited from Nippon Railway in Japan. Thanks to the hard work of Gotō and others, the railway linking the north and south of the island was completed two years ahead of schedule, in April 1909, though by then Gotō was already in mainland China as president of the South Manchuria Railway. Taiwan's train system contributed greatly to the colony's political and economic unification and development; it also did well as a business.

For Gotō, of equal importance to building the railway was constructing a harbor at Keelung. He expanded the original construction plan he inherited into a major project costing 10 million yen, but that was slashed to a mere 2 million yen when the funding plan failed to win legislative approval. Then, starting in 1902, he submitted repeated plans for the second phase of construction, which finally passed in 1906 on a seven-year schedule. When the second phase was completed in 1911, plans for the third phase were promptly approved, indicating that Gotō had been right all along in his ambitious vision for this undertaking.

Expanding Public Health Facilities

Along with developing the transport network, Gotō gave priority to expanding public health facilities—an area in which, as former head of the Public Health Bureau, he had considerable expertise. Taiwan was known as a hotbed of infectious disease: even at the turn of the twentieth century, there were two separate years when more than 4,500 people contracted the plague.

Gotō's policies had several hallmarks: they were systematic, exhaustive, and on a massive scale. His approach to the issue of public health was no exception. He realized that installing water supply and sewerage facilities would need to be the centerpiece of the program. When Japan annexed Taiwan, running water was available in only two locations, Keelung and Tamsui, and that was for military use. Gotō energetically pushed ahead with the project, recruiting one of his old subordinates in the Public Health Bureau, Takagi Tomoe, to oversee it, and completed it ahead of parallel efforts at home in Japan.

Meanwhile he actively engaged in urban planning in Taiwan's major cities, transforming their appearance as a result. Takekoshi Yosaburō described his surprise on first visiting Taiwan in 1904 thus:

In my imagination, the Taiwanese capital was a typical Chinese city: narrow roads twelve to eighteen feet wide haphazardly paved with cobblestones and flagstones, slops flowing down the street, drinking water and sewage intermingled, piglets darting in and out of the townscape. But when I saw it, the Taiwanese capital was a typical European-style city: it was clean and spacious, and the roads were as well macadamized as the streets of Tokyo or even more so, while between the roadway and the pavement there were Singaporean-style open gutters paved in cement and stone, each a foot or two deep, to carry off slops and rainwater. This is what urban renewal results in. Or rather, I believe, it must be a case of urban remodeling.[9]

Among the other major public health initiatives that Gotō spearheaded was the establishment of the Taiwan Medical School in 1899, a move almost unanimously opposed by public opinion at the time. Teaching medicine when Japanese language education had yet to get off the ground was seen to be utter folly. Having in his youth studied medicine in Japanese translation at Sukagawa Medical School, rather than in the original languages, what emotions did Gotō feel when he proposed establishing this institution? He was doubtless convinced that it would serve an important purpose. Until the school began graduating students, the system of "public physicians" introduced in 1896, under which doctors were recruited from Japan, remained in place. This too Gotō had recommended when still in Japan as head of the Public Health Bureau.

Industrial Development

Having installed the necessary infrastructure, the colonial authorities turned to promoting industry in Taiwan. Gotō focused particularly on developing the sugar industry. He famously invited Nitobe Inazō, the author of *Bushido: The Soul of Japan*, from the United States for that purpose, and made him head of the Industrial Development Bureau.

---

9   Tsurumi Yūsuke, ed., *Ketteiban: Seiden Gotō Shinpei*, vol. 3 (Tokyo: Fujiwara Shoten, 2005), 437.

Nitobe later recalled that as soon as he arrived in Taiwan, he was sent to Java, then a prosperous Dutch colony, to study the sugar industry there, and on getting back was promptly asked to submit his views in writing. When he said that he wanted to do some more research first, Gotō replied, "No, that won't be necessary. Write the thing while you're still unfamiliar with Taiwan. Once you get to know what Taiwan is really like, your eyes will be dimmed and you will no longer be able to come up with bold ideas for reform. Write the thing through refined eyes that have seen Java. Write anything, even if it can't be done, as long as you write it through eyes that have seen the best." The result was Nitobe's set of recommendations on improvements to the sugar industry, which became the basis of the Taiwanese sugar industry.

Such exhaustive research led to improved varieties of sugar cane and methods of cultivation. Manuring in particular was encouraged. It is, generally speaking, not easy to persuade farmers in a traditional society to adopt new methods, but thanks to subsidies and other generous protective programs and incentives, sugar cane production expanded dramatically as new varieties and methods of cultivation rapidly caught on.

Sugar mills were also modernized and expanded. This move aroused opposition among traditional small-scale native producers, fear of which discouraged Japanese investors from coming to the island. But Gotō recruited banker and future politician Yamamoto Teijirō and gave him a free hand while providing generous protections, thus transforming the Taiwanese sugar industry. Sugar production, which stood at around 30,000 tons in 1900, rose to 60,000 tons by the end of the Kodama-Gotō era. In 1937 it passed the million-ton mark, and during the Pacific War it reached a maximum of 1.6 million tons. It is also true, however, that in the process, native sugar producers were wiped out and their land forcibly bought up.

There is not space here to describe Gotō's other industrialization policies. Suffice it to say that the Taiwanese economy, especially the sugar industry, grew remarkably. Taiwan ceased to be an economic burden on Japan and, unlike Japan's other colonies, became highly lucrative.

"Civilizing" Taiwan

After accepting the presidency of the South Manchuria Railway in July 1906, Gotō enumerated what he considered to be the keys to running Taiwan in a set of notes evidently intended for an address to his subordinates. This may be considered his farewell message to Taiwan. The opening items, in classic Gotō style, stressed the importance of "physiographic" and "biological considerations." The final item in the list was, intriguingly, "Pursue development in good taste," a statement that seems to come out of the blue. What exactly did he mean?

On arriving in Taiwan, Gotō promptly built an official residence for the governor-general that was so magnificent it was nicknamed the Epang Palace of Taiwan after the sumptuous palace of China's first emperor. Gotō countered that he had wanted to build an opera house on the grounds as well. The idea was to cow the people of Taiwan with architectural grandeur. The possibility was also considered of significantly raising the standard of other government residences, on the model of the governor-general's. Otherwise, Gotō believed, it would be difficult to attract capable people from Japan. He was not, however, motivated solely by utilitarian considerations. He seems to have taken great personal delight in "civilizing" Taiwan.

The same can be said of his urban planning and other projects. Unquestionably, the construction of water supply and sewage facilities was a means of creating healthier living conditions and placing industry on a firmer footing. Urban development was also a means of flaunting the power of Taiwan's Japanese rulers. But that was not all. For Gotō, who had studied in Berlin and Munich and attended international conferences in London and Rome, an attractive, imposing cityscape was in itself a mark of civilization. As a longstanding admirer of Western civilization who had not been entirely successful in assimilating it, he doubtless took great pride and pleasure in civilizing a corner of Asia. He therefore rejected a purely utilitarian approach to developing Taiwan. What was needed was "development in good taste," without which Japan would be unworthy of joining the ranks of the civilized nations. It would be mistaken to overlook this point and view Gotō's policies as simply a shrewd means of exercising control over the population.

Gotō's Political Methods

What political methods did Gotō use to attain such spectacular success? How can they be characterized? To those questions we now turn.

First, he was careful to remain close to Governor-General Kodama. While Kodama recognized his abilities and gave him a free hand, Gotō for his part went to great lengths to reinforce Kodama's trust in him. Despite being known for his caustic tongue and sometimes riding roughshod over others, Gotō was always impeccably polite to Kodama; even the language in which he addressed him was a model of courtesy. It is said that he never slept with his feet pointing in the direction of the governor-general's residence, because that would be disrespectful. Further, he always obtained Kodama's approval even when making relatively minor decisions. He had of course earned Kodama's trust for his policymaking ability, not for his obsequiousness, but he was well aware nonetheless that retaining Kodama's trust was vital and took every care to do so.

Kodama, it is said, intended to resign as governor-general of Taiwan on several occasions, most notably when he became deputy army chief of staff in 1903, and make Gotō his successor. To that end he even considered revising the regulation requiring that the governor-general be a serving general or lieutenant general. But Gotō firmly refused the position. Later, in 1916, when it was suggested to him that being a civilian should no longer be a bar to becoming governor-general of Taiwan, Gotō pointed out that "a military man comes in most handy both for showing the new subjects a commanding figure and for stopping party politicians from interfering." Indeed, having a military man as powerful as Kodama serving as governor-general was also advantageous in securing funding and so forth from the cabinet and legislature, and it kept the army in check.

It was especially important to stop the military from getting out of control. We have already seen how effective Kodama's strong leadership was, for example, in withdrawing the army from the front lines, a move absolutely essential to success against the guerrillas. No one but Kodama could have criticized the three-tier security system as he did in his speech of June 1898. In sum, the best way to keep the military under control was to enlist the cooperation of an influential officer who saw the big political picture.

That undoubtedly was the primary reason why Gotō subsequently formed close ties with senior army leaders like Katsura Tarō and then Terauchi Masatake, much as Yoshida Shigeru (who was to become prime minister after World War II) later befriended the likes of Terauchi, Tanaka Giichi, and Ugaki Kazushige. Whereas most military officers of the late 1920s through the 1940s were essentially army bureaucrats who did not see beyond the army's interests and concerns, Katsura, Kodama, and Terauchi, who enjoyed the backing of the Chōshū clique, were military statesmen of far greater caliber, having borne the nation's fate on their shoulders during the Sino-Japanese and Russo-Japanese Wars.

When dealing with entities other than the army, too, Gotō always targeted individuals who wielded great power. Getting them on his side and thus overcoming the opposition of the organization behind them was his usual modus operandi. For that reason he had an aversion to people who always spoke and acted as loyal members of their organization. He did not, for example, see eye to eye with Hara Takashi, despite his considerable influence as a senior figure in the Seiyūkai (Association of Political Friends) in that Hara never veered from the party line. Nor did he agree with most finance ministry bureaucrats in that they always insisted on a balanced budget with only a few exceptions.

In other words, political power was for Gotō something to be borrowed when required. He was relatively uninterested in building his own power base. This explains why he chalked up a string of successes virtually unmatched by any other Japanese politician; it also explains why he never reached the summit of political power.

Just as Gotō was personally loyal to Kodama, he took a thoroughly personalistic approach to choosing his own subordinates. He searched all over Japan for capable people and often blatantly poached them. He would offer them the best employment conditions he could and then leave the job entirely to them, trusting in their abilities. After recruiting Nitobe Inazō, Gotō was only able to award him fifth rank in the civil service for official career reasons, but he browbeat the finance ministry into paying him a first-rank salary anyway, a move that was unprecedented.

On the organizational front, Gotō boldly tore down old administrative structures and built new ones in their place. When embarking on a major project, he would typically set up a temporary organization and assume its helm himself, the Taiwan land survey being a case in point. By nominally taking personal charge, he prevented outside interference and thus enabled his subordinates to do what they did best. It was projects like these at which he excelled.

Conversely, Gotō appears to have constantly been on his guard against the bloating of ordinary bureaucratic structures. On first arriving in Taiwan, he streamlined the administrative service by discharging many personnel, in part to save money for hiring more capable people, in part to reinvigorate the bureaucracy by changing its way of thinking. Organizations were for Gotō a means of executing projects, and he thought nothing of completely remaking them to match his goals. To ensure the success of his projects, he constantly had to fend off bureaucratic turf wars and combat the tendency of bureaucratic organizations to become overstaffed.

His emphasis on personal ability must, conversely, have appeared callous to men of mediocre talent. A network that could be called the Gotō faction later emerged centering on Taiwan, Manchuria, and the Japanese Railway Agency. All its members were technocrats who excelled in their own particular field, and they were motivated more by a determination to make a project succeed than by loyalty to their organization. They therefore had less organizational leverage than their fame might suggest, and that in turn limited Gotō's political influence as their leader.

Gotō's Personality

During his Taiwan years, Gotō was 163.6 centimeters tall and weighed 72.4 kilograms—short and plump by today's standards, but back then an imposing build indeed. Kodama was only about 150 centimeters tall, so Gotō had quite a physical presence in comparison. This bothered Kodama so much that he disliked being photographed with Gotō. On one occasion he stood on a crate that happened to be at hand so that he looked the same height.

Gotō prided himself on his good health and was full of vim and vigor. He always got up between four and four thirty, even when he went to bed after midnight, and he enjoyed taking a walk early each morning. He had a hearty appetite, very seldom drank, and was always bursting with energy.

Gotō was a handsome man with a fair complexion; he grew a great bushy beard during his days in Nagoya to camouflage his youthful good looks, about which he was shy. That unkempt beard looked terrible on him, people thought, and when he was in Germany, some friends cropped it as a joke; thus he ended up with a *Spitzbart* (a Vandyke beard), then the latest fashion. It suited Gotō surprisingly well, and he sported it for the rest of his life, visiting the barber every other day for a trim. When he was in Taiwan, he got into the habit of wearing a pince-nez, which was likewise the latest fashion.

Gotō was quite a snappy dresser. In Sukagawa, Fukushima where he went to medical school, his appearance had been downright squalid because of his poverty, but after moving to Nagoya he became more particular about what he wore. During his years with the Public Health Bureau he looked somewhat like a country squire, and in Germany his appearance was rather scruffy. Taiwan, though, was where he really came into his own fashion-wise: he cut a dashing figure in full uniform adorned with his medals. But he was not genuinely stylish or refined. He was in essence an unsophisticated man with a childlike fondness for the new and unusual and all that glittered.

One example of Gotō's fondness for new things was his fascination with bicycles. Back when there were only two or three bicycles in the whole of Taiwan, he promptly had a pair delivered, and for a while an early-morning ride with his wife became part of his daily routine—evidently much to her consternation. She had to practice cycling at night, since it would not do for the wife of the civilian governor to be seen falling off her bike.

Another example of his fondness for new things was his introduction of the phonograph to Taiwan. He wrote two songs for schoolchildren, "Mount Niitaka" and "Friends of the World," and, at his own expense, had a record of them cut by Columbia Records in the United States, which he then distributed throughout the island. That took some nerve. Moving pictures were a further case in point. Gotō ordered several from the United States when they were still a rarity in Japan and had them shown in various locations. Senior officials with the colonial government were assigned the job of providing live narration.

At any rate, Gotō was immensely curious about all things new. Just as he believed in the "biological principle," he believed in the progress of civilization and constantly strove to keep up with it. That enterprising spirit was the source of his many brilliant ideas.

He liked to meet people and engage in discussion in the quest for new ideas. Once he organized a reading group, though he appears primarily to have listened to others summarize what they had read. It is doubtful whether he was an avid reader himself. There were reports that he often read works in German, but that is highly unlikely.

While Gotō excelled at coming up with new ideas, he was not good at systematically explaining them to others. Most of his policy memoranda are replete with overblown language and longwinded expressions and leaps of logic that make them extremely difficult to read. While they brim with brilliant ideas, those ideas are jumbled together in confusion. And nowhere was his lack of communication skills more evident than in his speeches. Recordings of him speaking survive from the 1920s, and they demonstrate that he was an unusually poor speaker for a politician of that era.

Gotō displayed a similar lack of interpersonal communication skills. He was notorious for bawling people out, but then he would act as if nothing had happened. On the other hand, he was known for caring deeply about his subordinates. Once, when a young man to whom he had assigned a difficult task reported back, he rewarded him for his toils by taking him out for a bath at the public bathhouse. Stories like that abound. In short, Gotō was not the kind of man who could patiently explain his thoughts. Even when it came to commending a subordinate on a job well done, all he could manage was bathing together.

Whether it came to reading or public speaking, Gotō's great weakness was, in a word, his lack of learning. Journalist and historian Tokutomi Sohō hit the mark when he said that Gotō lacked a "trained mind." Gotō was a dashing, larger-than-life figure in all he said and did, almost to the point of being uncouth. That was why, when he was made a baron (*danshaku*) in April 1906 for his achievements in governing Taiwan, people sarcastically but affectionately nicknamed him the "Barbaron" (*banshaku*, a pun on the Japanese words for "baron" and "barbaric").

3. Relations with China and the United States

Relations with China

Taiwan was not Gotō's sole concern during these years. While talking about civilizing Taiwan, he was thinking globally, and in the course of governing the colony, he started to become involved in the actual intricacies of diplomacy.

Taiwan was often regarded more as a stepping stone to mainland China than as an economic asset in its own right. The second governor-general, Katsura Tarō, for example, was strongly inclined to that view. Gotō, by contrast, was less prone to such thinking. He was initially concerned with establishing order in Taiwan and developing its economy. But that, ironically, brought him face to face with the problem of the mainland by highlighting the closeness of Taiwan's relations with it. In the course of grappling with the issue of the Taiwanese economy, he came to realize that it was controlled by the landed gentry on the mainland, especially in Fujian Province, and formed part of the mainland Chinese economy. In a memorandum that appears to date from around autumn of 1898, he wrote, "Now, as a result of my investigations . . . I have concluded that it would not be wrong to say that the Taiwanese economy is actually centered on the opposite shore, namely in Qing China."

Gotō therefore decided to attempt to detach the Taiwanese economy from the mainland while, on the other hand, taking advantage of existing ties with the mainland to expand there. For instance, not only did he argue for immediately establishing a branch of the Bank of Taiwan in Amoy (Xiamen), he also thought that more than half the bank's assets should be deposited there. Thus the mainland became of concern to him for specifically economic reasons. He accordingly paid his first visit to Fujian Province in April 1900.

But within a few short months, the question of relations between Taiwan and the mainland was to become brutally political as the Boxer Rebellion escalated and spread to the south of China. In the face of this development, Governor-General Kodama hoped to "take advantage of this incident in northern China to preserve the peace, at least in Fujian Province, with the boon and might of our Empire, make this province Japan's sphere of influence substantially, and thus lay the foundations for addressing international issues in the future." Gotō, it is fair to assume, was basically of the same opinion.

The unrest also spread to Fujian. When the Japanese Honganji temple mission in Amoy was burned down, the Japanese used it as a pretext to send naval land forces (the equivalent of marines), and at one point decided to occupy the port of Amoy. But when Gotō secretly sailed to Amoy on August 23 to make the necessary preparations, a sudden order calling off the plan awaited him there. The government, yielding to the arguments of Itō Hirobumi and others who feared becoming embroiled in a dispute with the Western powers, got cold feet at the last moment. The Honganji temple had in fact been set on fire by the Japanese, and the British and Americans had already found out. Thus Gotō's plans to expand to the mainland foundered on the harsh reality of international relations.

The Amoy Incident was Gotō's first taste, as it were, of diplomacy in the conventional sense of the term. It held or reinforced several lessons for him.

First, he regarded the Amoy Incident as a Japanese defeat by the Western powers. Mainland China was the scene of ruthless international competition, and the Japanese had lost and the British and Americans had won. It strengthened his belief that overseas expansion was the direct expression of the vitality of the state and the nation, and neither retreat nor stasis was an option when expanding overseas.

Second, Gotō became acutely aware of the difficulty of military expansion without powerful economic backing. Though he remained an expansionist, he almost never advocated the use of military force. After the Amoy Incident he reverted to his old policy of establishing closer economic ties with the mainland. He concentrated on setting up and running a joint Sino-Japanese venture called the Sango Company, producing camphor in Fujian, and operating a railway in Canton (Guangdong) Province called the Chao–Shan Railway. In so doing he gave priority to developing de facto economic ties that would drive overseas expansion in accordance with his "policy of working with the local gentry." He did not insist on establishing a nominal monopoly.

American Imperialism

The Amoy Incident also made Gotō conscious of the importance of the United States. His interest in that country was subsequently fundamental in defining his foreign policy. Let us therefore take a moment here to describe the rise of the new American empire in East Asia.

The decisive turning point in the United States' evolution into an imperialist power was the Spanish-American War of 1898. Along with strengthened influence in the Caribbean and throughout the Americas, the US acquired the Philippines and Guam, thus advancing deep into Asia and the Pacific. Because the US had originally been founded on anti-colonial principles, there was strong resistance inside the country to the idea of building a formal empire possessing its own colonies—though having an informal empire by exerting what was in effect imperialist influence over neighboring regions, without actually colonizing them, was another matter. Domestic resistance was all the stronger because what was at issue was colonizing a region that, geographically and racially, was highly unlikely ever to be integrated into the United States. Therefore, from the summer of 1898 until the presidential election of fall 1900, a debate raged over colonial rule—what is known as the imperialism debate. But after the reelection of William McKinley (whose vice president was Theodore Roosevelt) and the defeat of William Jennings Bryan in the fall 1900 election, American imperialism was for the moment vindicated at home.

The American annexation of the Philippines occurred only three years after Japan acquired Taiwan in the Sino-Japanese War and, coincidentally, in the same year as Gotō arrived in Taiwan. The Philippines are, needless to say, immediately south of Taiwan across the Bashi Channel. The United States subsequently had to crush the Filipino independence movement, and it did not finally assert control over the archipelago until 1902—the same year Kodama and Gotō suppressed the Taiwan "bandits." The new imperialist powers of Japan and the United States thus vied at close quarters to govern their respective colonies of Taiwan and the Philippines.

Meanwhile US secretary of state John Hay issued his famous "Open Door" note on China in September 1899, followed by a second one in July 1900, in the midst of the Boxer Rebellion. This second note included an additional principle, the importance of respecting China's "territorial and administrative integrity," that made even clearer American opposition to any further colonization of China. The dispatch of troops to Amoy planned by Kodama and Gotō, which was in fact to take place in the month following this second statement, directly clashed with American policy.

The United States, along with Britain, actually lodged a protest against Japan's plan to dispatch troops to Amoy and sent warships with the intention of landing marines there to restore order. It also lent funds to the Qing government. The American role in thwarting Japan's plan in Amoy was thus as significant as Britain's, though it would perhaps be an overstatement to say that it was more so. Britain had a long-established presence in China, and the prominence of its role was hardly surprising. What was noteworthy was the rapid expansion of American activity in the country. In that sense, Gotō was justified in believing that the Americans had been central in checking the Japanese dispatch of troops to Amoy. At any rate, Gotō must have become acutely conscious of the rivalry unfolding between Japan and the United States in Fujian and throughout China as they competed to develop their respective colonies in Taiwan and the Philippines.

McKinley was assassinated in 1901, the year after he won reelection as US president. Theodore Roosevelt, an even more vocal advocate of imperialism, became president, a development that could not have failed to interest Gotō. In fact, it was around this time that the United States came to feature prominently in various aspects of his life.

Nitobe Inazō, who had been educated at Johns Hopkins University, arrived in Taiwan to take up his position as head of the Industrial Development Bureau in February 1901, after spending a year on a study tour of Europe. Several years before he had resigned his professorship at Sapporo Agricultural College because of ill health and gone to convalesce in the United States, where he wrote (in English) *Bushido: The Soul of Japan*. Gotō had recruited him in the fall of 1899, during this stay in the US. Gotō and Nitobe were personal friends as well as professional colleagues, and their friendship was enduring. Nitobe later accompanied Gotō on his two trips to North America and Europe at the latter's request; and when Gotō with several others endowed a chair in colonial policy in memory of Kodama

Gentarō at Tokyo Imperial University, Nitobe was the first person to hold it.

Another old America hand with whom Gotō became acquainted at this time was Hoshi Hajime, a friend of Nitobe's who had graduated from Columbia University despite financial hardship and published a small English-language magazine. Hoshi first met Gotō in the spring of 1902, and the two formed a lasting friendship. Gotō called him "the American" and enjoyed listening to his stories of the United States. Later, in the Taishō era (1912–1926), others familiar with the United States joined Gotō's circle, including the politician and writer Tsurumi Yūsuke, who became his son-in-law, and news agency director Iwanaga Yūkichi. Not many other politicians of his day were acquainted with so many intellectuals knowledgeable about the United States. Gotō saw Germany as his mentor and later Russia as his friend, but in fact he appears to have been most intrigued and influenced by the United States.

In June 1902, Gotō departed on a tour of North America and Europe accompanied by Nitobe, having sent Hoshi ahead. Unfortunately, there are few records of what Gotō saw on his first visit to the United States or how he reacted; it is known, however, that he was almost completely uninterested in the natural scenery and concentrated on studying colonial policy while observing industrial civilization in general, the progress of which impressed him deeply. To Gotō, the United States, like Germany, appeared to be a life form bursting with vitality and evolving at breakneck pace. His fellow traveler Nitobe was strongly influenced by the social Darwinism of Herbert Spencer, the British philosopher and scientist, so it was perhaps inevitable that what Gotō observed was not the mature civilizations of Britain or France, but rather the rising powers of the Germany of Wilhelm II and the United States of Theodore Roosevelt.

Gotō and Theodore Roosevelt

Gotō was later to become a great admirer of President Roosevelt. In an article entitled "My View of Mr. Roosevelt" published in the November 1908 issue of the magazine *Jitsugyō no Nippon* (Business Japan), he wrote, "Observing the current president of the United States, Mr. Roosevelt, from day to day, I have come to admire him for bearing himself like a paragon of the fighting hero, and I readily express my deepest esteem for him." He then characterized Roosevelt's stance on the anti-Japanese immigration movement that swept California in 1906 as follows:

> Mr. Roosevelt was most indignant when the issue of excluding Japanese children from schools arose in San Francisco. He criticized the citizens of San Francisco for their unfairness, and explained why the Japanese people deserved to be respected, in a presidential message that was truly irresistible in its sincerity, dignified language, and unflinching spirit. I thought to myself at the time, this is a man who can rival the light of the sun and the moon in the beauty of his character and the sublimity of his mind. . . . Even if there are indications of a tempering of his views out of consideration for public opinion, anyone can see that, through the fairness of his attitude in admonishing his own people for their injustice and in respecting the honor of the Japanese, he displayed integrity in the truest sense of the term.

Saying that Roosevelt could "rival the light of the sun and the moon" borders on the extravagant. The only other men whom the sharp-tongued Gotō praised so highly were German chancellor Otto von Bismarck and the scholar Fukuzawa Yukichi. He was impressed by Roosevelt because in him he saw the ideal statesman: a consummate leader, a physician—never led astray by popular opinion—the uniformed views of his patients. And behind that quality he identified a kind of bushido.

> Mr. Roosevelt is just like a warrior of old in his bearing, attitude, and inclinations. . . . Whenever Mr. Roosevelt speaks, he talks of the American spirit—that is his bushido. Now, analyzed scientifically, bushido is the means by which all living creatures ensure their own survival. Biting a cat when cornered is how a mouse exercises its particular form of bushido. The English have their version of bushido, and so too do the Germans. The American bushido that Mr. Roosevelt speaks of consists of respecting freedom, honoring

justice, championing the fighting life for his people, and promoting mankind's spirit of self-improvement. Whenever a problem arises, Mr. Roosevelt does not stop until he practices what he preaches about fighting. You can tell how noble his character is, and how steadfast his ideas.

Here Gotō uses the term "bushido" to mean a willingness to fight in order to develop the life force of one's nation and advance human civilization as a whole. Each nation, he argues, possesses its own version of bushido with traits rooted in its history, and Roosevelt exemplified the American version. Although Gotō later advocated opposition to the United States, he did not view the two countries as irreconcilable enemies, but rather as rivals competing in accordance with the same principles and therefore worthy of mutual respect.

Just as Nitobe and the Boxer Rebellion were the twin catalysts for Gotō's discovery of America, they also catalyzed Roosevelt's discovery of Japan. Nitobe's *Bushido* made a profound impression on Roosevelt, as is well known, and the Boxer Rebellion led him to take a deep interest in Japanese foreign policy. The two rising imperial powers, despite being in competition, also had much in common.

The Russo–Japanese War

As we have seen, running Taiwan brought Gotō face to face with China, and the Boxer Rebellion brought him face to face with the US. Later, in the final years of his tenure as civilian governor of Taiwan, his mind was increasingly occupied, of course, by Russia.

Gotō's views on the Russo-Japanese War of 1904–05 are notable in several regards. First, from the start of the war, he argued for steering international relations in a direction favorable to Japan. Specifically, he advocated bringing about the intervention of the other powers in Japan's favor. Second, he argued that Japan should put itself at an advantage in raising foreign loans by courting international opinion. To that end he thought it particularly important to stir up anti-Russian sentiment among Jewish financiers in the United States by mounting a publicity campaign there. Third, apparently when the Portsmouth Peace Conference was in progress, he contended that Japan should make peace as soon as possible without being inflexible in its demands for territory and an indemnity, describing his policy as "the softest of so-called soft lines."

These policies were not particularly original. They were largely those that the government's leaders actually carried out. Nevertheless, Gotō's views, such as his idea of enlisting the support of Jewish financiers, reveal surprising insight for a colonial administrator. Most noteworthy was his advocacy of an early peace, which was motivated by more than Japan's dwindling ability to keep fighting. He argued, on a more positive note, that instead of incurring Russian resentment by imposing draconian peace terms and pressing its material interests too insistently, and thus losing the sympathy of the other major powers, it would be wiser to "raise the country's status and power to a critical place in international relations," something of which he felt "the shallow, avaricious hardliners are incapable." Gotō envisaged two men with the ability to oversee such a foreign policy: Otto von Bismarck and Theodore Roosevelt.

Here we can observe Gotō applying his "biological" view of politics to actual international relations. Moreover, as we have seen, the countries that were to remain of most interest to him in later years, namely Germany, China, the United States, and Russia, had by now all come to form part of his perception of the outside world. With the basic outlines of his foreign policy now largely in place, he was ready to become a foreign policy leader as president of the South Manchuria Railway.

CHAPTER 3

PRESIDENT OF
THE SOUTH MANCHURIA RAILWAY

1. Assumption of the Presidency

The Political Situation after the Russo-Japanese War

In November 1906, Gotō stepped down as civilian governor of Taiwan to become the first president of the newly created South Manchuria Railway Company (SMR). Before discussing his assumption of that post, it would be well to outline the international and domestic political situation at the time.

Japan's victory in the Russo-Japanese War was an event of great significance in world history. First, it kindled nationalism in non-Western countries. Many of the leaders of the wave of countries that gained independence after World War II were in their younger days galvanized by the news of Japan's victory in this earlier conflict. Second, the Russo-Japanese War escalated tensions in and around Europe. The unusually long period of peace that Europe had enjoyed since the 1870 Franco-Prussian War correlated with the aggressive expansion of European powers outside Europe. When their advance was checked by the Russo-Japanese War, however, their interest began to revert to Europe and its environs. The conflict was in that sense an indirect cause of World War I. In both regards the Russo-Japanese War heralded the start of Europe's decline.

The Russo-Japanese War was also a significant turning point in modern Japanese history. The greatest challenge Japan had previously faced was ensuring its own independence, which most politicians, officials, and ordinary Japanese believed would be imperiled if the Korean Peninsula fell under the control of a powerful third state (though whether in fact Japan's independence was seriously threatened is another question). In that sense Japan's

foreign policy agenda had been fairly clear and straightforward. Victory in the Russo-Japanese War, ironically, deprived Japan of this obvious objective.

Japan's political leadership, too, underwent a significant transformation. Until the Russo-Japanese War, the genro, or elder statesmen, whose formative experience had been the Meiji Restoration, were at the center of political power and could act in unison at times of crisis. But after the war the elder statesmen withdrew from the political front line and yielded way to a younger generation of politicians. Two of the latter, Katsura Tarō and Saionji Kinmochi, were eventually to be treated as elder statesmen themselves, but they were the creations of the Meiji state, so to speak, not its creators. Katsura and Saionji were, now that the bureaucratization of state institutions was well advanced, far more beholden to the interests of whatever organization lay behind them than had been their predecessors. This made it even more difficult for the political leadership to reach a consensus on national goals.

Next, let us examine the international environment in which Japan found itself after the Russo-Japanese War ended in September 1905. Russia, to begin with, remained a formidable rival of which Japan needed to be extremely wary. Fears that a second war with Russia could break out were widespread. Elder statesman Yamagata Aritomo, for example, opined in a memorandum on postwar policy written immediately before the

Portsmouth Peace Conference that "the present peace is most accurately viewed as a rather extended truce."[1]

Relations with Qing China, meanwhile, had deteriorated. China had been relatively favorably disposed to Japan during the Russo-Japanese War, but only because the Russian occupation of Manchuria was the greatest threat to the country. Qing China was hardly likely to continue being friendly after the war, when Japan's occupation of South Manchuria presented a new threat. Moreover, the rise of nationalism in the non-white world triggered by Japan's victory had affected China as well. Indeed, the Chinese found the incursion of the Japanese, who were of the same race, even more intolerable than that of the Western powers. In any case, China was even more intransigent than the Japanese had expected, and the two countries clashed constantly over Japanese policy in Manchuria.

Another significant development was the deterioration of relations with the United States. During the war, the United States had been sympathetic to the Japanese cause because Russia was intent on occupying Manchuria and shutting out the other powers, whereas Japan supported the Open Door. After the war, though, Japan dragged its feet over opening Manchuria to the outside world, a stance that increasingly frustrated the US State Department, as it also did Britain, which despite being an ally was likewise unhappy with Japan's closed-door policy in Manchuria.

Japan's international relations after the war with Russia were thus fraught with difficulties. In view of the Russian threat, the Japanese army was reluctant to lift military rule and open Manchuria to the outside world. In addition, adopting an open-door policy might promptly force Japan to give up much ground owing to its economic weakness. The state of affairs, however, would never be acceptable to the Chinese and was bound to make the British and Americans even more critical of Japan.

To cope with these difficulties, a conference on the Manchurian question was held in May 1906 and attended by all Japan's top leaders, including the elder statesmen, the prime minister, and the heads of the military. It was presided over by one of the elder statesmen, Itō Hirobumi, who was

---

1 Ōyama Azusa, ed., *Yamagata Aritomo Ikensho* (Hara Shobō, 1966), 287.

apprehensive about British and American criticism of Japan. Here the decision was made to lift military rule in Manchuria and promptly open it up to the outside world, but that did not mean that Japan was ready to retreat from Manchuria. A vehicle for the projection of Japanese power was needed in place of the army, and around that time plans to set up the South Manchuria Railway Company to serve that purpose rapidly began to take shape.

Origins of the South Manchuria Railway

What was the nature of the South Manchuria Railway? Under the terms of the Treaty of Portsmouth, the peace agreement between Japan and Russia signed in September 1905, Japan gained two important concessions in Manchuria as a result of its victory in the war with Russia: Russia's leases on Port Arthur (Lüshun) and Dairen (Dalian), and its rights to the railway connecting Changchun to both cities. Because these had been acquired by the Russians from the Chinese government, their transfer to Japan required Chinese approval. Japan and China therefore signed a separate treaty concerning Manchuria (the Peking Treaty) in December.

The history of the Manchurian Railway goes back to 1896, when the Chinese government granted Russia the right to build a railway across Chinese territory connecting the Trans-Siberian Railway to the Pacific coast and to operate it for eighty years. The Trans-Siberian Railway, on which construction began in 1891, was originally to run from Lake Baikal via Chita and continue directly east (Trans-Baikal Railway), then detour along the north bank of the Amur (Heilong) River forming the boundary between Russia and China (Amur Railway) before turning at Khabarovsk and following the Ussuri River south and reaching Vladivostok (Ussuri Railway). The Amur route, however, was a roundabout way to the Pacific and presented considerable engineering difficulties. The idea therefore arose of building the line across Chinese territory instead, which the Russians then acquired the right to do. The Chinese Eastern Railway Company was established in 1897 to exercise that right.

When Russia acquired its leases in the Liaodong Peninsula in 1898, it also acquired the right to build a railway connecting the peninsula with Harbin, the main hub of the Chinese Eastern Railway. Three years earlier, of course,

Russia had, with Germany and France, pressured Japan into returning the Liaodong Peninsula to China during the Tripartite Intervention. Now, on that very peninsula, Russia planned to build a naval port in Port Arthur and a trading port in Qingniwa (or Dalny, as Dairen was earlier called) and link both to Harbin by rail. This line would form the southern branch of the Chinese Eastern Railway. Russia thus achieved its longstanding dreams of reaching the Pacific and acquiring an ice-free port. This positioned it to assert control over Manchuria.

The 970-kilometer southern branch of the Chinese Eastern Railway, though only about two-thirds the length of the main line, was thus of vital importance. In fact, the main line west of Harbin was completed first, then the southern branch, and only then the main line east of Harbin (in 1903). In that sense the route from the Trans-Siberian Railway via Harbin to Port Arthur and Dairen could be considered the main line and that from Harbin to Vladivostok the branch line.

Furthermore, the Chinese Eastern Railway Company was able to acquire the roadbed for the tracks with a strip of land on either side along the entire length of the railway, as well as purchase an extensive area of land around each of the major stations, all for the nominal purpose of operating the railway. That land, known as the railroad zone, was under the company's administration and exempt from Chinese jurisdiction. Additionally, the company was allowed to operate mines and other businesses as well, and it had the right to station fifteen troops per kilometer, ostensibly to keep order in the railroad zone.

The Chinese Eastern Railway was, in sum, much more than just a railway. It was an industrial combine running a host of subsidiary businesses, a regional authority with administrative powers, and, inasmuch as it had its own army and handled certain aspects of diplomatic relations with China, virtually a colonial government.

Japan acquired the three-quarters of the Chinese Eastern Railway's southern branch between Port Arthur on the coast and Changchun—a distance of more than 700 kilometers—along with all associated privileges. Besides this line connecting Port Arthur and Dairen to Changchun, southern Manchuria had one other railway of considerable length, the Anfeng Line, a light railway

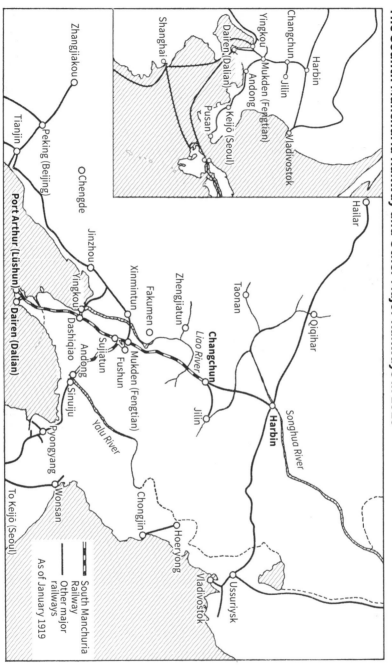

The Sounth Manchuria Railway and Other Major Railways in 1919

Zhangjiakou

Tianjin
Peking (Beijing)

Chengde

Jinzhou

Port Arthur (Lüshun)
Dairen (Dalian)

Yingkou
Dashiqiao
Andong
Sinuiju

Pyongyang

To Keijō (Seoul)

Wonsan

Xinmintun
Fakumen
Suijiatun
Fushun
Mukden (Fengtian)

Yalu River

Zhengjiatun

Chongjin

Hoeryong

Liao River

Jilin

Changchun

Taonan

Qiqihar

Hailar

Harbin

Songhua River

Vladivostok

Ussuriysk

South Manchuria
Railway
Other major
railways
As of January 1919

Shanghai

Dairen (Dalian)
Andong

Yingkou
Changchun
Jilin
Mukden (Fengtian)
Keijō (Seoul)
Pusan

Harbin

Vladivostok

over 200 kilometers long connecting Andong (present-day Dandong) on the Korean border with Mukden (Fengtian, present-day Shenyang), which Japanese forces had built for military purposes during the war. The rights to operate the Anfeng Line were one of the items on the negotiating table at the December 1905 Peking conference, where the Japanese got the better of the Chinese and won a concession for eighteen years (one year for repatriating troops, two years for upgrades, plus a further fifteen years).

On October 27, before this conference, the cabinet of Prime Minister Katsura Tarō decided that the Dairen–Changchun Line and the Anfeng Line should be operated by a single company modeled closely on the Chinese Eastern Railway. Some argued for nationalizing it, but that option was rejected at this stage. The establishment of the railway company was delayed because, as already mentioned, military rule continued for some time after, but the matter assumed urgency when in May 1906 the decision was made to put an immediate end to military rule. On June 7, an imperial ordinance was issued mandating the establishment of the South Manchuria Railway Company, which was to take the form of a joint-stock company partly owned by the government. And who was to be put in charge of it? Gotō, having accomplished so much in Taiwan, was singled out for the job that same month.

Assumption of the Presidency

There is a well-known story about how the idea for the South Manchuria Railway originated. In May 1904, when Japanese forces had finally crossed the Yalu River and just entered Manchuria, Kodama Gentarō allegedly instructed his subordinates to do research on the East India Company. He is said to have originally gotten the idea from Gotō. Gotō (so the story goes) had already started considering the possibility of managing Japanese interests in Manchuria through a railway company on the model of the East India Company, a non-government organization acting as a colonial government under the guise of doing business. It is somewhat debatable whether Kodama and Gotō were really thinking along these lines when the outcome of the Russo-Japanese War was still very much in doubt, but in Gotō's case it is not inconceivable.

At any rate, by the war's end at the latest, Gotō and Kodama had already agreed that the railway should be central to managing Japanese interests in Manchuria. Just before the Treaty of Portsmouth was signed, Gotō drew up a memorandum entitled "Outline of Policy for Administering Manchurian Affairs," which received Kodama's approval when Gotō submitted it to him on a visit to Manchuria at the beginning of September. It began, "The one and only key to postwar administration of Manchurian affairs is overtly to adopt the guise of operating a railway while covertly implementing a full range of measures."

At this time Kodama's prestige as the de facto supreme commander of the land campaign in the Russo-Japanese War had risen greatly. One purpose of Gotō's visit to Manchuria was, at Prime Minister Katsura's behest, to sound Kodama out about whether he was willing to form a new government.[2] The two men must also have had a lively discussion about how Japan's interests in Manchuria should be managed after the war. Kodama was subsequently appointed the head of the Manchuria Administration Committee formed in January 1906, which originally drafted the above-mentioned imperial ordinance of June 7 as well as other important documents determining the framework of the South Manchuria Railway. These included the order to the company issued by the ministers of foreign affairs, finance, and communications on August 1.[3] It is therefore fair to assume that the views of Kodama and Gotō were adopted by the government. For that reason, too, it was only natural that Gotō should have been recommended for the presidency of the railway.

Gotō for his part was already considering leaving Taiwan for new pastures. He and his immediate circle, it appears, vaguely had in mind Korea as his next destination. In a lengthy telegram of June 28 to Taiwan, political powerbroker Sugiyama Shigemaru explained that support for making Gotō president of the SMR was growing and urged him to go to Korea

---

2   Hara Keiichirō, ed., *Hara Takashi nikki* [The Diary of Hara Takashi], vol. 2 (Tokyo: Fukumura Shuppan, 1965), 152 (Oct. 6, 1905).

3   Harada Katsumasa, *Mantetsu* [The South Manchuria Railway] (Tokyo: Iwanami Shoten, 1981), 49.

after a stint in Manchuria. Gotō was eventually ordered back to Tokyo, where, on July 22, he met with Home Minister Hara Takashi and Prime Minister Saionji Kinmochi, as well as Army Chief of Staff Kodama Gentarō, who chaired the SMR Founding Committee formed on July 13, and elder statesman Yamagata Aritomo. All urged him to accept the presidency of the SMR. Kodama, who already agreed with Gotō on policy in Manchuria, was particularly insistent. On that day, however, Gotō firmly refused.

In a sudden turn of events, Kodama, having spent several hours trying to persuade Gotō to take the job, died suddenly the next morning. Gotō was determined to honor Kodama's memory by complying with what had turned out to be his dying wishes, and several days later, on August 1, he made clear his intention of accepting the presidency of the SMR.

Gotō, however, probably never intended to persist in refusing the post. He initially turned it down because, given the immensity and difficulty of the task it entailed, he wished to impose several conditions first. Even after the unexpected turn of events persuaded him to accept, he presented several conditions to Prime Minister Saionji and Yamagata. He also drew up a memorandum entitled "Circumstances of My Assumption of the Presidency of the SMR," which, between August 22 and 28, he submitted to Foreign Minister Hayashi Tadasu, Yamagata Aritomo, Army Minister Terauchi Masatake, who chaired the SMR Founding Committee after Kodama's sudden death, and Prime Minister Saionji. The document reviewed the background to his acceptance of the position with a view to securing the cooperation of these men.

Where did Gotō's concerns lie? In his memorandum, he wrote that he was troubled above all by the "lack of a center of colonial policy." It was unclear, in other words, who or what would play the central role in managing Japan's interests in Manchuria. More specifically, an organizational framework had yet to be created that placed the SMR at the heart of managing those interests.

He was particularly concerned about the army, which at the time had a free hand in Manchuria, and had strongly opposed the immediate lifting of military rule. The railway too was, needless to say, under army control. After military rule ended, the Japanese leasehold in Port Arthur and Dairen was named the Kwantung Territory, and the Kwantung Government-General (the organizational structure of which was announced on August 1, 1906) was set up to administer it. The Government-General was headed by a governor-general who was to be a serving general or lieutenant general of the army, an arrangement that ensured continued army influence. The governor-general also oversaw the SMR. That was why, after Kodama's sudden death, Gotō approached Yamagata, the most powerful figure in the army, and Army Minister Terauchi to seek a commitment of support from both. Having often relied on Kodama's influence over the army during his tenure in Taiwan, he now adopted the same tack in Manchuria, where again he thought it of decisive importance to keep the army in check. Indeed, such thinking had led him at one point to advocate appointing a military officer to the presidency of the SMR.

The army was not all that made the "lack of a center of colonial policy" such a serious concern. The SMR was subject not only to the governor-general of Kwantung Territory in Manchuria, but also to the Ministry of Foreign Affairs in Tokyo. The ministry was, despite the many consulates it had in Manchuria, not very enthusiastic about colonizing the region. This deeply alarmed Gotō, who wrote in his memorandum, "The foreign ministry's stance on colonial policy, it must be said, has long been hollow and ineffectual." In addition, the SMR had to obey the Ministry of Communications with respect to the railway's operations and the Ministry of Finance with respect to raising loans overseas and other financial matters. Gotō was naturally concerned that being subject to such controls would hinder the SMR's ability to play the central role in managing Japan's interests in Manchuria.

Gotō accomplished little in his attempt to alleviate the problem of the "lack of a center of colonial policy" other than securing an advisory role for the president of the SMR in the Government-General to ensure smooth coordination of responsibilities between the railway and the authorities. Disagreements between the three sides concerned—the army and the Government-General, the foreign ministry with its consulates, and the SMR—eventually became so serious that people spoke of the ills of tripartite rule in Manchuria. Gotō suggested various approaches to solving this conundrum, as will be described below.

The Launch of the South Manchuria Railway

Gotō's first task as president designate of the SMR was to find capable people to work under him. First, he appointed Nakamura Yoshikoto, director of finances and general affairs in the Government-General of Taiwan, to the post of vice president. Nakamura went to Taiwan after working in the Ministry of Finance and became one of Gotō's closest confidants. He faithfully assisted Gotō at the SMR and eventually succeeded him to become its second president. He was a friend of the novelist Natsume Sōseki at university. Sōseki visited Manchuria when Nakamura was president of the SMR and wrote about him in his account of his travels in the region, *Mankan tokorodokoro* (Here and There in Manchuria and Korea).

The company's directors, except Nonomura Kingorō from the Industrial Bank of Japan, who was selected on the recommendation of Yamagata Aritomo, were all Gotō's own appointments. They represented a unique combination of talent: Tanaka Seijirō and Inuzuka Nobutarō from Mitsui & Co., Ltd., who took charge of sales and marketing; Kubota Katsumi, an expert in accounting and finance from the Bank of Japan; Kubota Kiyochika and Seino Chōtarō from the home ministry, who applied their administrative and civil engineering expertise in the railroad zone; Kunizawa Shinbei, an engineer at the Ministry of Communications specializing in railways (later chairman of the company's board); and legal expert Okamatsu Santarō of Kyoto Imperial University.

Gotō was personally acquainted with only three of these men, Nakamura, Kubota Kiyochika, and Okamatsu; the rest he tracked down by gathering information from various sources in his quest for the right people. All of them were young. At the time of the company's establishment, Gotō was fifty, Nakamura was thirty-eight, and all the directors except Kunizawa and Nonomura were in their thirties.

Gotō stopped at nothing in his determination to get the people he wanted. He secured the services of the two Mitsui Trading men in the face of fierce resistance from their employer by asking Inoue Kaoru, an elder statesman with considerable influence at Mitsui, to intervene. He was equally ruthless in recruiting Okamatsu. Kyoto Imperial University and the Ministry of Education were reluctant to let him go, so Gotō resorted to the following argument: running the South Manchuria Railway on Chinese territory would require unraveling some complex legal tangles, and the only man capable of doing that was Okamatsu, who had spent six years studying Qing laws and customs at the behest of the colonial government of Taiwan. In short, there was no better place than Manchuria for him to apply the results of his research to date. It was, Gotō insisted, the most effective way to make use of government funds and real talent. Anyone could give lectures or write books. His words must have infuriated the university and the education ministry.

In August an imperial ordinance was issued prescribing that government officials working for the SMR would retain their government posts. Accordingly, upon joining the board of directors, Nakamura Yoshikoto remained director of finances and general affairs in the Government-General of Taiwan when he became vice president of the SMR, while Seino and Kubota Kiyochika retained their positions at the home ministry, Okamatsu kept his professorship at Kyoto Imperial University, and Kunizawa remained a railway engineer with the Ministry of Communications. This peculiar arrangement was Gotō's doing, designed to ensure that he got the people he needed.

Meanwhile, preparations for establishing the company proceeded apace. The SMR had capital of 200 million yen, half of which was the Japanese government's stake, all in the form of contributed assets. That made the SMR by far Japan's largest company. No other firm in the country at the time was capitalized at more than 100 million yen. The government was so concerned about the SMR's prospects that it guaranteed an annual dividend of 6 percent on shares other than its own for fifteen years from the company's establishment. The business community for its part was somewhat pessimistic about the outlook for a share offering, but when 100,000 shares worth 20 million yen were floated in September and October, the response was overwhelming, with more than a thousand applications per share—not out of bullishness about the SMR's future, but out of public expectations and support for the gains made in the Russo-Japanese War.

Buoyed by these expectations, the SMR was launched at the founding meeting held on November 26, 1906. Gotō, having officially become president several days before, on the thirteenth, was granted an imperial audience on the nineteenth and dined with the emperor, who gave him the unusual honor of addressing him personally: "The South Manchuria Railway is a difficult enterprise of great consequence. I expect you to make every effort." The vice president and directors were likewise granted an audience with the emperor before departing for Manchuria and served tea and cakes, again an unusual honor. All this reflected the high level of public expectations for the railway's future.

2. The SMR's Initial Policies: "Dairen-centrism" and Military Preparations in Civilian Garb

"Dairen-centrism"

The chief characteristic of the operating policy initially followed by the South Manchuria Railway Company after it commenced operations in April 1907 was what was termed "Dairen-centrism." Traditionally, the mainstays of transportation in Manchuria had been the junks that plied the Liao River and the seaport of Yingkou. Dairen-centrism was the idea of developing the harbor of Dairen, and the railroad connecting it to Mukden, into the backbone of the Manchurian transport network instead, and focusing the SMR's business efforts on that goal.

The basic elements of this policy had already been put in place by the Russians when they controlled the Liaodong Peninsula. They had invested massive amounts in increasing the port capacity of the harbor of Dalny (Dairen), and had set cheap freight rates between it and Harbin in a bid to attract cargo traffic to Dalny and the southern branch of the Chinese Eastern Railway. Whereas Yingkou was unusable for part of the winter, Dalny was ice-free and an excellent natural harbor; being a leasehold, moreover, it enjoyed several advantages under international law. The senior management of the Chinese Eastern Railway believed that by capitalizing on these strengths, it could prevail against the rival route via Yingkou and the Liao River.

The Japanese took over this policy of the Russians. The order issued by the ministers of communications, finance, and foreign affairs in August

1906 instructed the SMR to convert all railways under its management to broad gauge within three years of commencing operations. It also gave specific instructions to double-track the line between Dairen and Sujiatun (the second station south of Mukden, where the Fushun Line to the Fushun coal mines branched off). In March 1907, the three ministers further ordered a gradual upgrade of the harbor of Dairen so that it could accommodate a 10,000-ton steamship at low tide. Moreover, to ensure that the lion's share of Japan's exports to Manchuria were routed via Dairen, the Japanese government instructed the Yokohama Specie Bank (then Japan's only foreign exchange bank, later the Bank of Tokyo, which was merged into the present-day MUFG Bank in 2018) to offer a special low-interest documentary bill between Kobe, then the chief center of trade with Manchuria, and Dairen, and arranged for the Bank of Japan to support it.

The SMR applied itself to implementing Dairen-centrism in accordance with this government policy. Its first task was to convert the railway to a wider gauge. The Chinese Eastern Railway, as was usual for railways in Russia, had an extra-broad gauge of five feet. As the Russians retreated during the Russo-Japanese War, they took their locomotives and freight cars with them. In order to make use of the railway, therefore, the Japanese had to convert the tracks to the Japanese narrow gauge of three feet six inches and bring locomotives and freight and passenger cars from Japan for army use. But because a narrow-gauge railway had less carrying capacity, the tracks now needed to be reconverted to the gauge of four feet eight-and-a-half inches that was standard around the world (which in Japan is customarily referred to as "broad gauge," a term retained in this book).

Converting Russian broad gauge to Japanese narrow gauge was relatively straightforward, because the existing railroad ties could be left in place. It was simply a matter of laying an extra rail. Converting narrow gauge to standard broad gauge, however, often necessitated replacing the ties first, and operations could not be suspended for that purpose. Completing the conversion within three years as called for by the government therefore seemed a tall order, yet Gotō ordered the job to be completed within a year. By May 1908, almost the entire railway had been converted to broad gauge with the exception of the Anfeng Line, on which work could not begin owing to relations with the Qing government. On May 31, a bizarre farewell ceremony, the likes of which the world had probably never seen, was held in honor of the narrow-gauge rolling stock that had been rendered redundant. One of the company directors, Kunizawa Shinbei, declaimed on that occasion, "We weep copious tears of sorrow as we say adieu, but we cannot praise you at length. We simply offer a single parting word and wish you good fortune in the future on the merit of your services in the past." It was an emotional farewell to the trains that had made a signal contribution to Japan's victory in the Russo-Japanese War. The words were also filled with pride at the unexpected success with which the newly founded company had met its first major challenge. This episode offers a glimpse of what the SMR was like in those days.

The double tracks between Dairen and Sujiatun were completed in October 1909. Like the track gauge conversion, it was a significant achievement in world railway history. Meanwhile ambitious plans for developing the port of Dairen were formulated and gradually implemented. In October 1907, moreover, a multitude of regulations was drawn up on the handling of vessels and cargoes, and stevedoring operations were placed under the company's direct control. These changes greatly increased Dairen's port capacity.

Besides these infrastructure upgrades, also noteworthy was the special freight-rate program for goods transiting seaports introduced in July 1907. This program set a virtually uniform rate for certain goods traveling between either of two ports—Dairen and Yingkou (with the later addition of Port Arthur and Andong)—and Mukden and points further north. The railway to Yingkou branched off from the main line at a place called Dashiqiao, which was 22 kilometers from Yingkou but 240 kilometers from Dairen. Almost the same freight, however, was charged on both routes, indicating how much Dairen was favored to the detriment of Yingkou. The British and the Americans, who had hitherto generally used Yingkou, were later to lodge a protest against this policy.

It is unknown to what extent Gotō was involved in the government's decision to pursue Dairen-centrism. But considering his achievements in Taiwan, the circumstances behind his assumption to the presidency of the SMR, and the fact that the SMR actually went beyond the government's instructions in implementing Dairen-centrism, there can be no doubt that the policy reflected his views. Already in Taiwan he had shown himself to be an avid builder of railways and displayed an enthusiasm for large-scale harbor construction.

Dairen-centrism made excellent economic sense, at least in the early days of colonial administration. As a result of the policy, the SMR was, from its first year in business (FY1907), able to pay a dividend of 6 percent to private investors after setting aside a special reserve. By its third year, FY1909, it was also able to pay dividends on the government's stake. In its seventh year, FY1913, the SMR paid a 7-percent dividend, and from its eighth year, FY1914, an 8-percent dividend. These results exceeded virtually all forecasts. The success of Dairen-centrism was evidenced above all by the meteoric rise of Dairen's port. In FY1907, Dairen handled just 20 million yen worth of trade, less than 40 percent of the 54 million yen in trade that went through Yingkou. Nine years later, in 1916, that figure had jumped to 147 million yen, 2.7 times that for Yingkou, which had barely increased at all.

Thus Gotō, having already demonstrated his entrepreneurial abilities in Taiwan, succeeded magnificently when he was given a bigger stage at the SMR on which to display them. But he constantly insisted that the SMR was more than a moneymaking venture. Its initial economic success was merely a first step for him. We must now turn to the question of how he intended to build on that success.

Military Preparations in Civilian Garb

When discussing the SMR's operations, Gotō frequently spoke of "the Empire's special mission in South Manchuria," which the SMR was tasked with carrying out. He never fully spelled out what that mission was; all he left behind were abstractions. He spoke, for example, of "making Manchuria a place where peoples of all countries can come together to do business for mutual profit" in a speech delivered in Kōrakuen Garden, Tokyo, in April 1907. Were such phrases mere flowery rhetoric, or did they mean something specific? Or did "the Empire's special mission" lie somewhere else entirely? To answer that question, I would like to examine the idea of military preparations in civilian garb (*bunsōteki bubi*) that Gotō repeatedly espoused as the cornerstone of policy for managing Japanese interests in Manchuria.

The term was originally used by Gotō in contrast to "effeteness in arms" (*busōteki bunjaku*). During the Russo-Japanese War he had already argued that the South Manchuria Railway should be given the central role in managing Japanese interests in Manchuria. That contention stemmed from his belief that, rather than allow the army a continued say in Manchuria by stationing large numbers of troops in the region and strengthening military readiness, it would be more effective—even from the military standpoint—to make the railway the centerpiece of efforts to promote Japanese interests there, while developing agriculture and livestock farming and settling large numbers of Japanese immigrants. After all, a railway capable of instantly providing military transport on a large scale, and an immigrant population that could instantly be transformed into a militia, were both forms of military potential.

Gotō also put considerable effort into establishing large hospitals. These, he explained, could be promptly converted into field hospitals, for which reason the hallways had been made extra wide for the placement of stretchers. One of the first projects he undertook was setting up the Port Arthur School of Engineering, which was conceived in a similar spirit. Port Arthur had been of great value to the Russians as a base of operations against Japan, but it was of no use to Japan as a base of operations against Russia; hence it was doomed to decline as long as it remained simply a naval port. It would be better, Gotō thought, to build a large school there housing many students, which, in case of a crisis, could quickly be converted into a base capable of providing barracks and supplying rations on a large scale. The term "military preparations in civilian garb" thus meant, first of all, the development of non-military facilities that were instantly convertible to military use.

This idea of Gotō's was attractive to the army's senior leaders, who were well aware, given the state of Japan's economic power, of the difficulty of building up the country's military strength. Both Yamagata and Terauchi supported it, as did of course Kodama, who was particularly close to Gotō. Even Tanaka Giichi, who was far more optimistic about the military balance of power with Russia than were Yamagata and Terauchi, concurred that the transportation network was a key military asset. Indeed, the development of a transportation network on the mainland was deemed one of the cornerstones of Japan's defense strategy against Russia in the imperial defense policy for 1907, which these officers were instrumental in formulating. With their backing, Gotō was able to overcome the opposition of the army in Manchuria. In fact, the very term "military preparations in civilian garb" was, one suspects, from the start intended to gain the army's support.

Gotō also used the term in a slightly different sense. He often spoke of "practicing the art of hegemonism under the flag of righteous government," that is, introducing the so-called conveniences of civilization (righteous government) and thus establishing a relationship with the local Chinese population that inhibited opposition to the Japanese presence in Manchuria (the art of hegemonism). This too he described as a form of military preparations in civilian garb. The level of local support for the Japanese presence in Manchuria would undoubtedly be a decisive factor in any future conflict between Japan and Russia or China. It was therefore important to win over the hearts and minds of the local Manchurian populace during peacetime. Gotō used this pet phrase of his in the sense of utilizing the conveniences of civilization to that end.

The idea dated back to his days in Taiwan. The secret to life, according to Gotō, was to exploit human weaknesses, and the most skilled practitioners of that art were doctors and lawyers. People depended on them, paid them money, and generally did not hold it against them when they bungled. In government too, especially colonial government, it was vital to make the population dependent by exploiting its weaknesses. The colonial policy of the European countries, Gotō asserted, illustrated that principle. It had historically been based on the triad of "the church, the hospital, and the water supply," while more recently it had evolved to give priority to "the church, the hospital (public hygiene—including the water supply), and the railway." Since Japan could not of course expect to achieve much through religious proselytism, he argued, it should focus all the more on bringing the benefits of public hygiene, transportation, and schools to the local population and winning its loyalty thus.

Gotō therefore attached importance to establishing hospitals and sanitation facilities as he had done in Taiwan, a policy that yielded impressive results during the Manchurian plague epidemic of 1910–11. The Qing governor of Mukden Province, Tang Shaoyi, who was attempting to resist growing Japanese control in Manchuria by working with the Americans, tried to stem the outbreak by recruiting physicians from the United States, but they were no match for the Japanese in providing treatment, and Japan's growing presence in the medical field was subsequently welcomed by the population. The construction of the South Manchuria Medical School in Mukden in 1911 was enthusiastically greeted by the local people, if not the local government. To quote Gotō, "The medical school in Mukden has a halo. Where that halo shines, people are starting to look up to it for light." Thus the term "military preparations in civilian garb" assumed a second meaning: "practicing the art of hegemonism under the flag of righteous government."

It further evolved to assume a third meaning. Throughout his career, from his days in Taiwan until becoming mayor of Tokyo, Gotō was renowned for setting up large research institutions and conducting ambitious research projects. While at the SMR he established the East Asia Economic Research Bureau, organized a geographical and historical survey of Manchuria and Korea, and founded a central laboratory and other facilities dedicated to the natural sciences. These too he described as forms of "military preparations in civilian garb," and in a broad sense they were, because they helped ensure that Japanese policy in Manchuria was implemented on a scientific basis over the long term.

In light of the above, "military preparations in civilian garb" could be taken to mean essentially the use of nonmilitary facilities to strengthen military power in the broad sense. That indeed is how Gotō outwardly defined the term. But a deeper reading casts doubt on the notion that the policy of military preparations in civilian garb was intended ultimately to serve military ends. Indeed, in a speech of April 1914, Gotō himself said of military preparations in civilian garb, "It would be a mistake to understand me to mean that they are ultimately for military purposes."[4]

Take the railway, for instance. Gotō considered transportation to play a crucial role in historical evolution. He therefore believed that the Japanese

---

4   "Nihon shokumin seisaku ippan" (see chap. 2, n. 5).

would never be able to develop their interests in Manchuria without developing the South Manchuria Railway, quite aside from the question of its military functions. He was convinced too that the railway would bring significant benefits to the region as one of the conveniences of civilization. He proudly believed that the SMR would constitute a major artery in the global transportation network, connecting East and West and contributing to the fusion of the two civilizations. That conviction led him to put considerable effort into making through service available to international destinations. He later recalled that he had hastened to convert the railway to broad gauge because the SMR performed "an important mission as part of the world's transportation system." If it had been "purely a matter of profitability," Gotō felt, narrow gauge would have been perfectly adequate. Conversely, he never once sought to enhance the SMR's specifically military functions as part of its management policy.

More significantly, the railway's operations were intended not so much to prepare for a confrontation with Russia or China as to eliminate the tensions that could lead to one. Gotō considered it of utmost importance, for example, to improve through-service connections with the Chinese Eastern and the Peking–Mukden Railways. While offering through service was desirable for business reasons, there was also a more fundamental idea behind it: ensuring that the operators of both lines profited and thus creating a bond between them. During the Boxer Rebellion, Gotō had said of the Trans-Siberian Railway, "The railway is a convenience of global transport. One should not yet jump to the conclusion that it will be a lethal weapon in the hands of one or two countries." That view diverged considerably from the general Japanese perception of the Trans-Siberian Railway as a dagger pointed at East Asia, and Gotō's subsequent thinking on the issue of railways essentially grew out of it.

Much the same can be said of the second category of military preparations in civilian garb, such as schools and hospitals. Whether or not military tensions existed, schools and hospitals were needed, Gotō believed; and the civilizational benefits that they conferred on the region were invaluable, whether or not those benefits increased support for Japan. For example, while some criticized educating the Chinese as "tantamount to lending a dagger to the enemy," Gotō rejected that criticism outright, arguing that "as a Japanese, bringing neighboring countries the blessings of Japanese culture is truly in the Japanese spirit." Despite his talk of "practicing the art of hegemonism under the flag of righteous government," he in fact almost never pressed "righteous government" into the service of "hegemonism." Needless to say, his policy of building schools and hospitals was intended not to prepare for conflict but to defuse it.

Nor was particular priority given to military matters in the third category of military preparations in civilian garb—research institutions and projects. Such projects were carried out on a scholarly basis to provide basic research data so that policy in Manchuria could be implemented more scientifically, and Gotō took pride in thereby adding somewhat to the store of human knowledge. In the later Taishō years, he proposed the establishment of a major think tank to study and formulate national policy in the aftermath of World War I, which he dubbed the Industrial General Staff and described as another form of cultural armament. But what he envisaged was economic, not military, warfare.

It is interesting, too, that such research projects also took into account foreign relations. The materials collected by the East Asia Research Bureau, for example, were made available abroad, and surveys and studies were published in abundance. This was encouraged in order to "prevent the mis-understandings that can all too easily arise with others and thus promote mutual understanding" by informing non-Japanese of conditions in East Asia. Gotō recruited influential Western scholars like Karl Thiess and Kurt Wiedenfeld in the hope of facilitating unprejudiced acceptance of such research findings in the West. In brief, he expected the SMR's research arms to play a role in bringing Japan and other countries closer together through scientific research and eliminating mutual misunderstandings. He was confident that because Japan followed rational, scientific methods in implementing policy, other countries would support it.

As the above discussion shows, this set of policies on military preparations in civilian garb was not primarily military in nature, even if it unquestionably concerned national security in the broad sense. Gotō was more interested in using the railway to "civilize" Manchuria. He took great pride in granting the blessings of civilization and contributing to world civilization. Moreover, many of the policies he pursued under the name of military preparations in civilian garb actually had the function of transforming Japan's confrontational relationship with Russia and China into one of mutual dependence.

When Gotō spoke of "the Empire's special mission in South Manchuria" and "making Manchuria a place where peoples of all countries can come together to do business for mutual profit," he was in earnest. Those statements were underpinned by policy. The SMR's considerable revenues were designed to fund the development of "civilized" infrastructure.

One aspect of "civilizing" Manchuria that cannot be left unmentioned is urban planning. Dairen had already been built up to some extent by the Russians, and on a massive scale to boot. One bridge, for instance, was designed to be 54 meters wide, three times the width of Ryōgoku Bridge in central Tokyo—and that in a city with a population of somewhat over ten thousand. It staggered the imagination of the Japanese of the day. But Gotō firmly resisted numerous calls to scale back the plan; indeed, he actually advocated widening some roads.

In Changchun, there were plans to build a new town in the wilderness some distance from the old city. The engineer in charge of the project, Katō Yonokichi, came up with an ambitious design on an impressive scale centering on a station square 90 meters in radius. But Gotō faulted the roads for being too narrow and instructed Katō to increase the width of the main avenues to 36 meters as in Tokyo. When Katō objected, Gotō told him to take a look at the Champs-Élysées in Paris and Unter den Linden in Berlin, and packed him off to Europe.[5]

Gotō already had experience of urban planning in Taiwan, but there he had proceeded on intuition, as it were. He was not yet completely sure what he was doing or why. In Manchuria, however, he became a true builder of cities. His innate imaginativeness and his experience in Taiwan, coupled

5   Koshizawa Akira, "Dairen no toshi keikaku shi" [History of Urban Planning in Dalian] in *Nitchū keizai kyōkai kaihō* vol. 134–136 (Oct.–Dec. 1984). Ibid., "Chōshun no toshi keikaku shi" [History of Urban Planning in Changchun] in *Nitchū keizai kyōkai kaihō* vol. 165–169 (May–Sept. 1987) and vol. 173 (Jan. 1988).

with the knowledge he had gained of Russia's large-scale plans, transformed him into an urban planner of rare ability.

His city-building projects had many different objectives. Ensuring convenience for the residents was important; so too was the political goal of displaying Japan's might as the colonial power. But Gotō seemed to feel almost a duty to build magnificent cities as the embodiment of civilization, and he took supreme pleasure in doing so. In deploring the blinkered vision of one of his engineers and sending him to see Paris and Berlin, he revealed his pride and sense of mission as a bearer of civilization.

It should not be forgotten either that he did not simply impose civilization from above. He strictly forbade the use of Japanese-style place names, for example, and ordered the exclusive use of Chinese names—a natural enough attitude in view of the "biological principle." Nor did he brook discrimination against the Chinese quarter, instead making a special effort to ensure that Chinese settled in large numbers. Only then, he believed, would the SMR thrive. Here too the "biological principle" and the concept of "military preparations in civilian garb" were put into practice.

Today it would be easy to view Gotō's determination to "civilize" Manchuria as an imperialist ideology. Indeed, his idea of military preparations in civilian garb could be called imperialism in its most Machiavellian form. But if the SMR had stormed like a conquering army into a region as hotly contested as Manchuria, it would surely have caused much mutual suspicion and distrust, leading to a far more horrific outcome. For that reason, too, Gotō deserves due recognition for his constructive approach.

3. International Relations and the South Manchuria Railway

The New and Old Worlds in Opposition

As we have seen, the SMR served in itself as a vehicle for diplomacy with China and Russia. The concept of military preparations in civilian garb was the unique means devised by Gotō to further that goal. Running the SMR also led him to develop his own distinctive view of Japan's international relations, what he termed the theory of the New and Old Worlds in opposition.

In a nutshell, this theory held that Japan, China, and Russia needed to form a close partnership in opposition to the New World, that is, the United States of America, which was destined to become immensely powerful. As was always the case with Gotō, however, the theory was couched in extravagant language with frequent leaps of logic, and its details changed over time. It is therefore necessary to examine carefully what he really meant when he spoke of the New and Old Worlds in opposition. What form was the confrontation between Japan and the United States expected to take? How should Japan prepare itself for it? Why was a partnership with China and Russia necessary, and how could one be brought about? Let us analyze Gotō's policy stances toward each of these three countries and explore what he really meant.

First, however, we should survey Japan's international relations between November 1906, when the SMR was established, and April 1907, when it commenced operations. Relations with China remained strained. The two countries frequently clashed over administrative issues in Manchuria, and their mutual distrust steadily mounted. The Qing government lodged protests against the establishment both of the Kwantung Government-General in September 1906 and of the SMR in November. It was openly hostile to the very existence of these institutions dedicated to managing Japanese interests in Manchuria. As soon as Japan lifted military rule in April 1907, the Qing government reorganized the three northeastern provinces that together constituted Manchuria, appointing Xu Shichang governor-general of the entire region and Tang Shaoyi governor of Mukden Province. Both were powerful figures affiliated with the senior official and military commander Yuan Shikai, and their appointment was an indicator of the Qing government's resolve.

Japan's relations with the United States were likewise strained. In November 1906, Willard Straight became US consul general in Mukden. Straight, a highly ambitious young man, was determined to prevent Japan from bringing South Manchuria into its own orbit by providing American aid to the Chinese government in developing Manchuria. He thus hoped to safeguard Chinese unity while enabling the United States to establish a foothold in the region. Tang Shaoyi, a graduate of Yale University, was well disposed to the United States. Together Tang and Straight were frequently to menace Japanese interests in Manchuria over the next several years.

There was, on the other hand, one welcome development for Japan. In November 1906, France put out feelers about negotiating an agreement between the two countries. France, an ally of Russia, was anxious lest Russia become too embroiled in the Far East. It considered it vital to its own interests for the Russians to focus on their western border and strengthen their ability to fight Germany. Convinced that stable Russo-Japanese relations in Manchuria were a prerequisite to directing Russia's attentions west, the French approached Japan about closer ties and offered to mediate an agreement with Russia as well.

This was most opportune for Japan, which had feared that Russia might embark on a war of revenge for its recent defeat. Moreover, the prospect of closer relations with France, a major source of capital, was tempting indeed, given Japan's precarious position in the international financial market. After a series of negotiations, an agreement was concluded with France in June 1907 and with Russia in July. The Russo-Japanese Agreement still did not guarantee strong ties, because Russian advocates of a partnership with Japan did not yet have a sizeable voice. It was significant nonetheless in that it allayed Japanese concerns about relations with Russia.

Soon after, in August 1907, the Anglo-Russian Entente was concluded. As a result, the Anglo-Japanese Alliance and the Franco-Russian Alliance, which had at the time of the Russo-Japanese War been on opposing sides, became linked in an entente that, while not a close partnership, was nonetheless important. The four countries concerned were to curb Chinese and American claims in East Asia at the end of the Meiji era and form the core of the alliance against Germany and Austria in 1914.

Policy toward China

Gotō first landed in Dairen as president of the South Manchuria Railway in May 1907, immediately after the Qing government reorganized its three northeastern provinces. The most serious and urgent task facing him, therefore, was how to cope with the Qing government's uncompromising attitude.

First Gotō travelled to Peking, where on May 29 he had an audience with the Emperor and the Empress Dowager Cixi. He then visited Yuan Shikai in Tianjin on June 3. In his meeting with Yuan he proposed a "chopstick alliance" between their two countries, both users of chopsticks. While the concept of a Sino-Japanese partnership rooted in a common race and writing system was nothing new, it is interesting to note that this conference took place as the movement in the US to exclude Japanese immigrants from California was still raging. Because the Chinese had long been banned from immigrating to the United States, Gotō's advocacy of this chopstick alliance was intended to make the point that the rumored Chinese alliance with the United States was out of the question. It is worth noting too that when tensions between Japan and China were beginning to manifest themselves, Gotō did not exert pressure on Yuan, who was at the center of efforts to reassert Qing interests, but rather urged him to conclude an alliance.

Similarly, in dealing with Xu Shichang and Tang Shaoyi, Gotō recommended not coercion but rather aiding and working with them. Their anti-Japanese policy was, according to Gotō, not based on definite convictions or a clear national vision. It was rather an expedient that they pursued to advance their careers. Therefore, he argued, "if our government identifies Xu's and Tang's weaknesses . . . and by helping them achieve fame and influence, enables them to establish a foothold in Qing political circles, they will be in no position to resist our power or gloat in our disappointments." He thus advocated coaxing the two men to change their policy by giving them backing. Gotō put little stock in beliefs and ideology. This occasionally proved a stumbling block, but more often enabled him to perceive the harsh truth about people.

An interesting case in point of Gotō's approach to dealing with the Chinese was the issue of the Hsinmintun–Fakumen Railway project, a plan to build a fifty-mile-long railway running northeast from Xinmintun (Hsinmintun), west of Mukden, to Fakumen, almost parallel to the South Manchuria Railway (see the map of the South Manchuria Railway and Other Major Railways in 1919 on p. 80). This project was motivated by the American and Chinese desire to check the expansion of Japanese power in Manchuria. There were plans to extend the railway as far as Qiqihar (Tsitsihar) one day and turn it into a major trunk line running parallel to the SMR. The grave implications of that policy should be obvious in light of the principle of Dairen-centrism described above. The Japanese government's response was to try to scuttle the project on the grounds that it violated the prohibition on parallel railways in the annex to the Peking Treaty of December 1905.

Gotō, however, took a different tack. In July 1908 he sent a letter to Yuan Shikai, who appeared to be behind the Hsinmintun–Fakumen Railway plan, explaining that the project was illegal and, in the context of international relations, doomed to fail, and reiterating the need for China and Japan to cooperate rather than clash. He then suggested altering the route of the railway so that it ran from the Fakumen region to the SMR, which would enable the Chinese to develop that region while providing the SMR with a valuable branch (feeder) line. Having pointed out that both China and Japan stood to profit, Gotō said that Japan would be willing to cover any liabilities that China might incur to foreign companies as a result of the route change. He thus sought to alter the course of Chinese policy by creating an inseparable bond between the two countries using means that were lucrative for China, instead of simply condemning its position.

Another interesting example is provided by Gotō's meeting with Tang Shaoyi on November 1, 1908, soon after he stepped down as president of the SMR. Tang Shaoyi was, as already noted, one of China's leading pro-Americans and stood in the vanguard of resistance to Japanese policy in Manchuria. Indeed, he was in Japan at the time on his way to the United States to further that very goal. During their meeting, Gotō made three proposals: arranging ownership of SMR shares by Chinese nationals, arranging ownership of SMR shares by the Qing imperial family in particular, and having Chinese nationals serve on the company's board. These proposals were of course intended to mitigate Chinese hostility to the SMR, and the third would be especially advantageous to China. Tang was caught off balance and, while expressing interest in the third proposal, put off his answer and left for the United States. There, however, he was greeted by the news of the Root-Takahira Agreement (signed November 30) in which Japan and the United States promised to "strengthen the relations of friendship and good neighborhood." This came as a considerable shock to the Chinese, for it was taken to mean that the United States had rejected a partnership with China in favor of one with Japan instead.

In view of this development, Gotō must have been more or less aware, given the United States' attitude, that a Sino-American partnership could be forestalled. Yet he made the above proposals to Tang Shaoyi nonetheless. This suggests that they were formulated not simply with the goal of undermining China's anti-Japanese policies but, as in the case of his envisioned solution to the Hsinmintun–Fakumen Railway issue, with a more positive objective, namely to turn Japan and China into partners.

Not all Gotō's policies toward China were designed to promote cooperation between the two sides. Given the Qing government's reluctance to accept the Japanese presence in Manchuria, he also argued for pressuring China by isolating it in collaboration with the other powers. However, if promoting cooperation with China may be called the carrot and the threat of isolation the stick, Gotō clearly favored the carrot. Moreover, that carrot was not so much a means to an end as an end in itself. Gotō did not advocate a partnership between Japan and China simply with an eye to eliminating Chinese resistance so that the Japanese could develop their interests in Manchuria. His ultimate goal, it is fair to say, was to build an economic relationship around the SMR that was lucrative for both countries, and in that way bring them closer together. Of course, even if such a partnership had come into being, it could never have been an equal one under the circumstances of the day. But Gotō's stance was nevertheless noteworthy given the indignation at Chinese intransigence and calls for relentless pressure on the Qing government that generally characterized Japanese views at the time.

Policy toward Russia

In Gotō's view, relations with Russia were just as important as those with China. In April 1907, immediately before he first went to Manchuria, Gotō became personally acquainted with Russia's ambassador to Japan, George Bakhmeteff, and Financial Attaché Gregory Wilenkin. Gotō had many administrative issues to sort out with Russia in order to facilitate the SMR's operations, but that was not all. Cooperating with the Western powers would be essential to developing Japan's interests in Manchuria while avoiding alienating China, and Gotō believed that Russia would be the key partner.

Gotō, however, did not consider cooperation with Russia simply a means of facilitating development of Japanese interests in Manchuria and suppressing Chinese opposition. He fundamentally believed that Japan could not thrive without the friendship of its massive Russian neighbor, as is evident from the previously cited memorandum written during the Russo-Japanese War. Establishing a partnership with Russia was a vital objective worth pursuing in its own right.

Gotō's approach to dealings with Russia typically involved establishing good relations by engaging in working-level negotiations with the most senior responsible official on the Russian side. His negotiating partners in this case were Finance Minister Vladimir Kokovtsov and the Chinese Eastern Railway's vice president Alexandr Wenzel.[6] First Gotō attracted their attention by proposing to buy rails from Russia, and then visited Russia in May 1908 to sort out the details with them. That then led to the conclusion of a through service agreement with the Chinese Eastern Railway, as well as a tariff agreement to avoid unnecessary competition. These were not tremendous achievements in themselves, perhaps, but their indirect effect on Russo-Japanese relations as a whole was immense.

Gotō liked to deal personally with those in positions of influence, as seen in his visits to the Empress Dowager Cixi and Yuan Shikai. It was a strategy he often resorted to in the corridors of political power in Tokyo as well. He now dreamed of applying it at an even higher level as a means of strengthening the friendship between Japan and Russia. He hoped to arrange for a truly influential Japanese statesman to visit Russia for candid discussions with an equally influential Russian counterpart.

Itō Hirobumi was the man whom Gotō had in mind. In September 1907, when Gotō happened to run into Itō on a pilgrimage to Itsukushima Shrine on the island of Miyajima near Hiroshima, he tried to convince him of the urgency of establishing a close partnership with Russia and encouraged him

---

6   Wenzel was the de-facto president of the railway because the actual president was Chinese and had no real power.

to resign as resident general of Korea so that he would be free to visit Russia for that purpose. He later wrote a record of the encounter titled "Itsukushima yobanashi (Itsukushima Night Tales)," in which he claimed he spent three days and three nights explaining to Itō his theory of the New and Old Worlds in opposition until he finally won him over. This, however, was a typical case of Gotō exaggerating. The meeting surely lasted only a single night, and his account is suspect in several other regards as well. It nevertheless appears to be a fact that he asked Itō to visit Russia and did his part to set up a high-level meeting with the Russians. As a result, Itō left for Russia and arrived in Russian-controlled Harbin in October 1909. There he met with Kokovtsov, who had come to welcome him, but was assassinated immediately after.

Gotō nonetheless remained convinced of the importance of leading Japanese figures visiting Russia. Katsura Tarō's 1912 visit to Russia and Gotō's own 1927 visit to the Soviet Union, both described below, were in line with that conviction.

Gotō came to be seen as one of Japan's leading pro-Russians after his 1908 visit to Russia. In 1911 he became vice president of the Russo-Japanese Association under General Terauchi Masatake, army minister and governor-general of Korea. As such he transformed the organization and played an instrumental role in strengthening cultural and economic relations between the two countries.

Policy toward the United States

Perhaps even more critical than policy toward China and Russia was policy toward the United States. As president of the SMR, Gotō could not afford to ignore the American policy in Manchuria put together by Tang Shaoyi with Willard Straight, the US consul general in Mukden.

Characteristically, Gotō did not concentrate exclusively on undermining America's dollar diplomacy, but also attempted to relieve tensions with the US in various ways. First, for example, he had the idea of issuing SMR bonds in the United States with the intention both of raising funds and of thereby committing the Americans to the company's success. The Americans, however, showed little interest, and so the entire bond issue was ultimately floated in the United Kingdom in 1907 and 1908.

Second, Gotō purchased all SMR's freight and passenger cars from the United States despite the SMR's dependence on the United Kingdom for its foreign financing, a decision that surprised and upset the British. This move was motivated in part by the expectation of improved relations with the United States. Takahashi Korekiyo, financial attaché in Washington, indicated as much when, in February 1907, he wrote to Finance Minister Sakatani Yoshirō of the decision to purchase rolling stock from the US, "Using the American type on the SMR, ordering American supplies, and so forth will, I think, be a good thing for diplomatic relations between Japan and the US right now."

American perceptions of the SMR's operations remained a major concern for Gotō. In his view, the United States' interest in Manchuria was economic, and it was therefore concerned about the state of the SMR's business. For the Americans, the success or failure of the SMR was a barometer of the success or failure of Japanese policy in Manchuria as well as a leading indicator of the future of the Japanese economy. Hence it directly affected the price of Japan's foreign loans. As long as the SMR's outlook was promising, Japanese public bonds would retain the confidence of investors and escape the clutches of speculators, generating "pocket money" for ordinary citizens. The bonds would then be less vulnerable to price falls. Essentially, Gotō contended that demonstrating the SMR's growth potential would ensure Japan's position in financial markets and lead to more stable relations with the United States.

Gotō had similar reasons, it seems, for the considerable efforts he devoted to attracting foreign tourists, and not just Americans either. Attracting foreign tourists was an obvious business strategy, but Gotō went about it with uncommon zeal. For instance, he built accommodations such as the Yamato Hotels all over Manchuria, a policy that was criticized as extravagant, self-indulgent, and unprofitable. He believed, however, that attracting Western tourists was the duty of the SMR as a link in the global transport network, besides being of some political significance as well. Whenever Westerners criticized Japanese policy in Manchuria for being too closeddoor, he would refute it by citing this chain of hotels. "They're primarily for the use of Westerners, because we wanted large numbers of Westerners to come to Manchuria and join us in developing this new frontier," he said. Hotels were evidence of the "civilized," open nature of Japanese policy in Manchuria. Further, after stepping down as president, Gotō embarked on the compilation of a massive English-language guide to East Asia. This ambitious work, which took eight years to complete, consisted of five magnificently written volumes with a total of three thousand pages. It was considered by some to be the finest European-language publication ever issued by the Japanese government.

In asserting that the New and Old Worlds were in opposition, Gotō is usually understood to have meant that confrontation between Japan and the United States was inevitable and Japan needed to prepare for it by forming a bond with China, which in turn would require partnering with the Russians. This precisely reflects the state of international relations after the Russo-Japanese War. Our analysis so far, however, would suggest that while this was undeniably one aspect of Gotō's theory of the New and Old Worlds in opposition, its central meaning lay elsewhere. Gotō did not consider partnering with China and Russia so much a means of defending against American expansionism as an essential condition for Japan's future development. Moreover, he believed that these partnerships could be beneficial to both sides, especially economically. The United States was not an irreconcilable enemy. The US and Japan could be brought together through closer economic ties. In other words, Gotō's theory of the New and Old Worlds in opposition was not a balance-of-power theory focusing on causes of conflict in international relations; instead it focused on opportunities for integration. In this most important regard, it dovetailed with his theory of military preparations in civilian garb. The two were analogous ideas forming part of a single organic whole in his mind.

Gotō and Hara Takashi

To view the two ideas from a slightly different perspective, the theory of military preparations in civilian garb advocated making the SMR (with its subsidiary businesses) the central vehicle of Japanese policy in Manchuria, while the theory of the New and Old Worlds in opposition asserted that relations with the United States should be the main determinant of Japanese foreign policy. Seiyūkai politician and future prime minister Hara Takashi, who was a year older than Gotō and like him a native of Iwate Prefecture, basically agreed on both points, but with subtle differences. Here I would like to touch on the similarities and dissimilarities in their views, because these relate to the basic difference in the two men's foreign policy stance and are of considerable significance in the history of prewar Japan's foreign relations.

In 1906, when Hara was home minister and as such responsible for overseeing the Government-General of Taiwan, he was among those who supported Gotō for the presidency of the SMR. During a meeting with Gotō on October 28, Hara told him:

> Administration of Manchurian affairs must be rooted in the Manchuria Railway. . . . In that regard it is of prime importance to maintain the closest relations with the Chinese government and people. The shortcoming of the Japanese is a tendency to quibble. There is at present reportedly much talk among the Chinese about what they call expanding their interests, and the likes of Tang Shaoyi are calling above all for an expansion of state power. It would therefore be an error in long-term national policy to clash with them and thus allow another country to exploit the situation. Accordingly, we must strive to be as friendly as possible in all regards with the Chinese government and people and win their favor."[7]

The two men found themselves in complete agreement. Hara, believing that a diplomatic confrontation between Japan and China in Manchuria was unavoidable, viewed the SMR as a means of bringing the two countries closer together, hence the high priority he thought the railway should be given. In that regard Hara and Gotō saw eye to eye. It was in fact from this period that the two Iwate natives became close associates.

Their views on policy in Manchuria, however, were not identical. Of the three agents of so-called tripartite rule working at cross purposes in Manchuria—the Government-General, the SMR, and consular officials

---

7   Hara Keiichirō, ed., *Hara Takashi nikki* [The Diary of Hara Takashi], vol. 2, 204 (Oct. 28, 1906).

(the foreign ministry)—Gotō chiefly found fault with the foreign ministry, while Hara directed his criticism mainly at the Government-General. On June 6, 1911, Hara told Katsura, "To put it bluntly, foreign ministry bureaucrats, namely consuls and the like, understand diplomacy but do not understand commerce. The South Manchuria Railway understands commerce but does not understand diplomacy. As for the Government-General, it understands neither commerce nor diplomacy. That is the real reason things in Manchuria are not going well." Katsura responded, "One would hope that the consuls and the rest would be a bit more perceptive and not focus exclusively on official diplomacy, but that is not the way things are going." Hara replied that the rotation of diplomats made that impossible. He added, in defense of the foreign ministry and its officials, "It is better that they focus exclusively on official diplomacy." Thus for Hara the top priority in international relations concerning Manchuria was the conduct of diplomacy rooted in states' respective rights and duties, while commerce was a means of supplementing it. He clearly gave less weight to commerce than did Gotō.

What then were the two men's views of the United States? Hara departed on a tour of the West in August 1908 and spent about a month in the United States. On October 8, as he left New York for France, he wrote, "I have not had the opportunity to see America firsthand until today. It is truly a dynamic country, and although the economy is currently in a recession by which many places have been affected, I was able to clearly observe the emergence of activity nationwide. It is hardly necessary to reiterate that what this country will one day become to the world is a vital question warranting constant attention." Furthermore, Hara discovered in Europe that Americanization was progressing across a wide range of fields. "It is truly a source of amazement that America possesses such influence not only politically and economically but even culturally." Having thus awoken to the United States' immense influence, Hara was always to consider cooperation with that country of great importance. Gotō, on the other hand, while recognizing the United States' immense power, propounded his theory of the New and Old Worlds in opposition as a means of countering it, yet also worked to alleviate confrontation with it through economic ties.

For Hara, then, international relations were to be managed above all through diplomacy rooted in a broad view of global trends. Ordinary diplomatic negotiations he dismissed as "quibbling over fine points." In particular, Hara had a realistic understanding of the power of ideology in international relations. Gotō, by contrast, regarded commerce as the centerpiece of international relations. He knew that commerce had the ability to bring different parties together and alter the course of international relations. In that regard he surpassed Hara, but he was Hara's inferior when it came to recognizing the power of ideology. The cornerstone of Hara's diplomacy was cooperation with the United States, while the cornerstone of Gotō's was partnering with China and Russia. Both men had suffered great hardship in their youth because they were from domains that had fought against the imperial government immediately after the Meiji Restoration. Both had eventually worked their way up as technocrats, Hara as a foreign ministry bureaucrat and Gotō as a public health official and colonial administrator. That shared background was one of the reasons they possessed a breadth of vision that an ordinary foreign ministry official could never match. But they were never to work together on foreign policy.

CHAPTER 4

BUREAUCRATIC GOVERNMENT AND PARTY POLITICS

1. The Second Katsura Cabinet

Minister of Communications

When Katsura Tarō formed his second government in July 1908, Gotō resigned as president of the South Manchuria Railway to become minister of communications, and he was roundly lambasted for doing so. Nagao Hanpei, an adviser of Gotō and at the time head of the Public Works Bureau in the Government-General of Taiwan, sent a letter to him criticizing his decision to join the cabinet. "Your Excellency's assumption of this post (though people insist on calling it a promotion) was a silly move indeed, quite unworthy of your usual perspicacity. Abandoning a position of greater real prestige than a ministerial portfolio to occupy the thankless chair of humble communications minister is, it seems to me, taking your fondness for idle amusements too far."

Gotō did not sever his ties with the SMR, however. Before forming his new cabinet, Katsura had decided to transfer oversight of the SMR, excluding its diplomatic functions, from the Ministry of Foreign Affairs to the Ministry of Communications. His offer of the communications portfolio to Gotō was predicated on that condition. In December, when the Railway Agency was established within the cabinet and took over responsibility for railways from the communications ministry, it assumed oversight of the SMR as well, but since Gotō was also director-general of the Railway Agency, he remained in charge of the SMR. The presidency of the SMR was vacant for a while, but in December Vice President Nakamura Yoshikoto became president, while Director Kunizawa Shinbei was appointed vice president in his place. There was thus no significant change in Gotō's position as the man in ultimate control of the SMR.

The communications portfolio was considered, by the standards of the day, a second-rate post, a mere appendage to the cabinet. To Gotō, however, a cabinet post was a cabinet post, and he loved all things big and powerful. In that regard he was almost naively materialist, and he was delighted to have obtained a ministerial appointment while retaining control of the SMR.

A famous story is told of Gotō in those days. The mayor of Tokyo, Ozaki Yukio, on requesting an interview with Katsura, was kept waiting, since Katsura was with a visitor, namely Gotō. Katsura then met with Ozaki, but in less than ten minutes Gotō was back. Bemused, Ozaki asked, "Didn't Mr. Gotō just leave?" Katsura replied with a chuckle, "Well, this happens all the time. He leaves here, then on his way home something occurs to him, and he comes straight back. Sometimes he visits three or four times a day. He comes with a new and different idea each time, and when he's brought three or four ideas, maybe one of them is pretty good, so I do my best to see him." This story illustrates both Gotō's resourcefulness and the active role he played as one of Katsura's right-hand men. For Gotō, being a minister was more than merely a matter of heading an executive department; it was an opportunity to be involved in important affairs of state, something in which he greatly delighted.

Gotō was in fact in his element at the Ministry of Communications. He had a great fondness for anything new or scientific, as witnessed by how he loved to ride around on his bicycle in Taiwan. The Ministry of Communications offered much to satisfy his curiosity. Electricity was one case in point. He applied his penchant for study projects to conducting a massive survey project on hydroelectric power, passed the Electric Utilities Act, and oversaw a cut in electric lighting rates, all in an effort to develop and expand Japan's power grid.

Another example was the telephone, to further the spread of which Gotō championed a message-rate system, that is, charging for each call. At the time, customers were charged a flat rate for telephone service regardless of how many calls they made. This arrangement, which favored customers who made frequent calls, was a serious obstacle to the spread of the telephone. The message-rate system proposed by Gotō foundered on the opposition of heavy users like newspaper publishers and was not implemented until 1920, which goes to show how far behind Japan's telephone system then was.

In the postal field, express mail and a service known as content-certified mail were both introduced during Gotō's tenure as communications minister. It was his idea, too, to replace Japan's black wooden mailboxes with the iconic round, red metal ones. This was typical of the flamboyant Gotō. He also worked on setting up the postal life insurance program, inspired by the interest in social policy that he had first developed at the Public Health Bureau.

Gotō as communications minister

When he rose to answer questions in the Diet as a minister of state, however, Gotō frequently blundered. One member of the House of Peers, Kamata Eikichi, gave this account of Gotō's performance in the legislature: "On one occasion I asked Communications Minister Gotō five questions about light rail. When we met in the dining hall during the recess, he said, 'I wasn't listening to your questions because I thought you were just being facetious anyway. I listened to just one of them.' I was flabbergasted. No wonder his answer made no sense. Nobody knew what he was talking about, and so everyone was laughing and clapping. The man himself thought he was a hit and kept jabbering away, and the entire chamber burst out laughing."

Gotō often lacked a firm grasp of the minutiae of the bills tabled by the communications ministry. When the Electric Utilities Act was being debated, the Railway Agency opposed the ministry's plan to require government approval for power rates. Despite being responsible for the bill as communications minister, however, Gotō at one point expressed support for the plan's opponents as director-general of the Railway Agency. The vice minister of communications then angrily grilled him on the subject, whereupon Gotō remarked, "Well, don't get so upset. The communications ministry's position, the Railway Agency's position—it doesn't matter either way, right?" The vice minister was astonished.

Here is another revealing incident relating to the Electric Utilities Act. One morning at 6 a.m., Gotō summoned the bureaucrat in charge of the bill to his official residence to brief him for questioning in the legislature that day. After listening to the fellow for ten minutes, he began boasting about his achievements developing hydroelectric power in Taiwan, continuing until it was time to head to the Diet. Because of this cavalier attitude towards the Diet, he was often tripped up by questions, although that appears not to have bothered him at all.

It was not that Gotō lacked an understanding or sense of legislative detail, but his own priorities evidently differed from the focus of legislative debate. While he still deserves credit for his remarkable inventiveness, it was not enough to compensate for his shortcomings. The numerous plans he tabled in the legislature often came to nothing because his ideas were too advanced for ordinary minds to comprehend, but his inability to make a sustained, systematic effort to get legislation through the Diet should not be overlooked either.

Director-General of the Railway Agency

In December 1908, five months after the new government took office, the Railway Agency was established and Gotō was appointed its director-general while retaining the post of communications minister. Japan's railways had already been nationalized under the previous government and placed under the control of the communications ministry's Railway Bureau. The Railway Agency was set up under the cabinet's direct control to develop the train system into a single unified network. Gotō's appointment as director-general was more or less decided before the government was formed. After all, he had long been an advocate of nationalization and possessed extensive experience building railways in Taiwan and Manchuria.

The Railway Agency faced several challenges. To begin with, there was the problem of how to integrate what had until recently been seventeen separate companies into a single organization. Then there was the issue of how to bring Japan's still woefully underdeveloped railway system up to the standards of the advanced countries of the West.

In addition, there were two problems that inevitably resulted from operating a nationalized railway system. The first was how to prevent it from developing into a rigid bureaucracy in which individual workers had no latitude to be creative. The second was how to keep it from becoming a political football. (These two problems were ultimately to prove fatal to the Japanese national railway system, leading to its rapid decline since the late 1960s until it was finally split up and privatized in 1987.) In notes Gotō jotted down immediately after becoming director-general, he recorded his basic ideas for organizational reform. First, he wanted to make section managers the mainstay of the organization. Appointing men of ability as section and subsection managers and giving them the lion's share of operational authority and responsibility, he hoped, would eliminate the inefficiencies of the Japanese *ringi* system, in which draft proposals were prepared at the lower echelons of the organization and then had to be endorsed by upper management. It would rectify the tendency of section managers and their subordinates to rely on the judgment of their superiors and shift responsibility up the chain of command. And it would enable middle managers to supervise operations with the bigger picture in mind.

Second, Gotō made improving front-line operations his top priority. Wary of the unfortunate tendency of bureaucracies to become top-heavy, Gotō favored "putting individuals of exceptional ability in the position of working in direct contact with society and the public."

Third, he wanted each position filled by the best man for the job. That may seem obvious, but it is easier said than done. Regardless of the era, people with special skills working in a large organization, especially a government organization, often end up in positions unconnected with those skills, because personnel appointments are all regulated by identical criteria. Fourth, as a logical extension of this, Gotō advocated the principle of performance-based pay, in the belief that workers would lose their enthusiasm unless their remuneration was commensurate with their job. Finally, he considered it necessary to strengthen personal ties among staff in order to improve overall morale.

In the area of managerial policy, his first accomplishment was establishing a special, independent account for the national railway system, which would have been vulnerable to political interests if left in the government's general accounts. He not only eliminated this vulnerability, but also issued public bonds, which an agency with independent accounts was allowed to do.

Meanwhile Gotō was relentless in cutting costs. During his time as director-general of the Railway Agency, he reduced the workforce by more than 8,000 in three rounds of cuts, much as he had done in Taiwan. He also took a creative approach to purchasing supplies. The national railways had previously bought the very best of everything at the vendor's asking price, blissfully oblivious of costs. Gotō managed to get the price of cement, for example, reduced from 5.5 yen to 3.5 yen per barrel in return for purchasing a million barrels over three years. True to character, Gotō issued an order to be nice to customers. Handling goods with care was what the owners expected, he explained, and it would save money on compensating them for damage. He also pointed out that politely giving directions to passengers when asked would ultimately reduce the number of requests for directions.

One policy of Gotō's that generated much debate was his decision to prescribe a uniform for staff that at first glance might be mistaken for a naval officer's: gold buttons, gold braid, and a saber on ceremonial occasions. This drew a storm of criticism. The April 28, 1909 issue of the *Jiji shinpō* newspaper, for example, wrote, "The government is as bad at business as an ex-samurai anyway, so why not just give them a pair of samurai swords? Even better, dress them in formal samurai garb." Gotō rammed through the idea regardless of the criticism, and all staff wore the uniform until it was restricted to only station staff, train crew, and railway workers when Tokonami Takejirō became the agency's director-general in the Hara Takashi cabinet (1918–1921).

Gotō loved uniforms. As civilian governor of Taiwan, too, he had stirred up controversy by prescribing one. He had various reasons for doing so, among them saving on clothing costs, ease of movement, and safety. A uniform also symbolized the high priority he gave to front-line operations. But his primary motive, it seems, was to raise organizational morale. Gotō himself always wore his director-general's uniform. He cut a particularly striking figure on his tours of inspection to different regions of the country, strutting about clad in brown leather gaiters and wearing his Order of the Rising Sun, First Class, with a large retinue of subordinates in tow. Many ridiculed the spectacle for being like the procession of a feudal lord, but it must have greatly boosted the morale of Railway Agency staff. Gotō earned his nickname "the Japanese Roosevelt" when he made a tour to inspect the aftermath of the great flood of 1910 in the Kantō region attired in this fashion.

Fittingly for the former head of the Public Health Bureau, Gotō displayed great concern for the wellbeing of employees. He built hospitals and prioritized a sanitary environment. On his regional inspection tours, it was his habit to step suddenly into bathing facilities, to the astonishment of the employees using them, and peek into the lavatories. He also set up a mutual aid association for agency staff. Many of the practices associated with Japanese-style management and the idea of the company as family were first introduced by Gotō.

One goal that Gotō was ultimately unable to accomplish during his three terms as director-general of the Railway Agency, despite repeated attempts, was the conversion of Japan's trunk lines to broad gauge. To improve carrying capacity, and to enable through connections with continental railways, Gotō planned to upgrade the route between Tokyo and Shimonoseki to broad gauge. This enterprise had the support of the military, but was opposed by the political parties, especially the Seiyūkai, which called for channeling limited resources into building more rail lines. Party politicians were intent on developing the local economy and cultivating their electoral base by bringing the railway to their own constituencies. This was referred to as "drawing steel to your own paddy," a pun on the Japanese phrase "drawing water to your own paddy" (i.e., serving your own interests). Politicians blocked the conversion to broad gauge, which was not to be achieved until 1964 with the construction of the Tōkaidō Shinkansen (bullet train).

Many other projects undertaken by Gotō as director-general of the Railway Agency were ahead of their time. One example was the construction of an elevated railway in Tokyo. The December 1909 debut of the electric train on the city's Yamanote Line, until then a steam railway, created quite a sensation. Another example was the construction of the Atami Line,[1] a

---

1 Atami is a well-known hot springs town in a hilly area, 57 miles southwest of Tokyo. Tokyoites have long made the trip there to enjoy the hot springs; thus Atami was a popular train destination.

project to shorten the Tōkaidō Line—which in those days detoured to avoid the steep gradient on the way to Gotemba—while reducing the gradient by building a tunnel, the Tanna Tunnel, thus increasing carrying capacity. Owing to strong opposition, this plan was not officially adopted until 1912. Construction began in 1916, and the new line was finally completed in 1942. (The construction of the Tanna Tunnel, renowned as an epic feat of engineering, was once invariably featured in Japanese school textbooks.) It was Gotō, too, who initiated a massive plan to electrify the entire railway system, which was not however to be realized for many years. Gotō's plans thus frequently ran into intense opposition and were criticized for being newfangled and overambitious. Today, however, it is clear that he accurately foresaw the direction in which "civilization" would evolve.

Issues Relating to the South Manchuria Railway

As communications minister and director-general of the Railway Agency, Gotō was, as already noted, in a position to continue overseeing the South Manchuria Railway. Next, let us examine the situation at the SMR under the second Katsura government.

The initial phase of the SMR's establishment was finally over, but the company still faced many challenges. The first of these was the state of Sino-Japanese relations. When Gotō left Manchuria to join the Katsura cabinet, many Japanese interests in Manchuria granted by the Peking Treaty of 1906 remained unrealized. For example, work had yet to begin on refurbishing the Anfeng Line, which was slated to become one of the SMR's trunk lines. The lease on the Anfeng Line was far shorter than that on the main SMR Line: one year for repatriating troops, two years for upgrades, and then a further fifteen years until the end of 1923. Because the Anfeng Line was a light railway for military use, it was with its steep gradient inefficient for transporting heavy loads, making it almost useless in its current form. Despite the obvious need for immediate renovations, it had been left untouched because the Qing government objected to Japanese plans on the grounds that they went beyond the "improvements" provided for in the treaty and constituted "rebuilding." Many other questions likewise remained unresolved, including the problem of the Hsinmintun–Fakumen

Railway and the issue of Koreans living in the Jiandao (Gando) region in southern Manchuria along the Korean border.

These and a host of other unresolved issues in Manchuria were in fact among the causes of the collapse of the previous government headed by Saionji Kinmochi. The Katsura cabinet accordingly decided to resolve them all at once. In the summer of 1909, it negotiated aggressively with the Chinese and by September succeeded in concluding a five-point Sino-Japanese convention on Manchuria and a related agreement. Japan's hawkish tactics, coupled with the recent downfall of Yuan Shikai and other anti-Japanese hardliners in an unexpected political purge in China, thus led to a settlement.

The second noteworthy problem affecting the SMR under the Katsura government concerned relations with the United States. Even before this time, Americans such as railroad baron E.H. Harriman had planned to expand into Manchuria, while Far East hands with the State Department including Mukden Consul General Willard Straight had criticized Japan's closed-door policy in Manchuria and made notable efforts to pry the door open by establishing an American presence there. President Roosevelt, however, kept them in check. Given the problem of Japanese immigration to the United States, and aware that Japan considered Manchuria to be of vital interest, Roosevelt concluded that it was in America's fundamental interests to turn a blind eye to Japanese expansion in Manchuria, and he rejected the views of the State Department's Far Eastern Division. The result was the Root-Takahira Agreement of November 1908.

When William Taft became president in March 1909, however, the State Department's Far Eastern Division came to have a greater say in US policy in the Far East, and American plans for establishing a foothold in Manchuria picked up momentum. For example, a scheme to build a railway connecting Jinzhou (Chinchow) to Qiqihar (Tsitsihar) and beyond to Aigun (Aihui) further to the north—the Chinchow–Tsitsihar or Chinchow–Aigun (Chin-Ai) Railway—had by July 1909 made considerable progress. If this line was completed, it would inevitably be a formidable rival to the SMR. At the end of that year, a plan was proposed to "neutralize" the SMR, ostensibly with the goal of alleviating Russo-Japanese tensions over railways. Under this plan, the Qing government would purchase both the SMR and the Chinese Eastern Railway with loans from the United States. Barely had Japan asserted its rights in Manchuria vis-à-vis China when it found itself facing stiff competition from the Americans.

The United States' policy actually led to an improvement in Japan's third key diplomatic relationship, that with Russia. Russia likewise resented the American initiative and decided to reject it in tandem with Japan. The second Russo-Japanese Agreement of July 1910 was a de facto commitment to work together in opposing US policy in Manchuria. In the summer of 1909, many Russians had been wary of Japan's hardline foreign policy toward China, yet less than a year later Russo-Japanese ties were much closer, in large part because both countries saw as a provocation the ill-advised attempts of the United States to establish a presence in Manchuria.

Gotō must, one imagines, have played an important role in this aspect of foreign policy inasmuch as it affected the SMR. Although exact details are unknown, he frequently met with Gregory Wilenkin, Russia's financial attaché in Tokyo, and Russian ambassador Nikolai Malevsky-Malevich. Wilenkin even lived in Gotō's private home after the latter moved into his official residence. The two men appear to have been on very close terms indeed. Gotō discussed the question of the Chinchow–Tsitsihar Railway with Ambassador Malevsky-Malevich on four occasions between November 20, 1909 and the end of the year. Gotō stressed that Japan and Russia had common interests in Manchuria and maintained that they should coordinate their policy toward China. Since Gotō already had a reputation as an advocate of Russo-Japanese cooperation, his presence in the cabinet overseeing the SMR must have greatly reassured the Russians. At any rate, the conclusion of the second Russo-Japanese Agreement was the fulfillment of what Gotō had advocated all along, and he played no small part in bringing it about.

Foreign relations thus proceeded as Gotō envisioned insofar as the SMR was concerned. Surprisingly little progress was made, however, in developing a domestic institutional framework for managing Japanese interests in Manchuria. One issue that arose at this time was the question of setting up a special Manchurian financial institution. It was argued that the establishment of a special bank to supply long-term, low-interest loans was essential to the growth of Japanese businesses in Manchuria. With that goal, a draft

"Recommendation on the Establishment of a Financial Institution in the Manchurian Leasehold" was tabled in the Diet in 1909 and unanimously adopted almost unamended. The government accordingly began studying the issue, but the Ministry of Finance concluded that no such institution was needed. Instead, it decided to lend 3 million yen interest free to the Yokohama Specie Bank, which had already established an influential position in Manchuria, to use for low-interest business loans. These were termed special specie loans.

The president of the Yokohama Specie Bank, Takahashi Korekiyo, explained the rationale behind this as follows. The evolution of financial institutions in newly developed regions should proceed in a certain order. First usurers thrive; then respectable merchants and industrialists emerge and are unable to tolerate the usurers' abuses any longer. This leads to the third stage, the establishment of dependable financial institutions. But Manchuria, according to Takahashi, had not even reached the first stage.

Gotō was adamantly opposed to such thinking. "In Manchuria," he argued, "the potential of colonial management in all its forms must be cultivated through reliance on financial institutions. That is to say, finance in Manchuria is not simply a matter of facilitating the flow of income and expenditures in order to achieve the objectives of a particular enterprise; it must perform a central function in colonial management." He then attacked the finance ministry's plan as "liable to the charge of ignorance of Manchuria's economic situation, obliviousness to the true purpose of a colonial bank, and failure to take action to make our compatriots the economic masters of Manchuria in the future." Essentially, the finance ministry's plan was intended to address actual demand for financing among Japanese businesses in Manchuria, whereas Gotō's envisioned giving financial institutions the leading role in the Manchurian economy. His plan never saw the light of day, in part because of Japan's economic weakness.

His dream of establishing a unified institutional framework for managing Japan's interests in Manchuria likewise proved abortive. In 1910, the Colonial Office was created in the cabinet, with Katsura serving as director-general and Gotō acting as his deputy. But this office, which was designed to prepare for the annexation of Korea without attracting foreign attention, had only a minor role in policy in Manchuria. Katsura and Gotō resigned their positions at the Colonial Office in May 1911 after Korea was annexed in August 1910 and any related loose ends had been tied up.

It is interesting to consider what policies Gotō might have formulated if he had been involved in the colonial administration of Korea. In one memorandum he wrote, "Since we now have control over Korean foreign policy, it would be wise insofar as possible to leave the King and Korean bureaucracy to run domestic affairs as they like, and not attempt to intervene too much even if their actions are detrimental to the Korean people." With his constant advocacy of the "biological principle," he would surely have devised policies quite unlike the oppressive colonial rule that Japan actually imposed—though that is mere speculation.

2. Out of Office

Domestic Politics and the International Situation

When the second Katsura cabinet resigned in August 1911 and was succeeded by the second Saionji cabinet, Gotō found himself out of office for the first time in many years.

International relations in East Asia were at a turning point. First, the Xinhai Revolution broke out in China in October and the Qing dynasty fell the next year, in February 1912, eliminating one of the key assumptions behind Japanese foreign policy.

Second, the completion of upgrades to the Anfeng Line and the bridging of the Yalu in November 1911 created a direct link between the Korean Railway and the SMR, enabling through service from Pusan to Mukden. With this, the interests granted to Japan in Manchuria under the Peking Treaty of 1906 were largely realized, and the minimum goals of Japan's Manchuria policy were achieved.

Third, Japan's position in South Manchuria was further strengthened vis-à-vis the other powers. In 1911, the United States endeavored to prevent Japan and Russia from bringing Manchuria further within their orbit by loaning 50 million dollars to the Qing government to reform the country's currency and develop Manchuria. By November, however, that plan had collapsed due to opposition from Japan and Russia as well as France. This failure, following that of the Hsinmintun–Fakumen and Chinchow–Tsitsihar railway projects and the plan to neutralize the SMR, convinced powers other than the United States of the futility of opposing Japanese and Russian interests in Manchuria. One manifestation of this was the tacit agreement not to infringe on the two countries' special interests in Manchuria and Mongolia reached when, between the end of 1911 and June 1912, Japan and Russia joined the four-power loan consortium comprising Britain, France, Germany, and the United States to form a six-power consortium.

These changes in the international situation blurred Japan's foreign policy objectives. Japan had established a framework of sorts for managing its interests in Manchuria and secured the support or at least the connivance of the other powers. It had no other obvious goals left to achieve. The fall of the Qing dynasty, moreover, complicated the task of making foreign policy.

Japan was also at a turning point in its domestic politics. The two most influential forces on the political scene in the wake of the Russo-Japanese War were the Chōshū clique and the Seiyūkai, which were broadly speaking allies despite their frequent clashes. When Katsura, one of the leaders of the Chōshū clique, was in government, he was supported by the Seiyūkai party in the lower house (House of Representatives). When Saionji formed a Seiyūkai cabinet, he was supported by Katsura. In fact, in the six years between the end of the war and the fall of 1911, the House of Representatives was never dissolved; general elections were held only when its term expired. The two changes in government that occurred during that time were agreed on by the departing prime minister and his successor. Thus this era is called the Katsura-Saionji period.

During these years the influence of the Seiyūkai gradually increased. For example, the first Saionji cabinet, while underpinned by that party, had the character of a national unity government, but the second Saionji cabinet was more distinctly a party cabinet. In policy terms, too, Saionji gradually became more independent of Katsura's influence, while Katsura had to pay an ever higher price for the Seiyūkai's cooperation.

One reason the party was able to increase its leverage thus was because the second largest party, the Kensei Hontō (True Constitutional Party) and its successor the Kokumintō (Nationalist Party) remained hostile to the *hanbatsu* or "domain cliques"—the group of men from the four domains that played a central role in the Meiji Restoration who dominated politics in the Meiji era; they are also known as the Meiji oligarchs. Accordingly, oligarchic cabinets—cabinets headed by a member of one of the domain cliques, such as Katsura of the Chōshū clique—could implement their policies only by turning to the Seiyūkai for support, while the Seiyūkai could pressure the oligarchs by threatening to work with the Kensei Hontō or the Kokumintō.

The growth in Seiyūkai's power gave rise to various changes on the political scene. The Satsuma clique and the navy, which formed a minority among the oligarchy and the bureaucratic faction (and largely overlapped), began to seek closer ties with the party, which welcomed that development as a means of countering the Chōshū clique. This was among the reasons that the second Saionji cabinet gave higher priority to building up the navy than the army.

Naturally, this state of affairs displeased the army. Mid-ranking officers blamed it on the excessive compliance of their superiors, Katsura and Terauchi, and began to put pressure on them to take a firmer stance. Even the elder statesmen Yamagata Aritomo, who epitomized the Chōshū clique, did not hide his dissatisfaction with Katsura and Terauchi for their excessive readiness to cooperate with Seiyūkai. He was not then in a position of responsibility, which allowed him to criticize from the sidelines.

Discontent was mounting too in the second largest party. The Kokumintō felt that as long as it remained opposed to the oligarchs, it would simply be exploited by the Seiyūkai and never have its day in the sun. Reformists within the Kokumintō attained increasing prominence, arguing that the party's first priority should be achieving power. Its true rival in that quest was the Seiyūkai; it should therefore not hesitate to work with the oligarchs.

This domestic power struggle, significantly, was closely linked to foreign policy and therefore unfolded in step with the structural changes in Japan's foreign relations noted above. The Seiyūkai, the Satsuma clique, and the navy were against Japan overcommitting itself on the Asian continent, while militarily they gave priority to building up the navy. The Chōshū clique, the army, and the reformists in the Kokumintō, on the other hand, argued that Japan should become a continental power and were in favor of building up the army. The political elite was thus divided between gradualists and advocates of a more assertive policy on the continent.

Gotō too found himself at a major crossroads. His foreign policy initiatives had previously been successful because, first, a national consensus existed on the challenges to be met and, second, he had powerful backing from the Chōshū clique. It was no longer enough for him, however, simply to display his technocratic skills on the stage set for him. He now needed to be the one who set the stage.

The Chinese Revolution of 1911 and Gotō's Visit to Russia

The first upheaval that confronted Gotō was the Chinese revolution of 1911. The Saionji government hoped, in collaboration with Britain, to persuade the Qing dynasty and the revolutionaries to compromise on a constitutional monarchy. Britain, for its part, saw Yuan Shikai as the key to resolving the crisis and decided to support the establishment of a republic. The result was the complete failure of Japan's policy by the end of 1911.

Gotō meanwhile championed the Qing cause out of his belief in a partnership between Japan and Qing China, and criticized the government. Supporters of the Qing dynasty were not particularly uncommon at the time, but most of them expected that Japan would, in return for its support, be able to win concessions or station troops in Manchuria in readiness for its next move, a sentiment particularly widespread in the army. Gotō's pro-Qing stance was clearly of a different nature. He was genuinely committed to building a partnership with China.

This became obvious when Gotō renounced his pro-Qing stance and advocated an Asian version of the Monroe Doctrine instead. According to Gotō, neither the Chinese themselves nor the rest of Asia had anything to gain from internecine strife in China. If the fighting escalated, moreover, the opposing sides might in their determination to win even turn to foreign powers for support, with dire consequences. "This is why I believe that there is no other foundation on which we can stand secure than the Asian Monroe Doctrine or pan-Asianism," Gotō declared. He warned that internal conflict could leave China vulnerable to Western exploitation. On those grounds he asserted, "the conflict between republicanism and monarchy is merely peripheral." Japan should work with the actual Chinese people and their government, he argued, rejecting both the Saionji government's approach of waiting to see what the British did and the widespread Japanese desire to capitalize on China's internal struggles.

Later, during the second Chinese revolution of 1913 and the third of 1915–16, Gotō almost never took sides in the conflict or advocated exploiting it. Such an attitude was rare indeed at the time. Japanese observers of China were, whether from goodwill or ambition, typically fixated on that country's internal struggle and eager for one side or the other to prevail. But Gotō was generally uninterested in meddling in other countries' domestic affairs or form of government. In later years he was to describe such meddling as "folly." Believing as he did that each nation was a living organism, he considered it inadvisable and largely unproductive to take sides. That stance was the logical outcome of his "biological" worldview.

In July 1912, after the first revolution had run its course, Gotō departed on a tour of Russia and Europe in the company of, among others, Katsura Tarō and Wakatsuki Reijirō, former vice minister of finance. One purpose of the trip was, as Wakatsuki recalled, to investigate the state of party politics abroad. Katsura was thinking of forming his own political party, and he wished to observe how political parties were actually run, especially in Britain. But an even more important objective was to engage in candid discussions on China policy with men of influence in Russia, France, Germany, and Britain.

Russia was considered particularly important. Gotō had long believed that senior Japanese and Russian statesman should meet for a frank discussion of China policy, and he had earlier planned for Itō to visit Russia for that purpose. His dream had been cut short by Itō's assassination. Now he intended to realize it in the person of Katsura instead.

Upon landing in Dairen on July 6, Katsura and Gotō were met by Xu Shichang, former governor-general of the three northeastern provinces. Yuan Shikai, expecting that the Japanese delegation would discuss the issue of China with the Russians, had sent his confidant Xu from Peking to confer with them. That indicates how much interest this visit to Russia generated.

Katsura and Gotō arrived in St. Petersburg on July 21 and met with Prime

Minister Kokovtsov the next day to discuss the issue of China. Kokovtsov proposed temporarily occupying Manchuria and Mongolia on the grounds that the Chinese government was incapable of maintaining adequate order there. On another occasion the Russians suggested partitioning Manchuria and Mongolia. Katsura, however, demurred, simply stressing to Kokovtsov the need for Japan and Russia to work more closely together on addressing the situation. The Russians must have been rather disappointed by his restraint and lack of specifics, but the Japanese visitors were, not being official government representatives, unable to commit themselves further.

It would, however, be unfair to conclude that their policies lacked substance. In preparation for this journey, Katsura had been in close contact with Katō Takaaki, the Japanese ambassador in London, in order to size up the situation in Britain. It is therefore reasonable to conclude that he and his companions were exploring the outlines of a more moderate China policy, one agreeable to Russia, France, and Britain. Katsura and Gotō's goal was to establish closer ties of cooperation between those three countries and Japan on the Chinese question. Collaboration between Japan, Russia, Britain, and France had been the driving force behind international politics in the Far East around the end of the first decade of the twentieth century, and it seemed vital to strengthen that four-way partnership to address the volatile situation in China caused by the 1911 revolution. Such was the latest version of Gotō's theory of the New and Old Worlds in opposition. The China policy advocated by these men was, to be sure, short on specifics, but in those days the very act of senior government figures from different countries meeting to share their views was significant in its own right. If the delegation had met with other leading European statesman, and Katsura had then gone on to face a major crisis in China as head of another government, this trip would doubtless have proved to be of great import. Around the time of their arrival in St. Petersburg, however, the travelers received news from Japan that the Meiji emperor was gravely ill. They had no choice but to cancel the rest of the trip and, on July 28, set out on the return journey to Japan. They received the news of the emperor's death on the very next day. Gotō's plans were frustrated for the second time, just as they had been by Itō's assassination.

3. The Taishō Political Crisis and Katsura's New Political Party

The Taishō Political Crisis

On August 13, 1912, after arriving home from Russia, Katsura joined the imperial court as lord keeper of the privy seal and grand chamberlain, a move tantamount to retiring from politics. Katsura, who still had future ambitions, decided to accept the appointment only after much soul-searching, succumbing to the argument that the imperial court needed someone prestigious to oversee it after the accession of the new emperor. The decision proved a serious blunder, because Katsura's political activities were severely curtailed and Japan lost an able statesman.

Efforts to compile a budget for the next fiscal year, meanwhile, reached an impasse. While the cabinet aimed to streamline the bureaucracy and retrench public finances, the army demanded the formation of two new divisions in Korea and would not back down. For the army, this increase was significant in that it would mark a renewed commitment to expanding the Japanese presence on the continent, in contrast to the Saionji cabinet's record so far: giving priority to the navy, taking a passive stance on the 1911 Chinese revolution, and failing to come to grips with the Manchuria question.

Ultimately neither the cabinet nor the army gave ground. Army Minister Uehara Yūsaku resigned, and the army refused to nominate a new army minister (in accordance with the requirement that only an officer on active duty could serve in that post). The cabinet therefore stepped down on December 5. This provoked public outrage. It was described as the "poisoning of the Saionji cabinet." Choosing the next prime minister proved a difficult task, but in the end Katsura left the imperial court to form his third government.

Public opinion was scathingly critical of Katsura, because he was seen as the army's éminence grise. He was also condemned for immediately assuming power on leaving the imperial court and for his frequent use of imperial edicts. The popular groundswell that arose when the Saionji cabinet fell thus evolved into a massive campaign to protect "constitutional government."

It would be wrong, however, to see Katsura as the mastermind behind the fall of the Saionji government. The middle echelons of the army, typified by Tanaka Giichi, were deeply dissatisfied with the conciliatory attitude that

Katsura had taken toward the Seiyūkai and were not pleased that he would be heading the new government. Even though he had accepted the task of forming the next cabinet—in part because he was impatient to escape the confines of the imperial court—Katsura in fact had no intention whatsoever of falling in with the army's hardline views. On the contrary, he believed that beating the party politicians required policies with strong popular appeal. He therefore quietly developed a set of policies that, had they been implemented, would have caused panic within the army. They included postponing the army and navy's military buildup and abolishing the requirements that the army and navy ministers and colonial governors-general all be serving military officers. On January 20, 1913, he announced plans to set up a new political party, not as a stopgap measure but rather in an attempt to transcend the limits of bureaucratic government, of which he had become increasingly aware over the years, and be more responsive to public opinion.

Unfortunately for Katsura, all these efforts backfired. He tried to bring the situation under control by taking advantage of his long friendship with Saionji to detach the Seiyūkai from the popular movement and reach a deal. His establishment of a new political party, however, made the Seiyūkai more intransigent than ever, while the popular movement reached such a pitch that it was now beyond the control of the Seiyūkai's leaders. Katsura tried, but failed, to evade the Seiyūkai's criticism with an imperial order to Saionji. While he was able to prevail on Saionji, Saionji was unable to prevail on the majority of the Seiyūkai members. Saionji, branded guilty of disobeying the imperial command, then stepped down as president of the party, and the popular movement escalated even further, until Katsura was finally forced to resign as prime minister on February 11. His cabinet was the shortest-lived in Japanese history.

Gotō, having already established himself as one of Katsura's right-hand men, served in this third Katsura cabinet as minister of communications and director-general of the Railway Agency, as well as director-general of the cabinet's Colonial Office. Because the cabinet was so short-lived, however, he achieved nothing of note in his ministerial capacity. More significant was the role he played as Katsura's right-hand man, especially in trying to win over Saionji on his behalf.

Gotō met with Saionji on January 17, and requested his support for

Katsura, pointing out that he (Saionji) had been among those who had recommended Katsura for the premiership in the first place. Gotō then drew up a record of their conversation and showed it to Saionji, asking him to confirm the details. This was of course top secret, but it was scooped by a newspaper on February 1. Gotō must have leaked it himself, as he would go to any length if he believed the end was justified. This incident hurt Saionji. It also fomented deep distrust for Gotō in many circles, which helps explain why he never succeeded in becoming prime minister, especially after Saionji became the sole surviving elder statesman.

The New Political Party and Gotō's Decision to Leave It

Gotō joined Katsura's new political party (later called the Rikken Dōshikai or Constitutional Association of Friends) as one of his advisors and occupied an important position within it. Let us examine the nature of this party, starting with its membership.

Ninety members of the lower house joined the new party, including the majority of the Kokumintō (fifty of its ninety members, mainly reformists like Ōishi Masami) and all thirty members of the Chūō (Central) Club, a traditional "bureaucratic" (pro-oligarchic) party. Katsura's associates had expected a considerable number of defectors from the Seiyūkai as well, so this was far fewer than anticipated.

From outside the lower house, Katsura's Home Minister Ōura Kanetake, one of Yamagata Aritomo's senior advisors and the de facto leader of the Chūō Club, also joined the new party. Many other bureaucrats aligned with Yamagata supported Katsura's creation of a new party, but none actually joined, either because they disapproved of Katsura's decision to set up the party while prime minister or because public criticism was so severe that they got cold feet. The bureaucratic contingent of the new party, therefore, was somewhat younger, consisting exclusively of men who were close personal associates of Katsura and had been in his third cabinet. Gotō was the oldest among them. Others included Communications Minister Nakashōji Ren, Finance Minister Wakatsuki Reijirō, Vice Minister of Communications Hamaguchi Osachi, and Chief Cabinet Secretary Egi Tasuku. Foreign Minister Katō Takaaki joined a little later.

Given their diverse backgrounds, it was only natural that the members did not quite see eye to eye on the party's future. Gotō promptly exposed this. In May 1913, he drew up a pamphlet entitled "Questions for the Members of the Constitutional Association of Friends" and distributed it to the party membership. In it he contended that political parties were not vehicles for the transfer of political power but organs of public education, on the grounds that, under imperial constitutional theory, the cabinet was answerable to the emperor rather than to the legislature. If the new party became obsessed with expanding its base and attaining power, it would be no different from the Seiyūkai, Gotō maintained, and that was not the kind of party Katsura wanted to create. A party should educate the masses, not pander to popular opinion. Having made that point, Gotō then asked all the party members to declare where they stood on the issue.

This may have been what Gotō and the Meiji bureaucracy in general really believed. But for the former members of Kokumintō, who had long been proponents of party government, this denial of the need to expand the party base in the quest for power was anathema. The same was true for the former members of the Chūō Club, despite their bureaucratic sympathies. A party politician who lost an election was just another man in the street. The most splendid ideals were of no use whatsoever unless you listened to the electorate, met their expectations, and won the next election. For politicians, elections were wars and an electoral base was a fiefdom won with blood. Ōura too, despite coming from a bureaucratic background like Gotō, well understood how party politicians thought and acted, having spent years struggling as the leader of a small party himself.

The Rikken Dōshikai (or Dōshikai for short) was in a difficult predicament at the time. Party morale was low because of its unexpectedly small membership and rapid loss of power. What is more, Katsura had been taken ill. He had cancer, though that detail was kept secret. Moreover, the government of Yamamoto Gonbei, who succeeded Katsura as prime minister, seemed unassailable. The news of what Gotō had done naturally enough leaked out, so that the turmoil within the Dōshikai became public knowledge. Gotō's actions further damaged the party's reputation when it was already on the ropes, and this earned him the enmity of party members of all stripes.

In July 1913, with Katsura still seriously ill, the Dōshikai decided to establish a standing committee to run party affairs. Five men were appointed to the committee: Ōura Kanetake, Gotō, Katō Takaaki, and former Kokumintō members Ōishi Masami and Kōno Hironaka. Gotō with his impressive record of policy achievements and his close personal ties to Katsura was the best suited of the five to fronting the party. He himself, however, recommended Katō as head of the committee, and Katō was duly chosen. Gotō had been on bad terms with Ōura since the days of the second Katsura cabinet, while the pamphlet imbroglio had created an irreparable rift with party members from the old Kokumintō. He therefore abandoned the idea of heading the committee himself and backed the relatively neutral Katō instead.

Katsura died in October after many months on his sickbed. The Dōshikai's standing committee convened immediately afterwards to discuss the party's next move. Gotō proposed either raising 3 million yen to expand the party and rebuild the party organization from the bottom up or, if that proved impossible, disbanding it instead. This led to a bitter argument with the other four members. Gotō found himself completely isolated, and at the end of the month he left the party. The Dōshikai subsequently chose Katō as its leader and officially held its founding meeting in December.

What were Gotō's aims during this period? He was not really enthusiastic about forming a political party in the first place. Once Katsura died, he was not prepared to be just a party man. Gotō was in all respects a personalist, someone who put individual ability first. He disliked being a cog in a machine or acting as part of an organization. When it came to raising money to run a party, he was no match for Katō, who had married into the Mitsubishi clan. When it came to effectively creating a political organization, he was no match for Ōura. As Max Weber said, politics is a strong and slow boring of hard boards: it takes perseverance. This is especially true of party politics, and Gotō was bad at it. He was subsequently invited by Hara Takashi to join the Seiyūkai and, in the later Taishō years, was considered a potential leadership candidate by the anti-Katō faction of the Kenseikai (the successor of the Dōshikai). But there was little likelihood Gotō would have joined either party. Even if he had, it seems improbable that he would have been successful.

Gotō's proposal following Katsura's death, however, should not be seen as simply an excuse for bolting the party. Organizing a party such as Gotō envisioned—one that saw beyond its own narrow interests—would require, first of all, a source of funding with no strings attached. His last act was to propose freeing the party from its dependence on Katō's financial resources, and when that proposal was predictably enough rejected, he resigned his membership. He probably did not have what it took to be a successful party politician, but because his departure was seen as a betrayal of the beleaguered Dōshikai, it elicited strong public condemnation. Katō and Ōura must have found his conduct unforgivable. Katō in particular was to nurse a grudge against Gotō until his own death in 1926.

The Yamamoto Cabinet

Gotō's relations with the Yamamoto government, meanwhile, were tense. The Yamamoto cabinet was a coalition of the navy, the Seiyūkai, and the Satsuma clique, which, as already noted, were the main proponents of a gradualist approach to expansion on the continent.

The new government steadily carried out its policy program. For example, over the objections of the army and the Chōshū clique, it scrapped the rule that only officers on active duty could serve as army and navy ministers. It also revised the regulations on appointment of civil officials, narrowing the range of posts requiring formal qualifications and allowing greater freedom in making appointments. The Yamamoto cabinet thus undermined the power base of the Chōshū clique and bureaucratic faction while embarking on a massive naval buildup. On the other hand, it ignored the army's demand for two new divisions.

Of prime concern to Gotō was the Yamamoto cabinet's policy in Manchuria. He was especially perturbed by the new slate of appointments at the SMR at the end of 1913, when the old board's term expired. The government dismissed the current president and vice president, Nakamura and Kunizawa, and in their place appointed as president Nomura Ryūtarō, a technocrat from the Railway Agency, and two senior members of the Seiyūkai, Itō Daihachi and Oku Shigesaburō, as vice presidents. The dismissal of Nakamura, who had done more than anyone else to get the SMR up and running in its early days, came as a tremendous shock to employees on the ground in Manchuria.

When Nakamura left Manchuria on the night train, even clerical staff and ordinary railway workers lined the tracks to see him off. Six of the seven directors were also dismissed. Thus the original leadership of the SMR was almost entirely replaced. There was a minor change as well. The unusual arrangement whereby the SMR's executive officers all worked in the same room was abolished in favor of the practice followed at most companies, with the president, the vice presidents, and the directors each working in separate offices.

Hara Takashi was behind these personnel changes. A champion of party politics, he believed that as few areas as possible should be off-bounds to political-party intervention, and he could not make an exception for the SMR. In view of what was to happen in the 1930s, when the military used the independence of the supreme command as a springboard to achieving dominance, Hara's goal of fully politicizing government institutions seems prescient.

From Gotō's standpoint, however, political meddling in the SMR seemed an unforgivable act in blatant disregard of the national importance of developing Japan's interests in Manchuria. The change in working arrangements, too, seemed sheer folly in that it reduced the SMR, which had been vested with a special national mission, to just another company. All Gotō's painstaking efforts to prevent bureaucratization of the SMR were nullified overnight. Convinced that the Seiyūkai was intent on milking the SMR to its own advantage (which later turned out to be true), he fumed that it and the navy lacked the ambition to develop Japanese interests on the continent.

Gotō, however, was powerless. At loggerheads as he was both with the Yamamoto cabinet and with its rival the Dōshikai, he was more isolated than he had been since his imprisonment during the Sōma Affair discussed in Chapter 1.

The Ōkuma Cabinet and the Oriental Bank Initiative

The seemingly unassailable Yamamoto government, however, unraveled for an unexpected reason. At the beginning of 1914, the Siemens scandal[2]

---

2 Several Imperial Japanese Navy admirals and captains accepted bribes from the German conglomerate Siemens regarding the construction of warships. A month or so later, another bribery case concerning naval contracts came to light, this time involving the British company Vickers.

erupted, exposing corruption inside the navy. Turmoil again broke out on the political scene. Although Prime Minister Yamamoto was not personally implicated, he could not entirely escape blame, since he had dominated the navy for years as a senior naval officer. At the very least, the massive naval buildup that his government had planned was now out of the question. When in March, swayed by the tide of popular opinion, the House of Peers voted down funding for the buildup, the cabinet had no choice but to resign.

Finding a successor to Yamamoto proved difficult. Tokugawa Iesato, the president of the House of Peers, declined the appointment, and Kiyoura Keigo, a protégé of Yamagata, tried but failed to form a cabinet. Finally, Ōkuma Shigenobu[3] became prime minister on the recommendation of elder statesman Inoue Kaoru. Ōkuma, though long an avowed opponent of the oligarchs, was one of the architects of the Meiji state and an old friend of Inoue's; he was expected to rally the Seiyūkai opponents.

The second Ōkuma cabinet, which took power in April, depended primarily on the support of the Dōshikai and was backed by the Chōshū clique. Among the cabinet members from the Dōshikai was Ōura Kanetake, one of Yamagata's right-hand men. Ichiki Kitokurō was appointed education minister. Oka Ichinosuke, an influential member of the Chōshū clique, served as army minister. Whereas the Yamamoto cabinet had been a Seiyūkai government headed by an admiral of the navy, and had therefore taken a gradualist approach to continental policy, the Ōkuma cabinet was a coalition of the Dōshikai, the Chōshū clique, and the army, and therefore pursued a more assertive policy on the continent.

For these reasons Gotō was at first well disposed toward the new government. He and Ōkuma were similar in that they both thought big. But Ōkuma's cabinet was dominated by the Dōshikai, the party that Gotō had just abandoned. While Gotō might not have harbored any hard feelings, the Dōshikai certainly did. Gotō thought it possible that the advent of the Ōkuma government would lead to a more activist policy on the continent,

---

3   Ōkuma was the founder of the Kaishintō (1882), one of two major political parties in Japan that competed with the Jiyūtō. Ōkuma was a strong supporter of the Kokumintō, which originated from the Kaishintō, and critical of the Seiyūkai, which originated from the Jiyūtō.

and he hoped to play a role in furthering it, thus regaining his place on the political scene. There were, however, considerable obstacles to any rapprochement between Gotō and the Ōkuma cabinet.

Under these circumstances Gotō advocated establishing what he called the Oriental Bank. Specifically, he proposed using the money earmarked for the naval buildup derailed by the Siemens scandal to set up a bank capitalized at 100 million yen, with Japan contributing 50 million and China the other 50 million (borrowed from Japan). Gotō, while a proponent of closer relations with China, believed that "simply engaging in diplomatic negotiations and that type of thing [was] no longer effective" for achieving that objective. It was necessary, he argued, "to cooperate where figures allow of no deception, in the area of economic relations." With that goal in mind, he conceived of the Oriental Bank as an institution that, instead of seeking to "secure special rights," would foster recognition in practice "of the commonality of interests between China and our country." As a result, he contended, Japan would, "rather than having to fear a boycott in China, put them [the Chinese] in a position in the economic relationship where they are unable to implement a boycott."

This plan clearly incorporates the features of the policy Gotō advocated toward China as described so far. Its aim was to provide active assistance to China and thus favorably dispose the Chinese to Japan, or rather tie them so closely to Japan that antagonism was not a realistic option. In that regard, his envisioned Oriental Bank united the concept of military preparations in civilian garb with that of the New and Old Worlds in opposition. Gotō's subsequent policy toward China was to evolve along the same lines.

Gotō won the backing of elder statesmen Yamagata Aritomo and Inoue Kaoru for this idea and, in China, even sounded Yuan Shikai out about it. However, Katō Takaaki, now foreign minister in the Ōkuma cabinet, had taken a particular disliking to Gotō since his departure from the Dōshikai. As a foreign ministry mainstreamer, moreover, Katō was averse to the use of informal channels circumventing his ministry. On top of it all, Japan did not have much financial leeway. For these reasons Gotō's plan got nowhere.

CHAPTER 5

WORLD WAR I AND JAPAN

1. Critic of the Ōkuma Cabinet

The Outbreak of World War I

As we have seen, beginning around 1911, there was much political debate in Japan as to whether the country should take an assertive approach to expanding its presence on the Asian continent or pursue a more gradualist policy. This dispute was settled by the outbreak of World War I, which created the perfect conditions for Japanese expansion on the continent. In this chapter, we will examine where Gotō stood on the issue and what role he played.

The war, which began between Austria and Serbia on July 28, 1914, had by August 4 drawn in Russia, Germany, France, and Britain to become a conflict on an unprecedented scale. Consequently, the European powers no longer had the resources to intervene in the Far East and were forced to allow Japan a more or less free hand. As a result, the government of Yuan Shikai in China could no longer count on help from the European powers in its efforts to resist Japan. As the war dragged on, Japan's economic power grew dramatically. In sum, the constraints on Japanese policy on the continent rapidly disappeared, and a more assertive policy became possible for the first time. This is primarily what elder statesman Inoue Kaoru was referring to when he described World War I as "the godsend of the new Taishō era."

On August 3, just before entering the war, Britain requested Japan's help in the fight against Germany. The Japanese government readily complied. It decided to demand that Germany return its leasehold on Jiaozhou (Kiaochow) Bay in the Shandong Peninsula to China via Japan, and declare war if Germany refused. Japan was so bellicose, in fact, that at one point, relations with Britain became strained. In the end, Japan issued an ultimatum to Germany on August 15 and declared war on the twenty-third. The public strongly supported war with Germany, as the bitter memory of the Tripartite Intervention in 1895 still lingered.

But elder statesmen Yamagata and Inoue and the governor-general of Korea, Terauchi Masatake, were seriously alarmed by the cabinet's decision. They were deeply concerned that the cabinet might be exploiting the war as a means of gaining popular support. They also wondered how the government envisaged international relations unfolding during and after the conflict. They insisted that deciding the essentials of future China policy must be a prerequisite for going to war. Inoue, the self-proclaimed guardian of the Ōkuma cabinet, met with Prime Minister Ōkuma on September 24 and made several demands, including expanding the Anglo-Japanese Alliance to include France and Russia and dispatching a special envoy to China. This was exactly what Gotō had been espousing for years, and he was the man tipped for the post of special envoy.

Foreign Minister Katō Takaaki, however, disagreed. Staunchly pro-British, Katō rejected the expansion of the Anglo-Japanese Alliance on the grounds that it would be like putting too much water in your whisky. Coming from a conventional diplomatic background, he resented the elder statesmen's meddling and was averse to the use of non-institutional channels such as special envoys. As for sending his bête noire Gotō on a diplomatic mission, that was absolutely out of the question.

Ōkuma's Electoral Landslide

The elder statesmen, then, were unhappy with the Ōkuma government. They dared not go so far as to replace it, however, because they hoped that the Ōkuma cabinet would dissolve the House of Representatives and emasculate the Seiyūkai in general elections, and then once and for all resolve the issue of the two new army divisions in Korea, which for the past several years had afflicted politics like a cancer. Despite the opposition Seiyūkai's desperate efforts to avoid an election, the government dissolved the lower house at the end of 1914 and transferred Agriculture and Commerce Minister Ōura Kanetake, an old hand at elections, to the home affairs portfolio (previously held by Prime Minister Ōkuma) in preparation for the election campaign.

To digress for a moment, this election was one of the most interesting in Japanese history. Capitalizing on the surge in Ōkuma's popularity after his many years out of office, the government closed ranks, ran a brilliant campaign, and won by a landslide. Ōkuma stumped all over the country, stopping his train at various locations along the way to deliver a rousing speech. He sent telegrams to supporters up and down Japan. He even produced a record of an address entitled "The Power of Public Opinion in Constitutional Government" for nationwide distribution (on it can be heard the turn of phrase for which he was famous, "it is, it is, it is"). Alumni of Waseda University, which Ōkuma founded, formed the Ōkuma-haku Kōenkai (Count Ōkuma Support Association) and fielded independent candidates with Waseda ties. Even cabinet ministers took an active part in campaigning, which was unprecedented. In these and other regards this was without exaggeration Japan's first modern election.

The government won an overwhelming victory at the polls at the end of March. The Dōshikai dramatically increased its seats, taking the party from 95 to 153. And while the Chūseikai (Impartial Association) was reduced from 36 to 33 seats, the newly formed Ōkuma-haku Kōenkai won 12 seats. The government's total seat count thus jumped from 131 to 198. The Seiyūkai's seat count, conversely, plummeted from 184 to 108, and the Kokumintō was reduced from 32 to 27. The Seiyūkai had since its founding in 1900 always been the biggest party in the legislature and was for much of its history the majority party. In prewar Japan, the government often won big at the polls, but this was truly a historic victory for the government and an equally historic defeat for the opposition. The Seiyūkai naturally accused the government of meddling in the elections, which was likely true, but the new style of election campaigning described above appears to have been the decisive factor.

This election campaign strengthened Gotō's antipathy for the government. He had never seen eye to eye with Katō or Ōura. He found it unforgivable that when the country was at war and should have been united, the government resorted to fanning partisan conflict. It further galled him that the government appeared to be using foreign policy for political gain.

Criticism of the Twenty-One Demands to China

The infamous Twenty-One Demands were presented to China by the Ōkuma cabinet soon after the lower house was dissolved. This set of twenty-one articles was divided into five groups, the chief of which were the first two. Group 1 pertained to Japan's assumption of certain German rights on the Shandong Peninsula. Group 2 pertained to the strengthening of Japan's rights in Manchuria, including an extension of its leases on the Kwantung Territory and the South Manchuria Railway. Negotiations began in January 1915, and dragged on until Japan delivered an ultimatum in May and China finally capitulated.

The demands were backed by the implicit threat of military force, undoubtedly an act of diplomatic aggression. Yet the Twenty-One Demands were not blatantly aggressive by the international standards of the day. Germany's occupation of part of the Shandong Peninsula, Russian policy toward China, and British and French actions against China in the late nineteenth century were all far worse acts of aggression. Indeed, many of Japan's other policies toward China were just as aggressive as the Twenty-One Demands, if not more so. Japanese public opinion, with a few exceptions, such as the liberal magazine *Tōyō Keizai Shinpō*, was overwhelmingly in favor of the demands. Even the liberal scholar Yoshino Sakuzō, soon to become the champion of Taishō democracy and the international cooperation in the 1920s, basically supported them, although he later criticized himself for doing so. The political context of the Twenty-One Demands cannot be properly understood without an appreciation of that background.

It is therefore noteworthy that Gotō, along with the elder statesmen and Terauchi, was harshly critical of the Twenty-One Demands. His criticism was underpinned by the fundamental principles of the policy he advocated toward China. As mentioned in connection with his vision for the Oriental Bank, Gotō believed that Japan should first provide generous financial and other aid to China, thus establishing close ties between the two countries, and only then set about resolving the issue of Japanese interests there. The idea of sending a special envoy to China was rooted in the same thinking. Gotō doubtless agreed with the government on extending the leases on the Kwantung Territory and the SMR as called for by the Twenty-One Demands.

Nor can we ever know whether matters would have proceeded as Gotō envisaged had his own strategy been followed, with Japanese aid leading seamlessly to a cooperative relationship, leading in turn to a smooth resolution of the question of Japan's interests in China. It is fair to say, however, that Gotō's approach would have differed greatly from that embodied in the Twenty-One Demands, which China was forced to accept with little in return.

Gotō had at first been favorably disposed to the Ōkuma government because of his antipathy to the Seiyūkai. Indeed, he and Ōkuma were two of a kind in that they were among prewar Japan's biggest talkers. The 1915 election and the Twenty-One Demands, however, turned Gotō into a staunch opponent of the Ōkuma cabinet.

Criticism of the Government's Plans to Overthrow Yuan Shikai

In June 1915, after the issue of the Twenty-One Demands had been settled, the elder statesmen seriously considered replacing Katō with a new foreign minister. But it was evident that dismissing Katō, who led the governing Dōshikai and was deputy prime minister, would precipitate the fall of the Ōkuma cabinet. Still fearing a revival of the Seiyūkai's fortunes, the elder statesmen had no choice but to back down.

Katō, however, ended up leaving the government in July because of a corruption scandal involving Home Minister Ōura. It emerged that Ōura had, as agriculture minister in the legislative session prior to the election, been involved in a bribery scheme to win approval for the two new army divisions. Ōura ultimately resigned, and the charges against him were dropped on condition that he decline all honors and retire from politics. The entire cabinet also resigned, although many of its members secretly hoped to remain in office. Ōkuma remained prime minister, since no replacement for him could be found, and he reshuffled his cabinet, ousting Katō Takaaki and Finance Minister Wakatsuki Reijirō, who insisted on accepting joint responsibility for the scandal.

Yamagata's protégés in the bureaucracy, who had been tenuously linked to the Ōkuma government via Ōura, turned decisively against it due to his resignation, and they started working actively in the House of Peers to topple the cabinet. In November 1915, former bureaucrats among the members of the House of Peers who had gathered in Kyoto for the Taishō Emperor's enthronement ceremony began plotting to bring about the government's fall. Gotō was among their ringleaders.

In the meantime, the government embarked on an even more perilous course in China. In the summer of 1915, Yuan Shikai began planning to restore imperial rule and assume the throne himself. The Ōkuma cabinet initially assumed a wait-and-see attitude to this development, but then, between late 1915 and early 1916, changed course. It now started plotting to overthrow Yuan's regime, which had been a thorn in Japan's side, by exploiting and exacerbating the turmoil caused by his attempt to reimpose imperial rule. On March 7, 1916, the Ōkuma cabinet adopted an astonishing resolution calling for the overthrow of Yuan Shikai. It read in part as follows.

1. To consider the current situation in China, Yuan's loss of authority, his alienation of public opinion, and domestic unrest have become increasingly marked, and that country's future now truly contains elements of unpredictability. The course that the Empire should follow at this juncture is to establish predominance in China, make her people aware of the Empire's might, and thus lay the foundations of Sino-Japanese friendship.

2. Yuan's presence in power in China cannot but be an obstacle to the Empire's accomplishment of the above objective. Therefore his departure from the circles of Chinese power would be conducive to the execution of the above imperial policy. There can be no doubt that whoever replaces him would, compared to Yuan, be far more to the Empire's advantage . . .

6. There are private activists in the Empire who, being sympathetic to the activities of Chinese seeking to remove Yuan, seek to provide them with funding and other resources. While the Government shall take no responsibility for openly encouraging this, its connivance is consistent with the above policy . . .

Seldom had a Japanese government adopted such a blatant policy, at least before the Manchurian Incident of 1931. The government proceeded to implement this strategy in several ways. In Manchuria, it encouraged efforts to detach that region and Mongolia from China proper by establishing contact with the Zongshedang, an organization dedicated to restoring the Qing dynasty, with the Mongolian royal family, which sought independence from China, and with warlord Zhang Zuolin, who was attempting to consolidate his position in Manchuria. In the south, Japan furnished revolutionaries with weapons, funding, and many other forms of support. Elsewhere, it supported the Revolutionary Party in its efforts to organize anti-government uprisings. Indeed, the Japanese had no compunction about working with groups of any political stripe whatsoever, whether they sought to revive the Qing dynasty or establish a republic, as long as they opposed Yuan Shikai.

Gotō naturally opposed this policy, committed as he was to cooperating with whoever was in power in China. It was in his eyes the height of folly. Of the elder statesman, Inoue was already dead and Yamagata had fallen seriously ill in the winter of 1915–16. Gotō therefore sought to establish closer ties with Terauchi Masatake, governor-general of Korea and the man considered most likely to become the next prime minister, while plotting to topple the Ōkuma cabinet.

2. The Terauchi Cabinet Assumes Power

Negotiating the Transfer of Power

Gotō's campaign to overthrow the cabinet unfolded in the House of Peers during the legislative session that commenced at the end of 1915. His fellow plotters were the members of the Yamagata-aligned bureaucratic faction sitting in the House. Gotō himself was in a sense aligned with Yamagata as well, but not directly. Never having had much connection with organized power, he always had to rely on someone else's backing.

The efforts of Gotō and his fellows paid off. The cabinet found itself with its back to the wall. At the beginning of February, in a bid to get through the current legislative session, Ōkuma visited Yamagata and asked him to rein in the government's opponents, hinting that once the session was over, he would resign for reasons of old age (he was seventy-seven). Yamagata assented, and he and Ōkuma began negotiating the transfer of power to a new government.

Negotiations proceeded slowly owing to Yamagata's illness. In May, after the legislative session ended, Ōkuma announced his intention to recommend former foreign minister Katō Takaaki, leader of the Dōshikai, as his successor. Yamagata, taken completely by surprise, expressed opposition. Not only did he himself strongly disapprove of Katō's foreign policy, but even Ōkuma had once spoken of his disenchantment with him. Ōkuma therefore temporarily put aside the idea of handing over power to Katō and decided, in accordance with Yamagata's wishes, to throw his support behind Terauchi Masatake instead. He did, however, request that Terauchi maintain his cabinet's policies and form a Terauchi-Katō coalition government by collaborating with the Dōshikai. Terauchi came to Tokyo at Ōkuma's request, and negotiations between the two men commenced in July.

Many of Terauchi's associates argued in favor of cooperating with the Dōshikai, if not forming a coalition with it, most notably Yamagata himself and his close adviser Hirata Tōsuke. Yamagata, anxious to ensure that Terauchi's efforts to form a government proceeded smoothly, was afraid to clash with Ōkuma's supporters, who commanded a majority in the lower house. It was still too soon to allow the Seiyūkai to recover, he felt, and Ōkuma's influence was formidable, as the previous year's elections had shown.

Gotō, by contrast, was relentless in calling for confrontation with the Dōshikai and its allies. For him, the whole purpose of a change in government was to alter the course of China policy; otherwise it would be almost pointless. In a bid to engineer a decisive break with Ōkuma and the Dōshikai, Gotō prepared and circulated a secret pamphlet exposing the failures of the Ōkuma cabinet's China policy, particularly a clash between Japanese and Chinese forces at Zhengjiatun in Manchuria, a corollary of its anti-Yuan policy, and Japanese involvement in what were alleged to be Chinese Revolutionary Party operations in Shandong. While the pamphlet's claims were largely true, Gotō's methods were typically extreme. His opposition was one of the major reasons that the talks between Ōkuma and Terauchi in July and August failed to produce an agreement.

The Terauchi Cabinet Assumes Power

On October 4, 1916, Prime Minister Ōkuma tendered his resignation to the emperor, citing his advanced years, and recommended Katō Takaaki as his successor. It was unusual for a prime minister to refer to a successor in his resignation. Ōkuma did so because the three parties in his cabinet—the Dōshikai, the Chūseikai, and the Kōyū (Public Friends) Club—had been making plans to merge since mid-September. This three-way merger would create a massive political party with over half the seats in the lower house, a bloc that would be difficult to ignore when governing. The idea was to make Katō Takaaki, who was slated to be the leader of the new party, prime minister with its backing, and thus in effect keep the Ōkuma government in power.

After Ōkuma submitted his resignation, the four elder statesmen—Yamagata Aritomo, Ōyama Iwao, Matsukata Masayoshi, and Saionji Kinmochi—immediately visited the Imperial Palace and, in a conference with the emperor, recommended Terauchi as the next prime minister. The nature of the future Terauchi cabinet, however, was still a complete unknown. Terauchi proclaimed a government of national unity on the grounds that the country was at war, and for that reason it was thought that he would ask all parties to join the cabinet. He was expected to negotiate first with the Dōshikai, the largest party and one of the governing parties in the previous cabinet. If the Dōshikai agreed to join the new government, however, the other parties might refuse to do so out of hostility to it, in which case the cabinet would end up being a Dōshikai-based one. This was in fact what Yamagata and Hirata envisioned.

Gotō was determined to scuttle any such alliance between the new cabinet and the Dōshikai. He repeatedly stressed to Terauchi that the main point of the change in government was to alter the course of China policy, and everyone who had been involved in setting that policy in the previous cabinet needed to be ousted. The Dōshikai for its part could not accept Gotō playing a central role in the new cabinet when he had abandoned the struggling party three years earlier and had, just a month or two before, circulated a shady pamphlet attacking the Ōkuma cabinet's China policy. In the end, the Terauchi government and the Dōshikai did not cooperate.

The Terauchi cabinet thus took the form envisioned by Gotō, not that envisioned by Yamagata and Hirata.

That alone, however, was insufficient, to keep the new government in power. The Terauchi cabinet was a so-called "transcendental" (i.e., nonparty) cabinet as well as an oligarchic one. As such it could not expect much popular support, since transcendental cabinets were at the time considered a relic of the past. Public opinion was not implacably opposed to the Terauchi government only because of the failures of its predecessor. It would be a short-lived cabinet indeed unless it held elections while those failures were still fresh in memory and quickly struck a blow against the Kenseikai (Constitutional Government Association) party, which was formed on October 10 by a merger of the Dōshikai with the two smaller parties, the Chūseikai and the Kōyū Club.

The Fighting Home Minister

Gotō, who was home minister in the new cabinet, engaged in a series of provocations against the Kenseikai. In December, for example, he appointed Mizuno Rentarō vice minister of home affairs. Mizuno, who had previously served in that position under Home Minister Hara Takashi, had joined the Seiyūkai and was widely tipped for a ministerial post in the next Seiyūkai cabinet. Appointing a senior member of the Seiyūkai to this electorally important position, even if, as explained below, there were other reasons behind it, was a naked challenge to the Kenseikai in that it signaled the government's intention of allying with the Seiyūkai against the new party.

The Diet convened at the end of 1916, and in January 1917, the Kokumintō, led by Inukai Tsuyoshi, approached the Kenseikai about jointly tabling a no-confidence motion against the transcendental Terauchi cabinet. The Kenseikai agreed, but then in a speech, Inukai suddenly launched into a tirade against the Kenseikai. When the enraged Kenseikai tried to retort, the government dissolved the lower house. The Kokumintō then declared that it was severing relations with the Kenseikai and, in effect, went over to the government. The entire masquerade had, in fact, been a ruse to lure the Kenseikai into an election by exploiting the Kokumintō's hostility to it (since the core of the Kenseikai consisted of Diet members who had in 1913 defected from the Kokumintō to Katsura's new party). The man behind that stratagem was Gotō.

The Terauchi cabinet, which took office in October 1916
From right: Home Minister Gotō, Seiyūkai leader Hara, Kenseikai legislator Hamaguchi (fourth from right), Prime Minister Terauchi, Kokumintō leader Inukai, and Vice Minister of Home Affairs Mizuno

As home minister, the minister responsible for overseeing elections, Gotō put considerable effort into defeating the Kenseikai. In a speech delivered to a conference of prefectural governors in February, he spoke of the need to facilitate the natural expression of public opinion by vanquishing the "unnatural majority party," an implicit call to defeat the Kenseikai. Such a speech was most unusual for a home minister, who was supposed to be impartial. Gotō also cooperated closely with the Seiyūkai. He did not, however, stake the government's fate solely on that party. He also worked to bring the Kokumintō into the government and ran many independents in the election, hoping to manipulate them behind the scenes.

The Seiyūkai naturally objected to Gotō's ploy of running independent candidates. Gotō, however, parried the criticism by jokingly telling Seiyūkai leader Hara Takashi that he (Hara) was Japan's most consummate election campaigner, the equivalent of a grand master in the game of go, and it was hardly fair for the grand master to complain about where an amateurish, countrified player like himself placed his stones.

In the elections, which took place in April, the Seiyūkai won 165 seats, the Kenseikai 121, the Kokumintō 35, and independents 60. It was a crushing defeat for the Kenseikai. These results could to a considerable extent be attributed to Gotō. He had certainly proved himself a formidable operator. But Gotō always tended to go a bit too far, whether in his provocation of the Kenseikai, his exploitation of Inukai's hostility to the Kenseikai to trigger a dissolution of the legislature, or his blatant actions during the election campaign. At the very least, those who fell victim to his machinations did not easily forget their grudge against him, and that was often to have an unfavorable effect on his political career.

The crowning touch of this politicking was a new council on foreign relations. After the election, the government established the Provisional Research Council on Foreign Relations under the emperor's direct control for the ostensible purpose of achieving a national consensus on wartime foreign policy. It appointed senior figures from all sectors of the political elite to sit on the council with the status of ministers of state. In the end the only leading politician not to become a member was Kenseikai President Katō Takaaki. The Provisional Research Council on Foreign Relations, naturally, was expected to become a forum for criticizing the previous government's foreign policy, and the Kenseikai could hardly be expected to join it, especially after having savaged the government in the recent election campaign. Its nonparticipation, however, meant that it was for many years after to remain essentially an antiestablishment party. The council was the idea of privy councilor Itō Miyoji, though Gotō was also an enthusiastic proponent.

Home Affairs and the Railways

Gotō's administrative accomplishments as home minister, on the other hand, were few. The home ministry was a regulatory agency rather than a provider of public services; it did not implement programs itself. Besides, the home minister's most important task was, as we have seen, to formulate and execute the cabinet's political strategy as the prime minister's political lieutenant. In prewar Japan the home minister was often viewed as the deputy prime minister and frequently had to relinquish command of day-to-day operations. That was one of the reasons why Gotō had appointed Mizuno Rentarō, a heavyweight of ministerial caliber well versed in practical matters, as his vice minister.

Still, Gotō did manage to leave his mark on the home ministry. During his tenure, staff numbers increased considerably, the organization grew, salaries rose, and the overseas study program expanded. Throughout his life, Gotō did his best to develop new talent, and these moves at the home ministry were all essentially designed to secure and train able people and give them a stage on which to work.

Of particular importance was the overseas study program. The home ministry was deeply interested in what policies other countries were implementing in their efforts to fight a war of unprecedented scope while maintaining social stability. Many of the men who went on to run Japan's home affairs in the 1930s studied abroad with Gotō's blessing, including Gotō Fumio, Maruyama Tsurukichi, Tako Ichimin, Horikiri Zenjirō, Ōtsuka Isei, and Tsugita Daisaburō. Their primary field of activity was social policy. In addition, a relief section was established within the home ministry during Gotō's tenure, which later evolved into the ministry's Social Bureau and went on to become the Ministry of Welfare (now the Ministry of Health, Labour and Welfare). Gotō had been the first person in Japan to take an interest in social policy, back in his days as head of the Public Health Bureau during the Meiji era. It was certainly no coincidence that the personnel and organization that were later to run social policy were products of Gotō's term as home minister.

Another of Gotō's achievements was paving the way for the Urban Planning Act. Having been involved in building cities in Taiwan and Manchuria, he was eager to turn Tokyo and Osaka into modern, "civilized" metropolises. To that end he set up an urban planning committee, thus laying the groundwork for the Urban Planning Act. This set the stage for him to become mayor of Tokyo some years later.

Besides holding the home affairs portfolio, Gotō also served for the third time as director-general of the Railway Agency, with his trusted friend

Nakamura Yoshikoto serving as deputy director-general. Gotō again turned his attention to converting Japan's major railways to broad gauge. Thanks to technological advances, the project was now budgeted at around 60 million yen, whereas at the time of the Katsura cabinet it had been budgeted at over 200 million. Despite this, it again failed, primarily because of the government's relations with the political parties. The balance of power between the oligarchs and the parties had changed since Katsura had been prime minister. The Terauchi government basically had no choice but to work with the Seiyūkai, which had traditionally supported a narrow-gauge policy, while the Kenseikai was in favor of the broad-gauge plan. Terauchi and Gotō had higher policy priorities, and they could not afford to make enemies of the Seiyūkai over this issue.

3. China and Russia

Changing the Course of China Policy

For Gotō, the Terauchi government's highest priority was, as evident from his actions around the time that it came to power, changing the course of Japan's foreign policy. Another reason that he appointed Mizuno Rentarō vice minister was in order to leave the task of administering home affairs to him and concentrate on China policy. Motono Ichirō, who had been appointed foreign minister, was a seasoned diplomat but had little experience in Chinese issues; he was pro-Russian or pro-Franco-Russian. Gotō thus had a large role to play.

First, as the new cabinet was being formed, Gotō called for a purge of everyone who had been involved in China policy in the Ōkuma cabinet as a signal to domestic and international observers that the policy was now going to be different. The minister and vice minister of foreign affairs, the head of the foreign ministry's Political Affairs Bureau, the deputy chief of army staff, and the governor-general of Kwantung Territory were all on Gotō's hit list. Only two men survived the purge, Vice Minister of Foreign Affairs Shidehara Kijūrō and Deputy Chief of Army Staff Tanaka Giichi; the rest were dismissed.

The government's new China policy, which was adopted by the Terauchi cabinet on January 9, 1917, consisted of five main points: first, respecting and protecting China's independence and territorial integrity; second, advising on policy improvements to that end and further developing friendly bilateral ties; third, nonintervention in domestic affairs; fourth, advancing Japan's special interests in Manchuria, Mongolia, and Shandong; and fifth, cooperating elsewhere with the Western powers insofar as possible. This policy was clearly a complete repudiation of the anti-Yuan campaign in which the Ōkuma cabinet had engaged, especially during the latter part of its term in office.

This change in the course of China policy had two main thrusts. One was cooperation with the Western powers; the other was a commitment to a close partnership between Japan and China ("Sino-Japanese friendship," to use the slogan of the day), as articulated in the second point of the policy. The two were, strictly speaking, mutually exclusive, because the more closely interlinked Japan and China became, the less say the Western powers would have in China's affairs.

The written rationale for adopting the policy originally contained a section intended to rein in overzealous proponents of a Sino-Japanese partnership. It stated that there were those who argued that, by race and geography, the Japanese and the Chinese shared a common destiny, but, it went on to assert, the vicissitudes of Chinese history had in fact never affected Japan's national fortunes. Moreover, the notion of a shared destiny provided an excuse for intervention in China's domestic affairs, and could fan Western fears of the "Yellow Peril". In short, the section concluded, caution was in order.

Gotō objected to this section, and it was accordingly deleted. He was the most vocal advocate of the adoption and announcement of this new policy toward China, and his vision of a Sino-Japanese partnership pervaded this policy decision, trumping the wishes of the foreign ministry, which believed in the importance of cooperating with the Western powers.

Partnership with China and Cooperation with the Western Powers
After adopting this policy, the Terauchi government simultaneously pursued the goals of forming a partnership with China and cooperating with the Western powers. It actively assisted the Allies in the war effort and, in return, got them to agree to Japan's postwar claims. At the request of the British

and French, for example, Japan dispatched destroyers to the Mediterranean, and it subscribed to British, French, and Russian bond issues, all with the goal of helping the war effort. In return, in March 1917, those countries agreed to support Japan at the postwar peace conference if it made claims to German rights in Shandong and German island possessions north of the equator. This policy was in accord with the idea of an alliance between Japan, Britain, France, and Russia that Gotō had championed since 1914.

As for China policy, the government took definite action to bring China into the war as the British, French, and Russians were demanding. The preceding government under Ōkuma had refused to do so because it did not want China to become Japan's equal as an ally in the war. The Terauchi cabinet altered that policy in the interests of cooperating with the Allies.

Meanwhile, when the pro-Japanese Duan Qirui became premier of China in July 1917, the Terauchi cabinet adopted a second decision, this one relaxing the principle of nonintervention articulated in the January policy, and began taking active steps to build a Sino-Japanese partnership. Despite lacking strong support and facing domestic oppositions, the Duan government was internationally recognized as the legitimate government of China, and aiding it was regarded neither as intervention in China's internal affairs nor as a violation of the policy of cooperating with the Western powers.

The most serious question was how to channel funds to China. Japan was a member of a four-power loan consortium with Britain, France, and Russia. As such it was obliged to abide by the consortium agreement when making loans to China. This four-power consortium was originally formed in 1910 by Britain, France, the United States, and Germany to prevent excessive competition among lenders to China. Japan and Russia later joined, making it a six-power consortium until the United States and Germany withdrew. Its membership consisted of leading banks and banking syndicates from each country (in the case of Japan, the Yokohama Specie Bank). The consortium agreement had the binding force similar to that of a treaty and underwent several revisions. At the time, it required that "administrative loans" to China be jointly underwritten by all consortium members. The war had made Japan a creditor nation, and for the first time it could afford to lend large amounts to China, but it was prevented by the consortium agreement from immediately taking advantage of its financial wherewithal to acquire new rights or achieve other political objectives.

Already in December 1916, Gotō had, in a memorandum on this question entitled "Proposal on Policy toward China," asserted, "In order to relieve China's economic and financial difficulties, we should stand outside the four-power loan restrictions, lay the foundations of a national economic alliance, and, unconcerned with immediate petty interests such as guaranteeing our rights, abundantly demonstrate the Empire's magnanimity by investing massive amounts. We should thus take action to transform the psychological state of the Chinese, so that before they know it, they have spontaneously forgotten their previous suspicions and ill feelings." In short, Gotō argued that Japan should, instead of making the acquisition of rights and interests from China its primary objective, provide generous financial support and thus turn China into a friend of Japan. To that end he proposed devising a means unconstrained by the four-power consortium agreement.

The series of loans made to China under the Terauchi government known as the Nishihara loans were administrative loans categorized as "industrial loans," which were exempt from the consortium agreement. Gotō had, since the days of the Oriental Bank initiative, maintained that Japan should provide financing to China in exactly this fashion—"outside the four-power loan restrictions." He thus had a definite influence on the Nishihara loans, at least at the outset.

Relations with the United States

The most serious obstacle to the policy of simultaneously cooperating with the Western powers and establishing a Sino-Japanese partnership was the United States. The US had traditionally been the most sympathetic supporter of Chinese independence and unity, and its influence was growing with the rise of a new generation of Chinese educated in America. Moreover, not only could the US afford to lend large amounts to China, it was not bound by the consortium agreement. It had withdrawn from the consortium in 1913, on the grounds that the conditions of a 25-million-pound reorganization loan that the consortium was about to conclude with China were so severe that they would undermine Chinese unity and independence. The US therefore enjoyed a free hand and took advantage of it to arrange numerous loans to China in 1916.

Gotō had, since his days as president of the South Manchuria Railway and indeed as civilian governor of Taiwan, considered it important to compete and cooperate with the Americans in China. In his "Proposal on Policy toward China," written during the last days of the Ōkuma government, he stated that the government's greatest sin was its failed foreign policy, especially the deterioration of relations with China and the US. The shadow of the US is evident in his assertion about standing "outside the four-power loan restrictions."

Japan succeeded in squaring cooperation with the Western powers with a Sino-Japanese partnership insofar as relations with Britain, France, and Russia were concerned. The problem was how to draw the US into that relationship. The Lansing-Ishii Agreement of November 2, 1917 was an attempt to achieve that objective by capitalizing World War I on the golden opportunity afforded by the American entry into World War I in April of that year.

The first half of this agreement famously states, "The governments of the United States and Japan recognize that territorial propinquity creates special relations between countries, and, consequently, the government of the United States recognizes that Japan has special interests in China, particularly in the part to which her possessions are contiguous." The second half, however, seems to tone that statement down somewhat by declaring the two countries' commitment to respecting the independence and territorial integrity of China, the open door, and equal opportunity. The Americans afterwards denied that the quoted passage was of special significance, asserting that it was simply a declaration of a universally applicable principle. It was nevertheless an unambiguous acknowledgement of the especially close relationship that existed between Japan and China and of Japan's special interests in Manchuria and Mongolia; hence the US later made frantic efforts to annul the agreement after World War I was over.

At any rate, the China policy implemented by the Terauchi cabinet in the year or so after it took office achieved a fair amount, and most of its elements had long been advocated by Gotō. He had also been at least one of the main proponents of the Provisional Research Council on Foreign Relations set up to advance that policy, and he was a member of it along with the prime minister, the foreign minister, and the army and navy ministers. The success of the Terauchi government's China policy during its first year in office was largely attributable to Gotō.

The Shock of the Russian Revolution

In November 1917, immediately after the culmination of this series of foreign policy successes in the Lansing-Ishii Agreement, the October Revolution broke out in Russia, and with it collapsed the partnership with Russia that, along with the Anglo-Japanese Alliance, had been one of the two main cornerstones of Japanese foreign policy since the end of the Russo-Japanese War. It was a particularly severe blow for Terauchi and Gotō, who believed strongly in the importance of working with Russia. It left them with no choice but to dramatically alter the course of government policy.

The Russian Revolution was, needless to say, a fundamental challenge to the established political and economic order. At the time, however, it was regarded above all as a military setback, for it meant the collapse of the united front against Germany. On December 5, 1917, the revolutionary government signed an armistice with Germany and on March 3, 1918, it concluded the Treaty of Brest-Litovsk. This was a violation of the London Declaration not to make a separate peace with Germany. Moreover, the peace terms were highly favorable to Germany. Many observers on the Allied side accordingly believed that Russia had fallen under the control of a pro-German regime. It was feared that Russia had not only abandoned the Allies but would soon join the German camp.

The Allies therefore began discussing the possibility of sending a Japanese or joint Japanese-American force to Siberia to prevent Russia from allying with Germany and help the moderates recover, so that the Eastern Front could be restored. In December 1917, the French suggested that the Trans-Siberian Railway be placed under the control of Japanese and American forces. That marked the beginning of an intense debate on the dispatch of troops to Siberia that continued throughout the months before and after the

March 1918 signing of the Treaty of Brest-Litovsk. The Americans, deeply suspicious of Japanese ambitions, opposed the idea.

Opinions were divided in Japan as well. Observing the power vacuum in Siberia, many in the army, particularly in the General Staff Office, took a hawkish stance and argued that Japan should send its own independent expedition. At the other end of the spectrum, Hara Takashi and privy councilor Makino Nobuaki (both members of the Provisional Research Council on Foreign Relations) opposed sending troops out of a belief in the importance of cooperating with the US. The cabinet decided that it would consider sending troops if necessary for reasons of self-defense or if the Allies unanimously requested it. Even so, there were clashes between cautious voices such as Prime Minister Terauchi and hawks such as Foreign Minister Motono. Motono tried to browbeat the cabinet into uniting behind his plans for an expeditionary force but, having failed, resigned on April 23, 1918, partly for reasons of ill health.

His successor was Gotō. Previously, in January and February, Gotō had stood in for Terauchi, who was ailing at the time, by coordinating the government's lobbying efforts in the Diet. Indeed, the press had begun predicting that Gotō would be appointed acting prime minister. Instead, he became foreign minister in April and took on a massive workload, working almost nonstop despite losing his wife Kazuko at the beginning of that same month. Terauchi, meanwhile, often missed important cabinet meetings because of his continuing poor health. On April 29, Communications Minister Den Kenjirō, a senior cabinet member aligned with Yamagata Aritomo, met with privy councilor Itō Miyoji, one of the cabinet's most prominent outside supporters and a member of the Provisional Research Council on Foreign Relations. The two men agreed that if Terauchi's health did not recover, either Gotō or someone outside the cabinet (meaning Itō himself) should be his successor. Such was the importance of Gotō's position as foreign minister.

The Siberian Expedition

Gotō, long known for his pro-Russian views, was in favor of sending an expedition to Siberia. What disposed him to support the idea?

First, it should be noted that few Japanese politicians at the time accurately appreciated the nature of the revolution or the strength of the revolutionary government. Pro-Russians such as Motono and Gotō could not easily imagine the members of the Russian ancien régime with which they had long been on friendly terms suddenly being swept away. In fact, it was they, the pro-Russians, who were most in favor of an expedition. The skeptics were men like Hara and Makino who gave priority to cooperation with the British and the Americans and considered relations with Russia of less importance. For Gotō, with his "biological" view of humanity and the state, the revolution's principles such as the denial of private property must have seemed to go against the "innate character" of mankind. It seemed inconceivable that the new regime could survive for long. In a memorandum of May he wrote, "There are many elements in Russia secretly longing for the dispatch of an expedition by the Allies. The stance of the extremists, who are losing popular support by the day owing to their perfidy and savagery, is not worth of much thought during the formulation of a grand strategy for an imperial expedition." Gotō, convinced that the revolutionary regime rested on fragile foundations, believed that there must be widespread elements critical of it who were connected to the old Russia. Supporting such "moderates" was, for Gotō, part and parcel of the Russo-Japanese partnership.

Another important factor was concern over the Bolshevik regime's anti-imperialist diplomacy. The revolutionary government at one point hinted that it would return the Chinese Eastern Railway to China, promising to restore to that country "the interests that the old Russia had obtained using unfair pressure tactics," as Gotō wrote in a memorandum of 1924. Upon hearing that news, "I could not stop myself trembling from the depths of my soul," he recalled. "I agonized and groaned in solitude for several days and nights."

What was it that so shocked and dismayed him? The memorandum continues, "Why was that? Let me speak frankly. Is not the South Manchuria Railway—the main artery of continental development, vested with our great mission of uniting the civilizations of East and West—essentially a branch of the Chinese Eastern Railway? If, therefore, the Chinese Eastern Railway unconditionally came under Chinese control, not only would the functioning of the SMR of necessity have been gravely affected; it was not inconceivable that the very foundations of the Empire could have been shaken as a result. I feared that, given the tide of events, we might be confronted by a major upheaval incomparably more serious than the so-called Twenty-One Demands issue, one that could ultimately undo the gains from our two great wars [the Sino-Japanese and Russo-Japanese wars] and obliterate the momentous achievements of the great Emperor Meiji. That was why."

Gotō was, in sum, horrified because he saw in the Bolsheviks' foreign policy a set of principles that could nullify all his past accomplishments. He also recognized the possibility of Russia and China joining hands as anti-imperialist allies opposed to Japan, thus posing an existential threat to the SMR and Japan's other interests in Manchuria. If this was the case, and if the regime was weak and only regionally based, as Gotō thought it to be, then embarking on a campaign to overthrow it, or to isolate it from the Far East by establishing a buffer zone, must have seemed to him the obvious thing to do.

Furthermore, the Stevens Mission from the US had started running the Trans-Siberian Railway, having been commissioned to do so under the Kerensky government because of the power vacuum in Siberia. Gotō, long a believer in the role of the railway as a disseminator of civilization, proudly regarded the SMR as a global transport route. Hence he had, since Harriman's day, resisted American plans to acquire railways in Manchuria, seeing them as part of an effort to develop a global transport network. He was hardly likely to turn a blind eye to this state of affairs in Siberia.

So far as Japan's relations with Russia, China, and the United States were concerned, Gotō saw in the Russian Revolution the antithesis of his notion of the New and Old Worlds in opposition. His longstanding belief in establishing partnerships with neighboring countries built on economic ties had hit a dead end. So now he advocated sending an expedition to Siberia as a way to break the impasse. He did not support the immediate dispatch of troops, however. In view of Motono's failure, he intended to wait until a consensus emerged among the Allies and Japan's leaders.

Then in mid-May there was a major shift in global opinion as the plight of the so-called Czechoslovak Legion became an issue. The Czechoslovak

Legion, which had hitherto fought on the Russian side with the aim of gaining independence from the Austro-Hungarian Empire, was unhappy with the Bolshevik government's decision to make peace with Germany. It therefore headed east with the intention of returning to Europe via Vladivostok and rejoining the fight against Germany. The journey was long and extremely arduous, however, and the legionnaires frequently clashed with the Bolsheviks along the way. When these circumstances became known, there was a groundswell of popular support in the Allied countries for rescuing the Czechoslovak Legion, and Britain, France, and Italy again called on Japan to send troops. By July even the United States, which had until then consistently opposed a Japanese expedition to Siberia, proposed the dispatch of a joint Japanese-American force.

After Britain and France, concerned about the plight of the Czechoslovak Legion, approached Japan about sending troops to Siberia, Gotō became rapidly convinced of the need for immediate action. With Itō Miyoji he forced the Provisional Research Council on Foreign Relations into line. The American proposal called for the US and Japan each to send seven thousand troops. It limited the expedition's objective to evacuating the Czechoslovak Legion and restricted its geographical range of operations. The Terauchi cabinet, however, prepared a reply that, while ostensibly assenting to the American proposal, was in fact a declaration of intent to organize an independent expedition. The government won over Hara and Makino despite their concerns about relations with the US and in August went ahead with the deployment of troops to Siberia.

For Gotō, this was a once-in-a-lifetime opportunity, the fulfillment of a long-cherished dream. In his eyes, the point of the Siberian Expedition was to assist what he considered to be sound political elements in Russia with the endorsement of the Western powers, including the United States, and thus further strengthen relations between Russia and Japan while extending Japanese influence into north Manchuria.

The Siberian Expedition was, from today's perspective, one of the worst acts of folly in the history of modern Japanese foreign policy. The presumed Russian "moderates" were largely illusory, and Japan ended up alienating the entire Russian population. The expeditionary force ballooned in size, and left Japan with almost nothing to show for all the blood and treasure it had expended except lingering mistrust worldwide, especially in Russia and the United States. People are wont to stumble badly in the very field where they most excel. Gotō's Siberian Expedition is a case in point. Having assumed charge of foreign policy as foreign minister and linchpin of the cabinet, Gotō made a serious blunder in dealings with Russia, the very area that he was supposed to know best.

The Nishihara Loans

The Russian Revolution changed more than the Terauchi cabinet's policy toward Russia. It also led to significant changes in its policy toward China.

At first the Russian Revolution was, as already noted, regarded as the triumph of pro-German forces in Russia. It was feared that German power would soon advance east as far as Asia. Indeed, at the end of 1917, US President Woodrow Wilson told Japanese ambassador Satō Yoshimaro that the US and Japan needed to cooperate against the eastward expansion of German imperialism.

It was no wonder, then, that there were calls for changes in Japanese policy toward China. Even Hara Takashi, the most coolheaded and realistic observer among the political class of the day, saw the Russian Revolution and the Treaty of Brest-Litovsk as symptoms of the steady eastward advance of German power. He therefore espoused a change in the course of China policy. "Because of the risk of Russia gradually falling under German influence, there is also a risk that Germany's reach could extend to China after the return of peace. China policy therefore needs to be decided at the present time."[1]

Such perceptions led the Terauchi cabinet to adopt a set of policies for fostering cooperation with China that were assertive to the point of high-handedness. First, in May 1918, it concluded a military agreement with China providing for joint defense against the Bolsheviks. Second, it decided to enhance the Nishihara loans. To that end, in March it passed a

---

1   Hara Keiichirō, ed., *Hara Takashi nikki* [The Diary of Hara Takashi], vol. 4 (Tokyo: Fukumura Shuppan, 1965), 363 (Feb. 22, 1918).

law giving government guarantees for up to 100 million yen in Industrial Bank financing. It then proceeded to implement an ambitious series of loans.

The immediate objective of the newly enhanced Nishihara loans was to strengthen the pro-Japanese Duan Qirui government and thereby help it unify China. A further goal was to establish an economic alliance with China that went beyond merely augmenting Japanese interests. On May 22, Prime Minister Terauchi, Foreign Minister Gotō, and Finance Minister Shōda Kazue met with Nishihara Kamezō, the arranger of the loans and the man after whom they were named, to instruct him on how to proceed with the new loans. Gotō was an early advocate of separate Japanese loans to China, as already noted. Soon, however, he was to have a change of heart.

The Nishihara loans were, above all, fraught with risk. Their objectives—the Duan government's military unification of China and the establishment of a Sino-Japanese economic alliance—were of dubious feasibility. They were also highly problematic in procedural terms. The method of financing violated the international consortium agreement. The negotiating channel used with the Chinese bypassed the foreign ministry and went via Nishihara and Finance Minister Shōda instead. And the main vehicles for the loans were the Industrial Bank of Japan, the Bank of Taiwan, and the Bank of Korea, while traditional lenders such as the Yokohama Specie Bank were shunted aside.

The staff of the foreign ministry, including Japan's minister to China, Hayashi Gonsuke, were united in their adamant opposition to this highly irregular arrangement. Gotō was all the less able to contain their opposition, ironically, because he held the foreign affairs portfolio. And with the Siberian Expedition consuming all his energy, he could not force the ministry to rally behind the Nishihara loans policy as well. Around July, the US and the other Western powers again began taking an interest in the loans to China, making it impossible for Japan to continue blatantly disregarding the international consortium agreement any longer.

There was a further problem. The enhanced Nishihara loans of 1918, if not the initial Nishihara loans of 1917, were in many regards incompatible with Gotō's foreign policy ideas. Gotō had never been much in favor of interfering in China's internal affairs. While he had been enthusiastic about collaborating with Yuan Shikai, he did not advocate building up a partner government robust enough to work with where none existed. Furthermore, the kind of economic alliance between China and Japan championed by Nishihara Kamezō was alien to Gotō's thinking. Nishihara envisaged establishing a self-sufficient economic zone by developing China's resources under Japanese tutelage and turning China into a source of raw materials for Japan. Although sometimes couched in language similar to Gotō's, that concept was not at all what Gotō had in mind. Gotō believed in linking Japan to the rest of the world through trade, as evidenced by his insistence on the importance of the international transport network. Autarky must have seemed a sorry, small-minded notion indeed to Gotō.

Gotō began to oppose the Nishihara loans on these grounds, which led to a deadlock. Then, in September 1918, during the Terauchi cabinet's final days, it was decided that the funds set aside for the loans would be handed over to China as an advance payment for the construction of railways in Manchuria and Shandong. The money was thus spent on securing railway rights in readiness for the end of the war. This move, the outcome of a compromise between advocates and opponents of the Nishihara loans, was more in keeping with Gotō's thinking. The idea of stabilizing international relations by working together on a concrete project like railway construction that brought benefits to both sides was typical of Gotō, as manifested in the concepts of the New and Old Worlds in opposition and of military preparations in civilian garb.

On the whole, it is fair to say that the Nishihara loans would have ended in an even worse debacle if Gotō had not turned against them in June. Still, by unwisely committing himself to enhancing the Nishihara loans in May and then suddenly changing his mind, he was undeniably responsible for throwing China policy into further disarray. His tenure as foreign minister was an utter failure. Whether in his insistence on sending troops to Siberia or his initial support for enhancing the Nishihara loans, his reading of the situation was badly off.

The root cause of this failure was the increasing difficulty of making sense of international politics within Gotō's frame of reference. His foreign policy was predicated on the assumption that states were living organisms that maintained their unity and acted in accordance with their "physiological urge." When states were motivated by ideology and became divided against themselves, Gotō had no clue how to respond.

This was in sharp contrast to Hara, who became an even stronger advocate of cooperation with the United States than he had been before World War I. He was, out of concern for relations with the US, in principle opposed to intervening in the struggle between the north and south in China. In Siberia he believed that Japan should insofar as possible cooperate with the US. This was because he perceived that American entry into the war and Russia's collapse had turned the conflict into a struggle between democracy and militarism—in other words, that ideological symbols had come to the fore of international politics. In that regard he differed greatly from Gotō. It was only natural, then, that Japanese foreign policy after the war should have been guided not by Gotō, who advocated countering the US, but Hara, who advocated cooperating with it. Gotō's days as a foreign policy leader seemed to be over.

CHAPTER 6

LOST OPPORTUNITIES

1. The Postwar World and Japan

Touring the West

The end of World War I brought about immense changes in international relations. Democracy had triumphed against militarism, it was believed, and new principles such as pacifism, international cooperation, and self-determination were now enshrined as standards to be respected. A fundamental reset was needed in Japanese foreign policy in order to adapt to the new reality.

During the war, in 1916, Gotō had written a book entitled *Nihon bōchō ron* (On Japan's Expansion), which analyzed patterns of conflict among the world's peoples and espoused the need for Japan to expand overseas. In 1924, when the book appeared in a new edition, Gotō declared in the preface that none of his arguments needed revision. It is truly astonishing that, after the Russian Revolution, the end of World War I, and the emergence of the Versailles and Washington Treaty systems, he saw no need to alter either his views of the world or his foreign policy positions. Was this assertion true, and if so, why?

In March 1919, just over five months after the Terauchi cabinet resigned and just less than four months after the end of World War I, Gotō departed on a tour of the United States and Europe. It was his second trip to the West, excluding his studies abroad and his two trips to Russia. He was in the United States from March through June, in Europe from June through September, and again in the United States in September and October, arriving back in Japan in November.

Gotō took note of several developments during his travels. The first was

America's increasing prosperity and Europe's decline, both of which he had earlier predicted in his theory of the New and Old Worlds in opposition. The second was the failure of Woodrow Wilson's moral diplomacy. Gotō had at one stage lauded Wilson's visionary Fourteen Points underpinned by American power. "Mr. Wilson has, with rare genius, taken an absolute stand bearing a flag emblazoned with the Fourteen Principles, to which the world looks up. These are not of course of his own devising, yet he has convinced the entire United States, at least, of the need to embark on their implementation, and next intoxicated Europe and Asia with the idea. That must be described as a great achievement." But having seen the Fourteen Points founder on hard-headed calculations of self-interest, Gotō became more certain than ever of the powerlessness of ethics and ideology in international politics. Third (a related point), he was struck by the despotism of the powerful and the tragic fate of the weak. The draconian peace terms imposed on Germany convinced him that the world was as much as or more than ever a desperate battleground for survival between different peoples. Fourth, Gotō considered the Versailles system an unnatural, precarious arrangement, for it went against the grain of European history in its unfair treatment of the great German people.

These convictions had all been part of Gotō's existing views on international politics. Having observed postwar America and Europe, he remained firm in his belief that the world was a battleground for survival between different peoples, except the struggle was now less military and more all-embracing in the methods employed. How should Japan adapt to this new global reality? That was the question that Gotō brought home from his travels in the West.

Plans for a Major Think Tank

Upon returning to Japan, Gotō began advocating the establishment of a major think tank. At the beginning of a recommendation on the subject apparently written in early 1920, he observed that amid the current economic, social, and political turmoil, intellectuals in each country were endeavoring "to win the crown of victory in the new international great war." To that end they were formulating policies for building up the national economy against foreign rivals, and for developing and controlling industry and achieving harmonious class relations at home. Gotō's major think tank would be designed to study these global trends and promptly develop basic policies in response. It was, in other words, to serve as the "Industrial General Staff" in Japan's struggle to remain a player in the rapidly changing postwar world. Gotō carried out extensive research whenever he undertook a project. He sometimes referred to this by the term "military preparations in civilian garb," as we have seen. The idea of a major think tank was one of many ambitious research plans he pursued. Indeed, it was the most ambitious of all in that it concerned the nation's very economic foundations.

Gotō took the idea to Hara Takashi, Terauchi's successor as prime minister. Hara heard him out and in June 1920, after that year's elections, proposed to Gotō the establishment of a provisional research council on national industrial policy with 10 million yen in funding. Hara was motivated in part by a desire to avoid antagonizing Gotō, a political dark horse, and keep him in line, but it is also true that he sympathized with Gotō's idea. Gotō, however, rejected Hara's proposal. Many thought it strange that he did not accept it at least as a start; after all, he had originally suggested a five-year program with total funding of 30 million yen and then pared that back to 20 million. Gotō's reply to Hara of June 28 reveals the differences between what the two men had in mind and thus the essence of Gotō's idea.

Gotō pointed out, first, that the proposed funding was not for multiple years. That would complicate long-term planning, especially when it came to hiring foreign experts. It is interesting that he constantly emphasized, even now, the need for Japan to learn from other countries. Second, Gotō criticized the proposed council for its bureaucratic structure. While accepting that the council's administrative arm had to be run by bureaucrats, he believed that there should otherwise be as little bureaucratic involvement as possible. New policies were then considered necessary in a wide range of fields, but as long as they were studied under bureaucratic supervision, it would not be possible, Gotō was convinced, to conduct fundamental research and make comprehensive policy recommendations. Third, Gotō harshly criticized Hara for cutting the publishing arm from his proposal. For Gotō, it was essential to translate and publish Japanese research findings and Japanese views on the issues for an international audience.

Gotō's son-in-law, Tsurumi Yūsuke, perceptively analyzed Hara's political mindset in his biography of Gotō:

> Hara was a shrewd politician. He was a man who went through life observing the realities of human existence with the precision of a mathematician. Hence, while occupying the difficult position of party leader, amidst a tangle of interests, in constantly changing times, he was unerring in his decisions and executed them without hesitation. His great concern was today, not tomorrow. Life in his eyes was an amalgam of short-term interests and emotions. It was not about dreamlike ideals conceived among the stars.

It would be wrong to see Hara Takashi as no more than a political pragmatist. He had his dreams and ideals as a politician. But over many years leading a party amid the realities of politics, he had ceased to take chances in pursuit of them. By the time he formed his own government, he was, he admitted to a close adviser, too old to embark on major reforms. He no longer had the capacity to sympathize wholeheartedly with Gotō's grand vision. Gotō's plans for a major think tank thus ran aground.

Mayor of Tokyo

In December 1920, Gotō became mayor of Tokyo. The previous mayor, Tajiri Inajirō, had resigned in November to take responsibility for a corruption scandal, and the municipal assembly had almost unanimously supported Gotō as his successor. Having kept a low profile for a few years, Gotō now began making waves on the political scene again.

Gotō's associates were adamantly opposed to his becoming mayor of Tokyo when he was considered a potential prime minister. The Tokyo municipal assembly was known as a hotbed of intrigue rife with influence peddling and political infighting. The mayor's powers were seriously curtailed, moreover, and many a politician of ministerial caliber had tarnished his career by serving in that position. Yet Gotō was to retain the job until April 1923.

He accepted the post because Tokyo presented a microcosm of the problems facing Japan. Its haphazard urban sprawl was entirely unsuited to the capital of a civilized nation. No one could have felt this more keenly than Gotō, who in Taiwan and Manchuria had built cities rivaling those of the West. Tokyo, furthermore, was a place of deep-seated party rivalries. It also suffered from severe bureaucratic gridlock and inefficiencies. In a memorandum of May 1922, after becoming mayor, Gotō wrote, "Once in a lifetime it would be nice to sacrifice oneself to one's country by drawing a very short straw indeed. Is not the mayoralty of Tokyo one step to achieving that longstanding desire?" For Gotō, running Tokyo was almost as attractive an outlet for his abilities as the prospect of reforming Japan as prime minister.

A comprehensive overview of what Gotō wanted and felt he needed to do as mayor was provided in the Outline of Tokyo Municipal Policy released in May 1921. This became famous as the 800 Million Yen Plan, named after what it was expected to cost. In those days the Tokyo city government had a total budget of 120–130 million yen, including municipal lighting and railways, while the central government had a budget of 1.5 billion yen. That gives an idea of the exorbitant cost of Gotō's plan. People were flabbergasted. Gotō was just talking big again, they thought.

What the program envisioned was, put simply, the remodeling of the city. It called for the development of an urban plan and, on that basis, the construction or expansion and paving of arterial roads; the consolidation, relocation, or removal of underground facilities and above-ground structures; the installation of water supply, sewage treatment, and garbage disposal facilities; harbor improvements, renovations to waterways, construction of and improvements to parks and other public spaces, and power and gas upgrades; and the building of a new city hall and public hall. Some criticized this list for containing nothing new, and they had a point. Everything that needed to be done to redevelop Tokyo was perfectly obvious, but it was no easy task to pull off.

The greatest obstacles to the plan, Gotō firmly believed, were party politics and bureaucratic inertia, the two main foes that he had been combatting at least since his days in Taiwan. He had several strategies for overcoming these obstacles: bringing in new blood to revitalize the organization, silencing critics by carrying out extensive scientific research, and obtaining strong backing from a powerful figure.

Gotō started by appointing as deputy mayors three highly capable individuals who were under his aegis: Nagata Hidejirō, a member of the House of Peers and former head of the Police Bureau of the home ministry; Ikeda Hiroshi, head of the home ministry's Social Bureau; and Maeda Tamon, a counselor with the home ministry and head of its Urban Planning Bureau. It had previously been the practice to select deputy mayors from among veteran officials, taking into account their party affiliations in the assembly. Yet Gotō chose to appoint men from his own circle with established reputations for competence. Considering how Tokyo had previously been run, that was in itself a dramatic break with the past.

The compensation package he arranged to acquire their services was similarly unprecedented. The mayor had hitherto received an annual salary of 15,000 yen, while the three deputy mayors had together been paid a total of 24,000 yen a year. Gotō hiked the mayor's salary to 25,000 yen and the deputy mayors' combined salaries to 37,000 yen, and then donated all his own salary to the city. The deputy mayors' pay thus increased by more than 50 percent, yet the city saved 2,000 yen overall. Although some may have been put off by such grandstanding, Gotō had always believed in generously paying men of ability.

Gotō also reorganized city hall and made major personnel changes. More than three hundred staff left the municipal government. He espoused the need for a wholesome atmosphere at city hall and made education a priority by, for example, setting up a training center for city officials. He had taken similar steps in Taiwan, at the South Manchuria Railway, and at the Railway Agency.

Among the most interesting of Gotō's personnel moves was his recruitment of many influential figures to work temporarily for the city government. This practice started with the appointment of six holders of doctorates as honorary advisers, including Kobayashi Ushisaburō, Ichiki Kitokurō, Oka Minoru, and Minobe Tatsukichi. Not only were these men well known—Ichiki was a privy councilor and Minobe a professor at Tokyo Imperial University—but they were also leading experts in their respective fields, Kobayashi in finance, Ichiki in municipal policy, and Oka in social policy. Seventy-five such appointments had been made by September 1922. The presence of such minds provided intellectual stimulation at city hall, so much so that individuals who previously would have been uninterested in working for the city government decided to join it.

The recruitment of such intellectuals was also a preliminary step to the introduction of scientific methods, Gotō's second strategy for combatting the adverse effects of party politics and countering bureaucratic inertia. A well-known example of this strategy was the municipal research institute he established.

In January 1921, immediately upon becoming mayor, Gotō wired his son-in-law Tsurumi Yūsuke, who was then in the United States, asking him to investigate corruption in US municipal politics and the campaigns to rectify it, and promptly report back to him. Tsurumi met with Charles A. Beard, an authority on the subject, and requested his advice. Beard explained that attempts at municipal reform rooted in ethical arguments and emotional appeals had for years proved unsuccessful, whereas the New York Bureau of Municipal Research, which had been established for the purpose of scientifically studying municipal government and recommending specific policies, had been achieving results. He encouraged Tsurumi to pay it a visit.

When Tsurumi arrived back in Japan in May 1921, having completed his investigations in New York, work had begun on setting up Tokyo's own municipal research bureau. Funding was a problem, but financier Yasuda Zenjirō agreed to cover all the costs. Yasuda was assassinated by a terrorist in September, but the promised 3.5 million yen was duly donated, and the establishment of the Tokyo Institute for Municipal Research in Tokyo's Hibiya Park was completed in June 1922.

The institute's charter may be summarized as follows. Urban sprawl was a global phenomenon and a trait of modern civilization. Although cities were not states in their own right, a state's central nervous system ran through its cities, and the fate of those cities determined the fate of the nation. Japan's cities, however, having only recently been granted autonomy, were still plagued by many ills. There were those who "factionalize and collude to monopolize the citizens' interests," as well as those who "clinging to the old ways . . . become so preoccupied with the minutiae of the moment that they lose sight of larger plans for the city's long-term future." There were in extreme cases, the charter continued, even those who were so corrupt they stooped to crime. The best way to eliminate these abuses was to make municipal government itself the object of scientific observation and thus ensure that self-government was underpinned by scientific knowledge. Therein, the charter concluded, lay the mission of the Tokyo Institute for Municipal Research.

Despite Gotō's efforts, the 800 Million Yen Plan made little headway. Two of his three strategies achieved a degree of success. The problem was the third, namely enlisting the backing of a powerful individual, which in those days meant Hara Takashi. While it seems unlikely, as we have seen, that Hara was fully committed to the project, he does appear to have promised some support. Hara, however, was assassinated in November 1921. The government of his successor Takahashi Korekiyo (in office until June 1922) was ineffectual because of infighting within the Seiyūkai, and the next cabinet, that of Katō Tomosaburō (in office until August 1923), cut back on spending, a policy incompatible with Gotō's plans to redevelop Tokyo. Yasuda Zenjirō, who had displayed great interest in those plans and was committed to supporting them, was assassinated as well. The redevelopment of Tokyo was too big a project for the city to handle alone. It required strong backing at the national level. Throughout his career, Gotō struggled to find powerful backers for his visionary grand designs. That problem in this case proved insurmountable.

Gotō and Beard

At the time of the launch of the Tokyo Institute for Municipal Research, Gotō invited Charles Beard to Japan to advise him. Beard was one of the most influential American political scientists and historians of the first half of the twentieth century, and one of the intellectual giants of his day.

Gotō had no intention of letting Beard concentrate exclusively on studying how Tokyo was run. Rather, he expected him to play a role in stimulating public interest in urban problems. To that end he arranged for him to give talks all over the country. Beard kept busy with other undertakings as well. He offered recommendations on the running of Tokyo, introduced various methods from the United States, and advised the Institute for Municipal Research on its activities. His findings were summed up in a set of recommendations on the administration and politics of Tokyo later published in both Japan and the United States.

Beard arrived in Japan in September 1922 and stayed for six months, until March 1923. He then toured Taiwan and China and put in at Yokohama before returning to the United States. What he saw in Taiwan and Manchuria only increased his admiration for Gotō. In a letter of April 1 addressed to Gotō from Canton, he wrote, "Everywhere we go we discover signs of your genius. Your plans for the future are so truly comprehensive that there is nothing left to do but carry them out. What has especially struck me are the broad avenues, public buildings, marketplaces, parks, hospitals, railways, schools, and waterworks in each city . . . I was particularly impressed by the central research institute that you have established in Taipei. Later I intend to write a paper on your projects in the field of scientific research." (This letter now exists only in Japanese translation, which has been retranslated into English here.)

Beard's praise was no mere courtesy. When he arrived in Japan, he declined any compensation, honors, or decorations, grateful simply for the opportunity to study the country. Not being beholden in any way, he explained, would make him a more convincing spokesman for Japan upon his return to the United States.

Indeed, back in the United States, Beard asserted at one point that the US had no right to criticize Japanese policy in Manchuria and China while itself claiming dominance in the Americas under the Monroe Doctrine. Later, he stirred up much controversy when he published the theory that President Franklin Roosevelt exploited the raid on Pearl Harbor as a pretext to enter World War II despite having known that the Japanese were going to attack. The FDR conspiracy theory is not widely accepted today, but at least Japan could, thanks to Gotō, count one of the outstanding intellectuals of the day as a sympathizer.

Immediately before returning to the United States, Beard donated 2,000 yen in public bonds to the Tokyo Institute for Municipal Research, which he suggested be used to help fund an essay contest for teachers and students to be called the Viscount Gotō Awards. That suggestion was gratefully accepted and acted on.

The planned paper mentioned at the end of Beard's letter took the form of a short piece entitled "Japan's Statesman of Research" published in the

September 1923 issue of *American Review of Reviews*. In this Beard admiringly described Gotō's bold policies underpinned by scientific research. Such praise by one of America's greatest scholars must have been gratifying indeed for Gotō, who had dedicated his life to helping "civilize" the world by adopting Western ways. That mission had never left his mind for a moment, whether at the Public Health Bureau, in Taiwan, at the South Manchuria Railway, at the Railway Agency, or wherever else he applied his talents.

2. Negotiations with Joffe and the Rebuilding of Tokyo

Flaws in the Washington Treaty System

After two somewhat unproductive years as mayor of Tokyo, Gotō suddenly launched into action again. In early 1923, he set the stage for the restoration of diplomatic relations between Japan and Russia, now the USSR, by inviting Soviet diplomat Adolph Joffe to Japan. In addition, immediately after the massive earthquake that struck Tokyo later that year, Gotō became home minister again and applied himself to rebuilding the devastated city. Thus 1923 marked the final flourish of his political career.

First, let us examine international developments in Asia, which formed the backdrop to Gotō's decision to invite Joffe to Japan.

The Washington Conference held between November 1921 and February 1922 resulted in the establishment of the so-called Washington Treaty System in the Asia-Pacific region, which complemented the Versailles System in the West. Here the United States, which had often found itself isolated in East Asia before the war, assumed the initiative. The conference accepted the principles of the open door and equal opportunity advocated by the US and rejected spheres of influence. Among the agreements concluded at the conference was the Nine-Power Treaty, which committed the signatories to respecting the sovereignty, the independence, and the territorial and administrative integrity of China and ensuring equality of opportunity there for the trade and industry of all nations.

The Washington Treaty System, however, had three serious flaws. First, it basically allowed the powers to maintain their vested interests in China in order to achieve a consensus among them. It was, in other words, built on the suppression of China's growing nationalism.

Second—and this was a related problem—China was seriously divided against itself. In the south, the Canton government headed by Sun Yat-sen refused to accept the Washington Treaty System. The government in Peking, on the other hand, while on the whole far more powerful than its southern counterpart, was an unstable coalition of warlords. China was among the signatories to the Nine-Power Treaty and had rights and obligations under it, but it was too weak and disunited to fulfill them. That disunity threatened to undermine multilateral cooperation.

Third, the Washington Treaty System ignored Soviet Russia. The Soviets, having demanded a seat at the conference and been refused, condemned the Washington Treaty System. They championed anti-imperialism and called for the abolition of imperialist rights and privileges in China.

These three flaws suggested the possibility of an alternative system of international relations emerging in East Asia, one involving China, Soviet Russia, and their partner states. Under this system, imperialist rights and privileges would be rejected, making all parties equal. The first step in that direction was the restoration of diplomatic relations between China and Germany in May 1921. Germany, having lost its rights in China owing to its defeat in World War I, reestablished a presence in East Asia by forming a new, equal relationship with China. If the Washington Treaty System was to survive in the face of the possible emergence of such an alternative system, China would need to be convinced in practice that it could achieve prosperity within the Washington framework. That would require the other signatories to join together in giving China an economic boost.

The Washington Treaty System, however, was not so much an active attempt by the great powers to work together on establishing a new and more stable international order as a rejection of the old approach to international relations. It was in that sense proscriptive. While it was fairly clear what the signatories were forbidden from doing, it was not clear how they were supposed to cooperate. The Nine-Power Treaty called for promoting the unity of China, but it was short on specifics.

Gotō had long believed that Japan, China, and Russia should work together, and considered cooperation with Britain and the United States of secondary importance. To him, the Washington Treaty System seemed badly misguided in that it meant allying with the British and Americans while keeping the Chinese and the Soviets in check. In Gotō's mind, excluding the Soviet Union from the community of nations in Asia violated the natural order of things, just as excluding Germany from the community of nations in Europe did. The very act of inviting Joffe to Japan and engaging in preliminary talks on restoring diplomatic relations between Soviet Russia and Japan was, as explained below, a criticism of the Washington Treaty System and antithetical to it.

An Envisioned Partnership between Japan, China, and the Soviet Union

Japanese-Soviet relations had been in turmoil since the Siberian Expedition. The Dairen talks beginning in August 1921 and the Changchun talks beginning in September 1922 had ended in failure. At both conferences, Japan's negotiating partner had been the short-lived Far Eastern Republic. After Japan withdrew its troops from Primorsky Krai and the north of Sakhalin in September and October 1922, however, the Soviets annexed the Republic. The elimination of a buffer state between the Soviets and the Japanese had the potential to further complicate efforts to break the impasse in relations between them.

Progress was meanwhile being made in furthering Sino-Soviet relations. In the wake of Georgy Chicherin's declaration of 1918, the Karakhan Manifesto of July 1919 offered to return the Chinese Eastern Railway to China, along with Russia's other rights there, and proposed establishing diplomatic relations on equal terms. Despite backtracking on this policy in the second Karakhan Manifesto of 1920, the Soviets sent Joffe to China in the summer of 1922 to initiate negotiations with the Peking government. Joffe also made contact with Sun Yat-sen, who was then in difficult straits in the south. While the Soviets' main concern was the Peking government, they also considered the possibility that the Kuomintang could grow stronger. Soviet talks with Peking bogged down on the terms for restoring the Chinese Eastern Railway to China and the withdrawal of Soviet troops from Outer Mongolia. Sun Yat-sen, however, welcomed Joffe's overtures, and in January 1923 the two men issued a joint statement.

Gotō was deeply concerned about these developments. If Japan cooperated with Britain and the United States, and the Chinese and the Soviets formed an anti-imperialist alliance in response, what would happen to Japan's interests in South Manchuria and its plans to expand from there to other parts of the continent? The outcome might be the polar opposite of his ideal of the New and Old Worlds in opposition.

On the other hand, Gotō noted several promising developments favorable to the improvement of Japanese-Soviet relations. First, the Soviets, despite offering to relinquish the rights and privileges held by imperial Russia in China, showed little intention of actually doing so. Most significantly, the unconditional offer to return the Chinese Eastern Railway contained in the first Karakhan Manifesto of July 1919 was deleted from the second Karakhan Manifesto, and Sino-Soviet negotiations became deadlocked over the issue. The second promising development was the Soviet adoption of the New Economic Policy (NEP). Gotō had already predicted, during his tour of the United States and Europe several years before, that the Soviet state was doomed to fail if it insisted on "adhering to the principles of communism." A course correction in some form was inevitable, he believed. The incorporation of capitalist elements in the NEP indicated to Gotō that the Soviets were resuming their "innate character" as members of the human race. He approvingly compared that change to the way in which the Meiji government, which was made up of men once fervently committed to eliminating foreign influence from Japan, had switched to a policy of westernization and modernization.

In short, the Soviet state, by seeking to maintain its overseas interests and reviving elements of capitalism at home, had in Gotō's eyes proved itself to be a unified, living, thriving organism, just as Russia had been. He concluded that it was perfectly possible to work with such a state.

Having reached that conclusion, Gotō invited Joffe, who was then in China, to Japan in January 1923 and commenced private negotiations on restoring diplomatic relations. The move was harshly attacked by many rightists fearful of the "Red Peril." The foreign and home ministries were decidedly unsympathetic as well and occasionally tried to thwart his efforts, but public opinion strongly supported Gotō. Under pressure from the business community of the Osaka and Kobe region, which was eager for a revival of trade with Russia, and from the North Pacific fishing industry, which employed well over ten thousand people, the foreign ministry did an about-face and started following the Gotō-Joffe talks closely. As a result, the talks achieved a degree of success, leading to the opening of informal negotiations by the foreign ministry in June.

Gotō's efforts to restore diplomatic ties with the Soviet Union were thus rooted in the public's desire for normalized relations. In that regard he was successful, and he has been favorably judged by history for it. But breaking the impasse in Japanese-Soviet relations was not his only aim. He hoped also to replace the Washington Treaty System with a new international order in the Far East by establishing a trilateral partnership between Japan, China, and the Soviet Union. That desire arose from his awareness of the Washington Treaty System's fragility and his realization that it was leading China and the Soviets to form an anti-imperialist alliance in reaction. Gotō's concerns about the clash between those two systems, and his fears that Japan could be left isolated between them, led him to envision a third system, namely an alliance between Japan, China, and the Soviet Union that would be less anti-imperialist to the extent that it would recognize Japan's existing rights and interests in Manchuria. If it had been simply a matter of forestalling a Sino-Soviet alliance, it would have been possible to do so within the Washington Treaty System, by strengthening cooperation with Britain and the United States and putting pressure on China. But Gotō was not interested in using balance-of-power politics to manage the conflict between the Washington Treaty System and the Soviet Union, which for Japan boiled down to confrontation with the Soviets in China. As he put it himself, his methods were "not the old-fashioned balance-of-power ones." On the contrary, he sought a mutually beneficial arrangement between Japan and the Soviets. "I would go so far as to argue not merely that the two countries have nothing to steal from each other," he declared, "but that they have much to give each other." In a nutshell, Gotō's approach was to eliminate international tensions by establishing a new, integrative relationship. His ultimate goal, of course, was to preserve Japan's interests in Manchuria, but his position was still a unique one to adopt in those days.

Japan and the Soviet Union restored diplomatic relations in January 1925, two years after Gotō invited Joffe to Japan and a year and a half after he handed over negotiations to the foreign ministry. I would like to summarize developments in the interim.

After issuing the joint statement with Joffe in January 1923, Sun Yat-sen adopted three major policies in November: cooperating with the Soviets, working with the Chinese Communist Party (CCP), and helping the workers and peasants. Then, at the first national congress of the Kuomintang (KMT) in January 1924, the KMT formed an alliance with the CCP. The Peking government, alarmed at the rapprochement between the Canton government and the Soviets, also made overtures to the latter. As a result, an agreement between Wang Zhengting and Lev Karakhan was announced on March 24, and diplomatic relations were established on May 31. The USSR relinquished the special rights that tsarist Russia had enjoyed in China, including its extraterritorial rights, and renounced the indemnity due from the Boxer Rebellion. It was also decided, however, that the question of the Chinese Eastern Railway would be settled by the two sides at a later date, and that Soviet troops would withdraw from Outer Mongolia after certain conditions were met. The rivalry between the Peking and Canton governments thus resulted in a Sino-Soviet relationship that, while avowedly anti-imperialist, favored the USSR in that it left certain important Soviet rights intact.

In this context Sun Yat-sen's famous speech on pan-Asianism delivered on his visit to Japan in the fall of 1924 assumes special significance. In this speech, which he gave in Kobe on November 28, he contrasted the righteousness of Oriental civilization, which was rooted in benevolence and virtue, with the hegemonism practiced by Western civilization, which advocated utilitarianism and force. The Japanese people, he continued, had already mastered the hegemonistic ways of the West, but they retained the essence of the culture of righteousness. The choice that lay before them was whether to be the pawns of Western hegemonism or the guardians of Oriental righteousness. This speech was, in light of the new Sino-Soviet relationship, not simply an abstract moral appeal but a call to abandon the Washington Treaty System. Given the actual nature of the Sino-Soviet relationship, the new system of international relations it embodied was potentially compatible with what Gotō had in mind. Japan, however, chose to remain within the Washington Treaty System, and the restoration of diplomatic relations with the Soviet Union was delayed. The opportunity to realize Gotō's vision of a partnership between Japan, China, and the Soviet Union was accordingly lost.

The Yamamoto Government and the Rebuilding of Tokyo

In August 1923, Prime Minister Katō Tomosaburō died from illness, and finding a successor proved difficult. The Seiyūkai, despite enjoying an overwhelming majority in the lower house, was divided against itself. For that reason it had had no choice but to support Katō when he formed his government. The second largest party, the Kenseikai, was too weak to make a difference. Powerful non-party actors like the old Yamagata faction had ceased to exist.

Yamamoto Gonbei was ultimately appointed prime minister, returning to power after a nine-year hiatus. He had previously headed a powerful but short-lived government for about a year in 1913–14, as we have seen, until he was forced to step down by the Siemens scandal. Those who knew Yamamoto from the old days thought he had what it took to break the impasse in party politics. He attempted to form a powerful cabinet by asking the heads of the three major parties, the Seiyūkai, the Kenseikai, and the Kakushin (Reform) Club, to serve as ministers, along with several men who were considered prime ministerial material.

These efforts to put together a powerful team, however, actually impeded the process of forming a government. Then, on September 1, a massive earthquake struck Tokyo. The new cabinet took office in the midst of the crisis, and Gotō was appointed home minister for the second time. The cabinet included several other heavyweights as well, among them Tanaka Giichi as army minister, the Kakushin Club's Inukai Tsuyoshi as communications minister, and Den Kenjirō of the old Yamagata faction as minister of agriculture and commerce.

Gotō's mission within the Yamamoto government was, predictably, the rebuilding of Tokyo. On September 2, immediately upon returning from the cabinet's investiture at the Imperial Palace, he drew up the following four-point program:

1. The capital should not be relocated.
2. Three billion yen should be invested in reconstruction.
3. A new capital worthy of our nation should be built by employing the latest urban planning techniques from the West.
4. Landowners must be firmly dealt with so that the new urban plan can be implemented (in the past, landowners have received illicit profits, without making such sacrifices for the sake of urban improvements as the principle of equity demands).

At the same time, Gotō sent Charles Beard a telegram requesting that he immediately come to Japan. This crossed with one from Beard advising Gotō, "Lay out new streets, forbid building within street lines, unify railway stations." Gotō was of the same mind.

Gotō's plans for rebuilding the city were drastic. They called for buying up all burnt-out lots, constructing broad new roads, and adjusting property boundaries. He now had a golden opportunity to execute the radical overhaul of Tokyo that he had been unable to carry out when mayor. The 800 Million Yen Plan from those days could serve as the basis for the task of reconstruction.

Gotō thus rejected the idea of simply restoring the imperial capital and forged ahead with plans to rebuild it completely, and he intended to establish a ministry of reconstruction for that purpose. When that idea fell through, he established a reconstruction agency instead, headed by himself, on September 29. Previously, around September 8, he had, to the astonishment of all concerned, called for 4 billion yen to rebuild the city, a figure he eventually reduced to 1 billion. People criticized him for his typical big talk and hyperbole. It was not, however, as big a climbdown as it seemed, since his initial figure of 4 billion yen had been idealistic anyway, and it included money required by local governments and state ministries.

In the end, the government budgeted a total of 700 million yen for reconstruction. With the addition of 200 million in fire insurance subsidies and aid to prefectural governments, plus 500–600 million to restore state-owned buildings and other facilities, the plan was to spend a grand total of 1.5–1.6 billion yen over several years.

But Gotō's plan was harshly criticized for its colossal scale when, on November 24, it was presented to the Imperial Capital Reconstruction Council chaired by Prime Minister Yamamoto. Itō Miyoji, hitherto a close associate of Gotō's, attacked it on several scores. The arterial roads were too broad, he contended; why not just widen existing roads? There was no need to adjust property boundaries; the property rights of landowners should be respected. Such criticisms set the tone of the meeting. It has been argued that Itō opposed the plan because he himself was a big landowner in Tokyo's upper-class Ginza neighborhood. True, if, as Gotō proposed, gutted lots had been bought up with government bonds, there would have been a glut of bonds on the market, causing their value to fall and dealing a serious blow to landowners. More importantly, Itō was probably unable to understand Gotō's idealism. Although the latter's plan had numerous flaws both legally and financially, at least it offered a vision of what the Japanese capital should look like. Itō, on the other hand, was a master of the bureaucratic art of uncovering tiny defects and inconsistencies and finding loopholes around them, but he was no visionary. Gotō for his part lacked the eloquence to prevail in the face of his criticisms.

The reconstruction plan was then tabled at the extraordinary session of the Diet beginning on December 11. With the council's recommendations incorporated and the road-building plan pared down, it was now budgeted at 597 million yen. A further 130 million was cut in an amendment introduced by the Seiyūkai. The Reconstruction Agency's entire office budget—a paltry 700,000 yen—was also eliminated. In effect, this was a vote of no confidence in Gotō's entire plan.

There were two reasons for the Seiyūkai's cuts to the reconstruction budget. First, the party was rural-based. In Tokyo, its ties were with powerful vested interests who were, for the same reasons as Itō, unenthusiastic about giving the city a complete makeover. Second, the Seiyūkai was deeply suspicious of Gotō, who had for several years been attacking the evils of party politics. He was also considering tabling a bill granting universal manhood suffrage, which the Seiyūkai was reluctant to support. Gotō had, when serving in the Terauchi cabinet, described the Kenseikai as an "unnatural majority." He now thought of the Seiyūkai in the same way and was planning to cut it down to size by introducing universal suffrage. That prospect frightened the Seiyūkai.

On December 18, the government finally caved in to the Seiyūkai and accepted its amendment. Until then, the men around Gotō had been divided into two schools of thought. One advocated dissolving the lower house immediately, taking on the Seiyūkai at the ballot box, and submitting a fuller bill to the next session of the Diet. The other advocated starting rebuilding efforts under the Seiyūkai bill in order to prevent any delay, and then dissolving the lower house, or adopting a supplementary budget, in or after January. Many of Gotō's associates took a hard line, but Gotō himself was more conciliatory, because he was confident that no one but he could successfully rebuild Tokyo.

Even today many regret that Gotō's ambitious reconstruction plan was not adopted intact. Although it was cut back in size and geographical scope, the core of his plan survived. One recent study concludes, "In sum, the reconstruction program, by skillfully bringing the existing urban landscape and its lifestyle traditions within the framework of systemic innovations developed in Germany (the Adickes Law, zoning) and technical innovations from America (small parks, modern bridges, land appraisal techniques, asphalt), marked Tokyo's emergence from the shadow of the feudal city of Edo to become a modern metropolis."[1] Even though Gotō suffered a political defeat, the pool of talent, research findings, and wealth of ideas that were his legacy lived on to transform Tokyo.

Gotō, however, was prevented from overseeing the rebuilding program when the Yamamoto government fell due to an unexpected incident: Nanba Daisuke's attempted shooting of the regent, Crown Prince Hirohito, on December 27 (the so-called Toranomon Incident). This led to the cabinet's resignation on December 29, only four months after it assumed office.

---

1 Mochida Nobuki, "Gotō Shinpei to shinsai fukkō jigyō" [Gotō Shinpei and the Rebuilding of Tokyo], *Shakai kagaku kenkyū* vol. 35, no. 2 (Mar. 1983).

3. Twilight Years

The Campaign for Ethical Politics

After the resignation of the Yamamoto cabinet, Gotō lay low for more than two years. Meanwhile, in June 1924, a three-party coalition dedicated to "protecting the constitutional politics" assumed government, inaugurating the era of party cabinets. Then, in 1925, the universal suffrage law, which had long been on the political agenda, was finally enacted. A man like Gotō with no party affiliation now seemed out of place on the political scene. He made the news but once, when in October 1924 he became director-general of the Tokyo Broadcasting Station, where he helped organize Japan's first radio broadcasts.

In 1926, Gotō suffered a cerebral hemorrhage. His first act upon recovering was to launch a campaign for ethical politics. He gave 183 talks on the subject in the course of a year, starting with one delivered in Aoyama, Tokyo, on April 20. People compared this campaign to the Midlothian campaign undertaken by William Ewart Gladstone when he was over seventy. Gotō himself likened it to Theodore Roosevelt's bid to take on the two dominant political parties in the US by forming the Progressive Party in 1911. Gotō's talks were always packed. The first one he gave was published as a hundred-page pamphlet, which only cost ten *sen* (one *sen* being one hundredth of a yen at the time, one yen was equal to about one dollar). A million copies were printed.

The campaign for ethical politics was also called the campaign to reform party politics. Gotō criticized party politics for succumbing to the evils of majoritarianism and being rooted in raw power. He argued that it should be rooted in ethics instead, hence the term "ethical politics." Years before, he had censured party politics and majoritarianism as a member of the Dōshikai in 1913. Later, when he was mayor of Tokyo and home minister in the second Yamamoto cabinet (1920–23), the savagery of interparty conflict in the assembly had made him even more critical.

Above all, Gotō argued, the tyranny of the majority caused people to lose sight of Japan's relationship with the world. He often spoke, in his typically clumsy phraseology, of Japan's Japan, the world's Japan, and Japan's world.

"Japan's Japan" meant understanding Japan. "The world's Japan" meant understanding the world. "Japan's world" meant fostering global understanding of Japan. Gotō's greatest concern was, as ever, the question of what form politics should take to ensure that Japan remained a successful player on the world stage.

Gotō built on the success of his campaign for ethical politics by organizing the Fusen Junbikai (Universal Suffrage Preparation Group), which signed up 250,000 members. People wondered about the nature of this movement. Some thought that it was a new political party, others that it was a campaign to do away with party politics altogether. In the end it remained purely a political education campaign and eventually petered out. It was not that Gotō lacked ambition, but there was a serious limit to how much support he could muster at this point in his career.

Nonetheless, Gotō's campaign exposed a serious flaw in Japanese party politics. It had failed to produce a statesman with a global perspective capable of overcoming the evils of majoritarianism. Even the introduction of universal suffrage would fail to change Japanese party politics much, and many people sensed if not consciously predicted as much. That was why his campaign initially attracted such a large following. Gotō discerned the mood of the times and tapped into a deep vein of public opinion, but he was too isolated and powerless to turn it into an effective political force.

Gotō as Mentor

During his campaign for ethical politics, Gotō would tell young people to keep up the good fight after he died. People, he believed, were everything. It is understandable that Gotō, aware of his own advancing years, should have become almost obsessed with mentoring others. He was unstinting in his support of anyone who possessed the kind of political vision that might help reform Japan, from anarchist Ōsugi Sakae on the left to ultranationalist Kita Ikki on the right.

As an example, let us take Shōriki Matsutarō.[2] Shōriki, who was head of

---

2   As described in "Geppō [Monthly Report]," *Gotō Shinpei* vol. 4, ed. Tsurimi Yūsuke (Tokyo: Keisō Shobō, 1967).

the Police Affairs Department of the home ministry under the Yamamoto cabinet, was forced to take responsibility for the attempted assassination of the crown prince (the Toranomon Incident) and dismissed from his post. Gotō, who felt bad for him, offered him 10,000 yen and urged him to spend a few years enjoying himself. Shōriki declined the money, but not long afterwards a friend suggested that he take over management of the *Yomiuri Shinbun* newspaper. He needed to raise 100,000 yen for that purpose, so he turned to Gotō for help. Hardly listening to what Shōriki had to say, Gotō immediately agreed to provide the money and told Shōriki to come back for it in two weeks. Running a newspaper was a dicey business, he warned, and Shōriki should wash his hands of it if things did not work out; he wouldn't need to repay the loan. Gotō further instructed Shōriki not to tell anyone where the funds had come from, since he did not want people constantly pestering him for money. Shōriki asked what he should do if the rumor got out that Gotō was the source of the funds. Gotō replied, "Tell people Gotō looks like a soft touch but he's really a skinflint." The entire conversation lasted barely five minutes. Shōriki was dumbfounded.

Shōriki suspected that Gotō had arranged for someone else to put up the funds, but after Gotō's death, Gotō's son Ichizō told Shōriki that his father had raised the money by mortgaging the land on which his house stood. The revelation moved Shōriki to tears. That was how determined Gotō was to help out young people.

Gotō's residence, incidentally, was a large estate covering some 23,140 square meters located in Azabu Sakurada-chō, Tokyo. After his death, the estate passed to other owners because of the massive debts he left behind. It later became the site of the embassy of Manchukuo and is currently the site of the Chinese embassy—a happy fate for the home of the man who played such a prominent role in developing the Manchurian economy and devoted himself to establishing a Sino-Japanese partnership.

In his old age Gotō took a great interest in the Boy Scouts. He first became involved in the movement in 1922, when a jamboree was held in Japan to honor the British crown prince's visit to the country. Gotō was acting chairman of the jamboree and later became the Chief Scout of Japan. He was such a scouting enthusiast, in fact, that he donated the entire

100,000 yen that he received in retirement pay on stepping down as mayor of Tokyo to the Boy Scouts of Japan. The association had a song entitled "Hail to Chief Scout Gotō," which began,

> Our beloved Chief Scout,
> White-bearded and pince-nezed,
> Uniformed and with a cane,
> Is always spry and smiling.

Some might have thought that the elderly Gotō, tearfully listening to this song, looked ridiculous dressed in his Boy Scout uniform complete with shorts (he had always been fond of uniforms). True, he had lost whatever influence he had once exercised on the political scene. But while he may have gone down to defeat in politics, he had chosen to devote the last years of his life to youth education, and no one could laugh at him for that.

China during the Northern Expedition

Gotō mustered his strength for one final effort when, between December 1927 and February 1928, five years after inviting Joffe to Japan, he visited the Soviet Union. Having already suffered two cerebral hemorrhages, he was virtually putting his life on the line by making the trip in the frigid depths of winter. What made him so determined to go?

To Gotō's disappointment, little progress had been made in improving Japanese-Soviet relations since the restoration of diplomatic ties. Negotiations on revising the fisheries treaty and concluding a commercial treaty had become bogged down. In 1925, Gotō had approached Prime Minister Katō Takaaki with the idea of a Siberian development initiative designed to foster Japanese-Soviet cooperation, but Katō showed little interest. In August 1926, the Soviets suggested concluding a treaty on the model of the German-Soviet treaty of friendship and neutrality, and in May 1927, they proposed signing a nonaggression pact. The Japanese government, however, was unwilling to go beyond concluding a series of sectoral agreements, and even negotiations on these made little headway.

One probable reason for the Japanese government's reluctance was

Visiting the USSR, 1927
Front row, third from the left: Tanaka Seijirō; fourth from the left: Gotō Shinpei

an increase in Japanese Communist Party activity under the aegis of the Comintern, especially after 1927, when several Japanese Communist Party leaders came home from Moscow with a policy platform known as the 1927 Thesis.

Earlier, in 1922, when the Germans strengthened ties with the Soviets in the Treaty of Rapallo, Gotō had viewed the move as a revival of Bismarckian diplomacy. He was therefore disappointed that a Japanese partnership with Germany as well as the USSR never materialized. After all, his old theory of the New and Old Worlds in opposition had embraced not only Japan, China, and Russia but also Germany and even France.

Needless to say, the question of China's future made strengthening Japan's ties with the Soviet Union even more important in Gotō's eyes. An alternative to the Washington Treaty System was, as we have seen, then emerging in China. If the Washington Treaty System was to survive in the face of the challenge it posed, the Western powers and Japan would need to join together in giving China an economic boost. The best opportunity for accomplishing this was the Peking Tariff Conference that began in October 1925. If Chinese tariffs were raised at the conference, the Peking government's financial position would be greatly strengthened.

The conference, however, ended fruitlessly, for two reasons. First, Japan, Britain, and the United States were working at cross purposes. Japan, for example, was amenable to the idea of China regaining tariff autonomy, but it insisted on low tariffs on cheap items so that Japanese products would remain competitive. Foreign Minister Shidehara Kijūrō was unyielding on this point despite his otherwise conciliatory approach to Britain, the US, and China. Second, the Peking government was unstable. It had never been more than a motley coalition of warlords and was opposed by the Kuomintang government in Canton. There was accordingly relatively little support for negotiating a hike in tariffs, which if realized would benefit whoever held power in Peking. The tariff conference was in the end adjourned indefinitely in July 1926. The attempt by Japan, Britain, and the US to cooperate in nurturing a Chinese government able to work with all three had ended in failure.

The failure of the conference roughly coincided with the start of the Northern Expedition, the Kuomintang's campaign to reunify China. The expedition, which was officially launched in July 1926, achieved great success. By the end of the year nationalist forces had brought almost the entire area south of the Yangtze River under their control. This signaled the incipient triumph of the new China, and the Soviet-centered system of international relations of which it was a part, over the old China and the Washington Treaty System.

But the influence exercised by the Soviet Union during the first phase of the Northern Expedition intensified conflict within the Kuomintang, and in July 1927 the Chinese Communist Party quit the nationalist government, bringing to an end the alliance between the KMT and the CCP. Then, in December, the Nanking (Nanjing) government broke off diplomatic relations with the USSR. It was not only in the south that Sino-Soviet relations worsened. Earlier, in April, the Peking government had raided the Soviet embassy and the Chinese Eastern Railway.

The Northern Expedition's success and the deterioration of Sino-Soviet relations between 1926 and the summer of 1927 threw international relations with China into flux. The impasse in the Washington Treaty System, coupled with the impasse in the opposing Sino-Soviet relationship, presented Japan with at least three options. First, it could resume efforts to work more closely with the British and Americans. Second, it could develop a new relationship with China. Or third, it could court the Soviets.

The Japanese government, now headed by Tanaka Giichi, chose the second of these options. In November 1927, Chiang Kai-shek, who three months later was to seize complete control of the Kuomintang and resume the Northern Expedition, visited Japan and met with Prime Minister Tanaka. While declaring his intention to continue his march north, Chiang explained that this presented no threat to Japanese and Western interests, and he requested Japan's aid. The Tanaka government was thus so far successful in its aim of strengthening ties with the right wing of the Kuomintang.

Last Visit to Russia

It was around the time of this meeting that Tanaka's advisers approached Gotō about visiting the Soviet Union. The visit's immediate objective was merely to break the deadlock in the fisheries talks. Another consideration, of course, was the need to adjust Japanese-Soviet relations to accommodate the rapprochement with Chiang Kai-shek. But Gotō envisioned a broader partnership between the two countries. Although some in Tanaka's circle were alarmed by this idea, Gotō himself was raring to go.

What then did Gotō discover on his visit to the Soviet Union? First, with regard to the power struggle then rumored to be unfolding within the Soviet government, he unequivocally recognized Stalin's ascendancy. Stalin, he said, "with his conservative streak reminiscent of our own Ōkubo Toshimichi"—one of the leaders of the Meiji Restoration—"appeared to possess the character and ability to control the Soviets after Lenin's death." Trotsky, who had already left the government, was inevitably compared to Saigō Takamori, who was also a Restoration leader but later rebelled against the government. Gotō, who had once likened the New Economic Policy to the policy of westernization and modernization pursued during the Meiji

Restoration, similarly saw the Soviet government as the analog of the Meiji government. Second, he lauded the Soviet leadership headed by Stalin for its zeal and diligence. He saw it as embodying Soviet-style bushido, much as he had once described Roosevelt's fighting spirit as the American version of it. Third, he praised the Soviet leaders for focusing not on "general political theory" but rather on "concrete aspects of governance." Fourth, he considered their methods of governance to be based on "scientific foundations," with the State Planning Committee (Gosplan)—the Soviet version of Gotō's abortive think tank—at their heart. In these respects, Gotō concluded, the Soviet Union was a highly effective state developing under the "scientific" guidance of outstanding leaders.

It is significant in this connection that Gotō drew a sharp distinction between the Soviet Union and the Comintern. In talks with Gotō, People's Commissar for Foreign Affairs Georgy Chicherin denied that the Soviet Union had ever propagated communism in China. Premier Alexei Rykov too disclaimed any ideological influence, declaring that the ascription of the unrest in China to "Red propaganda" was "truly an excessive honor" for the Soviet Union. Gotō was inclined to believe these protestations. He was as skeptical as ever of the power of ideology. The Soviet Union was, in his eyes, a great power that deserved to be judged first and foremost on its actual strength.

Gotō wished to collaborate with this powerful new Soviet state in the area of China policy. This idea, which he already had in mind during his negotiations with Joffe, corresponded to the third of the options that became available to Japan in the wake of the nationalists' Northern Expedition in China.

When Gotō met with Stalin on January 7, 1928, he maintained that peace in the Far East should be based on a triple entente between Japan, China, and Russia, but in the absence of a dependable regime in China, he proposed "solving the China problem through Russo-Japanese consultations, based on a candid understanding." Although he provided no specifics, Gotō believed that reaching a bilateral agreement on the question of China was important because it would be the first step to extricating Japan from the Washington Treaty System, which required working with the British and the Americans. As he himself bitingly put it, "there are still adherents of Anglo-American policy in Japan." He was convinced that Japan needed to stop toeing the Anglo-American line and establish its own independent foreign policy, and that required "shaking hands with Russia."

Gotō's meeting with Stalin was interesting in another regard. Each pointed out the supposed errors committed by the other's country in China. The Soviets' first blunder, according to Gotō, was that they had been "in too much of a hurry to achieve results," the "communization campaign" being a case in point. Their other blunder was being ill informed about China. "The old civilization is so deeply rooted in China," he remarked, "that new social movements have little chance of success." What looked like success was in fact superficial, as exemplified by Sun Yat-sen. This had consistently been Gotō's view since the wave of nationalism that swept China after the Russo-Japanese War.

Stalin for his part asserted that Japan's essential error was "having failed to understand the true nature of the Chinese social movement," which basically originated in nationalism. The Japanese, he argued, having once been oppressed by unequal treaties themselves, should have understood that movement better than anyone else. Stalin further criticized Japan for its habit of sending troops at every juncture, noting that America's more flexible policies were beginning to yield success. Gotō did not respond directly to these criticisms, except to observe that Japan's "ill-considered dispatch of troops was the result of its policy of following the British and Americans." Stalin made no attempt to respond to Gotō's criticisms either. As always, Gotō refused to acknowledge the power of ideology, and so the two men ended their discussion at cross purposes. Despite their differences, however, Gotō must have found such frank mutual criticism instructive.

With the Washington Treaty System at an impasse, the great powers, including Japan, faced a difficult choice between multilateralism and bilateral cooperation with China. The Tanaka government inclined toward the latter. Soviet influence in China, meanwhile, had waned. Nonetheless, Gotō contended that in the area of China policy, Japan should first and foremost cooperate with the Soviets. That was a most unusual contention at the time and therefore attracted little support. Some Japanese disliked the Soviet

Union out of fears of "Red" influence, while many, especially in the army, were wary of Soviet military might in the Far East. Yet despite such potential sources of tension with the USSR, or rather because of them, Gotō believed that, historically and geographically, Japanese-Soviet cooperation could and should be the cornerstone of Japanese foreign policy. For that reason, it was perhaps inevitable that the last real political act of his life should have been to visit the Soviet Union.

What Might Have Been

After World War I, there were two schools of thought in Japan on the subject of global diplomacy. One held that it had entered a completely new era; the other asserted that it was as rooted as ever in national interests. Gotō of course belonged to the latter school. In his eyes, only two things had changed in the Far East: American power had grown, and countries now took a more economic approach to advancing their interests. This was exactly what he had predicted in the late Meiji era.

None of Gotō's writings from this period particularly emphasize the American threat. He was relatively dispassionate even on the fraught subject of Japanese immigration to the United States. His advocacy of a bilateral partnership with the Soviet Union, or a trilateral partnership with the Soviet Union and China, was therefore not directly motivated by a desire to counter the United States. Rather, his belief in the need for the Japanese, Chinese, and Soviets to work together arose from his longstanding conviction that "international relations must always accord with geography and history." Japan's ability to expand its interests abroad, Gotō believed, could not be guaranteed under the Washington Treaty System, which involved working with the British and the Americans but did not allow for cordial relations with the Chinese and the Soviets. "Establishing better trilateral relations between Japan, Russia, and China" was "what the Providence of Nature demands."

Gotō therefore gave highest priority to relations with the Soviet Union. That country was the fundamental cause of Japan's difficulties on the continent, because the ultimate threat to Japanese expansion there was the Soviet policy toward China originating in the first Karakhan Manifesto of 1919. He sought common interests between Japan and its Soviet rivals and explored the possibility of a partnership between them, much as he had done with the Russians before the war. His disdain for ideology made this possible. That disdain had previously embroiled him in the Siberian Expedition against the Soviets, but now it had the opposite effect. His thinking, however, had little influence on the foreign policy of the day. Neither the Tanaka government nor its successor led by Hamaguchi Osachi adopted his ideas.

What then, in the light of subsequent history, was the significance of the failure to implement the policy that Gotō envisioned? In November 1929, some six months after Gotō's death, the Chinese and Soviets clashed in North Manchuria over control of the Chinese Eastern Railway, and the Soviets won a crushing victory. The Soviet Union's reemergence as a major military power came as a grave shock to the Japanese army. China, meanwhile, began demanding the return of Japanese interests in Manchuria. The perception that those interests were under threat from both Soviet military power and Chinese nationalism prompted the Japanese Kwantung Army to invade Manchuria in 1931. That invasion (the Manchurian Incident) was strongly supported by the Japanese public, because the public shared the military's apprehensions.

The Soviets, seriously alarmed by Japan's actions, rapidly strengthened their military presence in the Far East. In 1935, the Kwantung Army, concerned about the Soviet buildup, advanced into other parts of northern China with the intention of securing Manchukuo's rear.

In short, fear of the Soviets underlay the series of expansionist moves by Japan that started with the invasion of Manchuria. Historians should generally avoid speculating about "what if." But what if Japan and the Soviet Union had agreed to recognize each other's interests in Manchuria, or indeed any relationship of trust had existed between them? The Kwantung Army might then never have invaded Manchuria. Even if it had, the invasion might not have gained the popular support that it did. Furthermore, the spiral of mutual fear and suspicion that followed might have been avoided, and Japan's reckless overseas expansion might have been checked.

In this light, Gotō's trip to the Soviet Union can be seen as an attempt to stabilize Japan's relationship with that country. He was motivated by the insight that the instability of that relationship was the greatest vulnerability in Japan's security. Years earlier, his urban policy had been motivated by the perception that the weakness of Japanese civilization lay in the uncontrolled sprawl of its cities. His campaign for ethical politics had been motivated by the perception that the weakness of Japanese party politics lay in the tyranny of the majority. His Soviet visit was another visionary act that took a similar leap of the imagination. The Japanese public must have felt, albeit vaguely, that in undertaking his final journey, he was indicating where Japan's challenges lay and what path the country should follow. This was why Gotō was remembered as a foreign policy leader, and indeed a national one. His death was truly an immeasurable loss for Japan.

EPILOGUE

Gotō Shinpei died in April 1929, somewhat more than a year after returning from the Soviet Union. In the end he never had the opportunity to lead Japan as prime minister, but that is not to be lamented, for his achievements far outnumbered those of the average prime minister. Indeed, he was ill-suited for that role, because he sorely lacked the level-headedness and constancy essential for a national leader.

He was for the same reason ill-suited to being foreign minister. What then does it mean to be a foreign policy leader? Perhaps the question should be rephrased. What is the most fundamental issue facing diplomacy? When diplomacy is considered in the broadest sense and over the maximum time span, it ultimately boils down to a question of what place one's country should occupy on the global stage and how it should deal with the rest of the world. This was a particularly acute concern for Japan, the first non-Western state to join the modern community of nations, in the late nineteenth and early twentieth centuries. It is above all in this regard, I believe, that Gotō cannot be overlooked as one of modern Japan's foreign policy leaders.

Gotō deserves recognition, first, for his adroitness in embracing various aspects of Western civilization. He was without peer when it came to importing to Japan such major "civilized" institutions as a public health system, the railway, and urban planning and transplanting them to Taiwan and Manchuria. He believed that "civilizing" Japan in this fashion, even more than achieving military superiority or economic might, was a way to claim a place of honor among the comity of nations. He likewise believed that "civilizing" Japan's colonies was a means of participating in global civilization. Indeed, he saw it as Japan's mission.

To that end, Gotō sought far and wide for Western knowledge, but what really set him apart was the way in which he exhaustively studied the history and customs of the society to be "civilized" and improvised accordingly. Further, he set up new organizational structures for that purpose quite unlike the regular institutions then existing in Japan. In sum, while believing in the universality of civilization, he followed biological principles in adapting it to local conditions. That was the key to his success.

For Japan's colonies, it was blatantly imperialist ideology. For all Gotō's talk about "civilizing" Manchuria being Japan's mission, in Chinese eyes it was an unwanted intrusion. Gotō left no real explanation as to why Japan needed to be in Manchuria. By the 1920s, liberal writers such as Ishibashi Tanzan and Kiyosawa Kiyoshi were arguing, based on a dispassionate tally of costs and benefits, that maintaining a presence in Manchuria did Japan much more harm than good. Gotō's views on the subject were thus in certain regards outdated. Indeed, by no means all Japanese who were deeply committed to the Japanese presence in Manchuria shared his policy positions, so his experiences as president of the South Manchuria Railway do not fully explain his attitude. Still, to those who played a role in Manchuria in the early days of the Japanese presence, the importance of Japan's interests there must have been so obvious that they hardly gave it a second thought. Nonetheless, it is a fact that Gotō, guided as he was by the universal standard of civilization, never became a narrow-minded racist or chauvinist. The institutions he established delivered many benefits over the decades, despite changes of regime.

In that respect Gotō resembled Theodore Roosevelt, another believer in the universality of civilization. Roosevelt, too, thought nothing of forcing neighboring countries to become more civilized, yet rose above racial and cultural prejudice because of his faith in civilized standards.[1] Gotō, however, faced a far more daunting task in Asia than did the United States, a great power and heir to European civilization, in its attempt to "civilize," say, the Caribbean. In that sense Gotō was no mere Roosevelt in miniature.

---

1   Frank Ninkovich, "Theodore Roosevelt: Civilization as Ideology," *Diplomatic History*, vol. 10, no. 3 (Summer 1986).

Gotō also resembled Fukuzawa Yukichi in calling for the adoption of Western civilization without falling into the trap of idealizing it. Gotō practiced what Fukuzawa preached. It is no coincidence that Gotō revered both Fukuzawa and Roosevelt.

Gotō's second legacy to Japanese foreign policy was his focus on opportunities for achieving closer integration with other countries, rather than on sources of conflict. To the superficial observer, he may appear to have regarded the world as a battleground between different peoples and to have offered lessons on how to prevail on that battleground. In the late 1930s and early 1940s, he was often remembered as an outstanding leader in exactly that regard. But the facts show he was a champion of cooperation with the Chinese and the Russians (or Soviets), not of balance-of-power politics. It is thus a mistake to see the 1940 Tripartite Pact with Germany and Italy, coupled with the 1941 Soviet-Japanese Neutrality Pact, as Foreign Minister Matsuoka Yōsuke's updated version of Gotō's idea of the New and Old Worlds in opposition.

Gotō, moreover, maintained that the only way for Japan to expand its interests overseas was by bringing benefits both to the regions to which it expanded and to the adjacent countries. In his mind, Japan's development of Manchuria, particularly the South Manchuria Railway, would contribute to "civilizing" the world, profit China, Russia, and Manchuria itself, tie all three to Japan, and thus guarantee the smooth progress of Japan's overseas expansion. This thinking made Gotō's approach unique. He sought to identify interests shared by parties that appeared to be at loggerheads, systematically coordinate and develop those interests, and thus sublimate a confrontational relationship into an integrative one. This can be termed an integrationist view of international relations.

That view can, of course, be criticized. Even if Japan and China had worked together, their relationship could never have been an equal one. It could be argued that Gotō's envisaged approach to overseas expansion was Machiavellian in the extreme. Nonetheless, his integrationist view of international relations is of the greatest significance in modern Japanese diplomatic history.

There is a confrontational side and an integrative side to every international relationship. The prewar Japanese state, in part because it emerged under foreign pressure, invariably focused on the confrontational side. The country's leaders in the early and mid-Meiji era were terrified that the Korean Peninsula would, in Chinese or Russian hands, become a dagger pointed at the heart of Japan. The Trans-Siberian Railway was in their eyes a lethal Russian weapon aimed at the Far East. Even in the last years of the Meiji era, when Russia and Japan were partners busy developing North and South Manchuria respectively, Yamagata Aritomo feared that Russia might be strengthened militarily as a result and worried that increased contact between the two countries could heighten the risk of a clash.

This fixation on the confrontational side of international relations gave rise to a kind of defensive proactivism, a desire to take some form of action before any confrontation took an unfavorable turn. To some degree, Japan's concerns about the Korean Peninsula led to the Sino-Japanese War, its concerns about the Trans-Siberian Railway led to the Russo-Japanese War, and Yamagata's fears led to the imbroglio over the two new army divisions in Korea. It is not necessarily a bad thing to seek to be undefeatable in case tensions escalate. But it was folly to attempt to establish a completely impregnable national defense perimeter in the face of all possible threats when the evolution of transportation technology and advances in weapons systems had already rendered unconditional viability (to use Kenneth Boulding's term) unattainable. No defense regime could be simultaneously invulnerable to Chinese nationalism, Soviet military power, and American economic might. The quest for one inevitably ended in disaster.

The foreign ministry, like the army, saw international relations primarily in confrontational terms. Japanese foreign policy in the prewar era was almost exclusively concerned with acquiring, reinforcing, and protecting interests and maintaining the balance of power by establishing alliances in case a conflict occurred. But confrontation remained confrontation. In other words, both the army and the foreign ministry regarded international relations as a zero-sum game, in which whatever was to the benefit of one side was to the detriment of the other. Although they thought about controlling tensions, the idea of turning them into something different hardly occurred to them.

In this context, the distinctiveness of Gotō's thinking becomes clear. He looked on the integrative side of Japan's tense international relationships, namely shared interests. He endeavored to systematically coordinate and develop those interests, primarily through business, and forge a common bond between the parties concerned, thus sublimating their confrontational relationship into an integrative one. He saw international relations as a positive-sum game. This integrationist view of international relations must have been why he struck his contemporaries as a foreign policy leader.

Japan today has close ties with countries around the world thanks to its remarkable economic growth, but this has actually heightened tensions due to a multiplicity of institutional and cultural differences. Recent talk of the need for Japan to open its doors to the outside world for a third time, as it did in the mid-nineteenth century and after World War II, is motivated by fears that it could be ostracized from the international community unless it once more reinvents itself. The challenge that Gotō faced is certainly not a thing of the past. Now as in his day, Japan can find a place for itself in the world only if it changes its ways.

The interplay of confrontation and integration often characterizes foreign relations today. Highly suggestive in this regard is the emergence of the term "trade war," a compound of two mutually contradictory words. "War" is the most extreme form of confrontation, and "trade" is something that benefits both parties. How can the element of confrontation be controlled so that the element of integration predominates? That was another question with which Gotō grappled, and far from being obsolete, it is now more pressing than ever.

Gotō's envisioned solutions to these two challenges have not lost their relevance for anyone interested in the fundamental direction of Japanese foreign policy.

Timeline of Gotō Shinpei's Life

Year	Gotō Shinpei	Developments in Japan and Abroad
1857	July: Born in Shiogama, Isawa County, in the province of Rikuchū (present-day Mizusawa, Iwate Prefecture).	
1867	March: Appointed *okugoshō* (personal page) to the Rusu clan.	
1868		January: Battle of Toba-Fushimi (start of the Boshin War). October: Sendai domain surrenders to government forces.
1869	March/April: The Gotō family forfeit samurai status and become farmers. October/November: Becomes a student boarder at the home of Yasuba Yasukazu, *daisanji* (senior counselor) of Isawa Prefecture.	
1871	March/April: Travels to Tokyo and boards with Sōmura Shōzō.	August: The feudal domains are abolished.
1872	February/March: Returns home.	
1873	May: Enrolls in Fukushima First School of Western Studies.	October: Saigō Takamori and Itagaki Taisuke resign from the government in a dispute over Korea policy.
1874	February: Enrolls in Sukagawa Medical School.	
1875	July: Becomes a medical student, 6th class, and deputy dorm head at Fukushima Prefectural Hospital.	
1876	March: Becomes supervisor of the junior and senior student dormitories. August: Becomes physician, 3rd class, at Aichi Prefectural Hospital.	
1877	September: Becomes a staff doctor at the temporary army hospital in Osaka. Granted a home ministry medical license. November: Hired as a staff doctor at the Nagoya Army Garrison Hospital.	February: The Satsuma Rebellion breaks out (lasting until September).
1878	March: Returns to Aichi Prefectural Hospital. October: Submits a recommendation on "health police medical officers" to Yasuba Yasukazu, now governor of Aichi Prefecture. December: Submits a recommendation on sanitary police to Nagayo Sensai, head of the home ministry's Public Health Bureau.	

Year	Gotō Shinpei	Developments in Japan and Abroad
1879	December: Becomes acting head of Aichi Prefectural Hospital and Medical School.	
1880	May: Becomes provisional head of Aichi Prefectural Hospital and Medical School.	
1881	October: Becomes official head of Aichi Prefectural Hospital and Medical School.	October: Ōkuma Shigenobu is expelled from the government.
1882	February: Offered a position in the home ministry's Public Health Bureau by Nagayo Sensai. April: Treats wounded Liberal Party leader Itagaki Taisuke in Gifu.	
1883	January: Appointed to a junior position at the home ministry, becoming deputy research director at the Public Health Bureau. September: Marries Kazuko, second daughter of Yasuba Yasukazu. October: Meets Nishigori Takekiyo and becomes involved in the Sōma Affair.	
1885		December: Japan's first cabinet.
1889	August: Publishes *Principles of National Hygiene.*	February: The Meiji Constitution is promulgated.
1890	April: Leaves to study in Germany.	July: First general election for the lower house of the Diet. December: First Imperial Diet.
1892	June: Returns to Japan. November: Appointed head of the home ministry's Public Health Bureau.	
1893	November: Arrested and jailed in the Sōma Affair. December: Suspended from government service.	
1894	May: Released on bail. December: Found not guilty on appeal.	August: Outbreak of the Sino-Japanese War.
1895	April: Appointed administrative director of the Temporary Army Quarantine Department. September: Reappointed head of the home ministry's Public Health Bureau. November: Submits a memorandum on the issue of opium in Taiwan to Prime Minister Itō Hirobumi.	

Year	Gotō Shinpei	Developments in Japan and Abroad
1896	April: Appointed public health adviser to the Government-General of Taiwan. June: Visits Taiwan with its new governor-general, Katsura Tarō.	
1898	March: Appointed director of civil affairs in the Government-General of Taiwan. June: Becomes civilian governor of Taiwan.	April: Outbreak of the Spanish-American War.
1899		September: US Secretary of State John Hay proposes the Open Door policy in China.
1900	April: Visits Amoy. August: The Amoy Incident.	January–May: The Boxer Rebellion spreads through northern China. July: John Hay issues the second Open Door Note.
1902	June–December: Tours North America and Europe.	January: Anglo-Japanese Alliance concluded.
1903	November: Appointed by the emperor to the House of Peers.	
1904		February: Outbreak of the Russo-Japanese War.
1905	September: Visits Kodama Gentarō in Manchuria.	August: Portsmouth Peace Conference. September: Treaty of Portsmouth signed.
1906	April: Agrees to stay on as civilian governor of Taiwan when Sakuma Samata becomes the new governor-general of Taiwan. Made a baron. June: Asked to become president of the South Manchuria Railway (SMR). July: Decides to accept due to Kodama's death. November: Becomes first president of the SMR.	May: Conference on the Manchurian question attended by the cabinet and elder statesmen.
1907	April: The SMR commences operations. May–June: Has an audience with the Qing Emperor and Empress Dowager Cixi and meets with Yuan Shikai. September: Meets with Itō Hirobumi on Itsukushima.	June: Franco-Japanese Agreement. July: First Russo-Japanese Agreement.

Year	Gotō Shinpei	Developments in Japan and Abroad
1908	April–June: Visits Moscow. July: Becomes minister of communications in the second Katsura cabinet (until August 1911). November: Meets with Tang Shaoyi. December: Concurrently appointed director-general of the Railway Agency (until August 1911).	November: The Root-Takahira Agreement.
1909		August–September: Five-point Sino-Japanese convention on Manchuria signed. October: Itō Hirobumi assassinated in Harbin. December: The US proposes "neutralizing" the SMR.
1910	June: Concurrently appointed deputy director-general of the Colonial Office (until May 1911).	July: Second Russo-Japanese Agreement. August: Japan annexes Korea. November: Four-power Chinese loan consortium formed by the UK, US, France, and Germany.
1911	August: Becomes vice president of the Russo-Japanese Association (under President Terauchi Masatake).	August: The second Saionji cabinet takes office. October: The Xinhai Revolution in China. November: Direct rail link completed between Korea and Manchuria.
1912	July–August: Visits Russia with Katsura Tarō, but the trip is cut short. December: Becomes minister of communications, director-general of the Railway Agency, and director-general of the Colonial Office in the newly formed third Katsura cabinet.	February: The Qing dynasty falls. June: Japan and Russia join the four-power consortium to form a six-power consortium. July: Third Russo-Japanese Agreement. December: The second Saionji cabinet falls, triggering a campaign to protect constitutional politics.
1913	October: Leaves the newly formed party upon Katsura's death.	January: Katsura Tarō announces the establishment of a new party. February: The third Katsura cabinet falls and is replaced by the first Yamamoto Gonbei cabinet. March: The US withdraws from the six-power consortium. December: Official founding of the new party, the Rikken Dōshikai.

Year	Gotō Shinpei	Developments in Japan and Abroad
1914	June: Lobbies for the establishment of the Oriental Bank.	January: The Siemens scandal breaks. March: The Yamamoto cabinet resigns. April: Ōkuma Shigenobu's second cabinet takes office. July–August: Outbreak of World War I. Japan also declares war.
1915		January: Negotiations begin on the Twenty-One Demands (lasting until May). March: The Dōshikai and other governing parties in the Ōkuma cabinet win the 12th general elections by a landslide. July–August: The Ōkuma cabinet resigns over a scandal involving Interior Minister Ōura, but ultimately remains in office after a reshuffle. October: Japan, Britain, and Russia advise Yuan Shikai to postpone restoration of imperial rule in China.
1916	October: Becomes home minister and director-general of the Railway Agency in the newly formed Terauchi cabinet.	March: The Ōkuma cabinet adopts a resolution calling for the overthrow of Yuan Shikai. July–August: Ōkuma and Terauchi Masatake negotiate the transfer of power. October: The Dōshikai merges with two smaller parties to form the Kenseikai.
1917	January: Works to defeat the Kenseikai after the lower house is dissolved. June: Becomes a member of the newly established Provisional Research Council on Foreign Relations.	January: The cabinet decides to change the course of China policy. April: The US declares war on Germany. July: The Duan Qirui government takes power in China, and the Terauchi cabinet decides to assist it. August: China declares war on Germany. November: The Lansing-Ishii Agreement. The Russian Revolution.
1918	April: Loses his wife Kazuko. Becomes foreign minister.	January: US President Wilson announces the Fourteen Points. March: Treaty of Brest-Litovsk. August: The Siberian Expedition. The rice riots. September: The Hara Takashi cabinet takes office. November: World War I ends.

Year	Gotō Shinpei	Developments in Japan and Abroad
1919	February: Becomes president of Takushoku University. March: Leaves for a tour of the United States and Europe (returning in November).	March: March 1st Movement in Korea. May: May 4th Movement in China. June: Treaty of Versailles signed.
1920	February: Becomes president of the Russo-Japanese Association. June: Confers with Prime Minister Hara on establishing a major think tank. December: Becomes mayor of Tokyo (until April 1923).	
1921	April: Tables the so-called 800 Million Yen Plan.	September: Yasuda Zenjirō is assassinated. November: Prime Minister Hara Takashi is assassinated. The Takahashi Korekiyo cabinet takes office. The Washington Conference begins (lasting until February 1922).
1922	June: Becomes head of the Tokyo Boy Scouts and then Chief Scout of Japan. September: Charles Beard comes to Japan at Gotō's invitation. Made a viscount.	June: The Takahashi cabinet falls and is succeeded by the Katō Tomosaburō cabinet. December: The Soviet Union is formed.
1923	January: Adolph Joffe comes to Japan at Gotō's invitation. September: Becomes home minister and director-general of the Imperial Capital Reconstruction Agency in the second Yamamoto Gonbei cabinet.	August: Prime Minister Katō Tomosaburō dies. September: Massive earthquake strikes Tokyo.
1924	October: Becomes director-general of the Tokyo Broadcasting Station.	January: The Kiyoura Keigo cabinet takes office, triggering the second campaign to protect constitutional politics. The nationalists and the communists form an alliance in China. May: The US enacts a law excluding Japanese and other Asian immigrants. June: The Katō Takaaki cabinet takes office, initiating the era of party cabinets. November: Sun Yat-sen gives a speech on pan-Asianism in Kobe.

Year	Gotō Shinpei	Developments in Japan and Abroad
1925	July: Speaks on the radio to mark the start of regular broadcasting in Japan. Proposes a Far Eastern development plan to Prime Minister Katō.	January: Soviet-Japanese Basic Convention signed, normalizing relations. March: Universal manhood suffrage enacted. October: Peking Tariff Conference begins.
1926	February: Suffers a cerebral hemorrhage. April: Launches the campaign for ethical politics.	January: The Wakatsuki Reijirō cabinet takes office. July: Chiang Kai-shek launches the Northern Expedition to reunite China.
1927	August: Suffers a second cerebral hemorrhage. December: Visits the Soviet Union (returning in February 1928).	April: The Tanaka Giichi cabinet takes office.
1928	November: Made a count.	February: First elections under universal suffrage. June: Chinese warlord Zhang Zuolin is assassinated by Japanese army officers. Nationalist forces enter Peking, marking the completion of the Northern Expedition.
1929	April: Dies on April 13.	

References

Materials

The most essential source documents are as follows:

Gotō Shinpei monjo [The Archives of Gotō Shinpei], owned by the Mizusawa Shiritsu Gotō Shinpei Kinenkan. These documents originally belonged to the Municipal Research Bureau in Tokyo, but are currently stored at the above-mentioned Gotō Shinpei Memorial Hall. They make up one of the most massive and best organized collections of private papers of politicians in modern Japan. The archives are on microfilm (87 reels, Gannandō Shōten), which are in the collections of several libraries in Japan.

Hara Takashi nikki [The Diary of Hara Takashi], compiled by Hara Keiichirō (Tokyo: Fukumura Publishing, 1965–1967). Hara, a rival of Gotō, wrote coolly, cynically and at length about Gotō in his diary. Tsurumi's biography of Gotō, which is listed just below, references some parts of Katsura's archives and other materials. Hara's diary is probably the most prominent source material it does not reference.

Katsura Tarō kankei monjo [The Archives Related to Katsura Tarō], *Terauchi Masatake kankei monjo* [The Archives Related to Terauchi Masatake], owned by the Modern Japanese Political History Materials Room of the National Diet Library. Letters and memoranda written by Gotō are naturally in the private archives of their recipients. Some of the most valuable such documents are found in the archives of Itō Hirobumi (most of his documents published), Yamagata Aritomo, Inoue Kaoru, and Itō Miyoji (all owned by the Modern Japanese Political History Materials Room of the National Diet Library). In these archives, particular attention should be paid to papers related to Katsura and Terauchi, who had close relationships with Gotō.

Biographies

Shinobu Seizaburō, *Gotō Shinpei: Kagakuteki seijika no shōgai* [Gotō Shinpei: Life of a Scientific Politician] (Tokyo: Hakubunkan, 1941). The book's coverage is more or less similar to that of Tsurumi's biography described. Shinobu writes about Gotō from the viewpoint of research and science. Though old, this book is worth reading.

Sugimori Hisahide, *Ōburoshiki* [Pipe Dreams] (Tokyo: Kadokawa, 1967). This book contains new interesting information about Gotō's relations with women, but it adds little to what we can learn from Tsurumi's biography. The book is about 700 pages long, of which 190 pages are about the Sōma Affair, thirty pages about Gotō's Taiwan period, and fifty pages about his work as the president of the South Manchuria Railway. Thus, the focus is not as well-balanced as might be expected for a politician's biography.

Tsurumi Yūsuke, *Gotō Shinpei* [Biography of Gotō Shinpei], four volumes (Tokyo: Gotō Shinpei Hakushaku Denki Hensankai, 1937–1938; reprinted by Keisō Shobō, 1967). This is an authentic biography written by Gotō's son-in-law, who was a politician and writer. Featuring abundant references and accurate, alluring descriptions, this biography of a politician is one of the most outstanding of its kind in modern Japan. Over 4,000 pages and replete with countless citations in tiny print, the biography is most probably too difficult for non-researchers to read from cover to cover. Tsurumi slightly overrates Gotō's roles and abilities and takes an antiquated view of the historical background—but this is only to a degree that seems unavoidable. Numerous events described in my book are based upon Tsurumi's biography, but citations are omitted to avoid cluttering up the text.

Research papers

This book was written based upon some of the author's writings and papers. Refer to them for more details and the evidence of descriptions in the book.

"Gaikō shidōsha toshite no Gotō Shinpei" [Gotō Shinpei as a Foreign Policy Leader], which appeared in *Kindai Nihon to Higashi Ajia* [Modern Japan and East Asia], compiled by the Kindai Nihon Kenkyūkai (Tokyo: Yamakawa Shuppansha, 1980).

Nihon rikugun to tairiku seisaku: 1906–1918 [The Japanese Army and Continental Policy: 1906–1918] (Tokyo: Tōkyō Daigaku Shuppankai, 1978).

Seitōseiji kakuritsukatei ni okeru rikken dōshikai kenseikai: Seikenkōsō to seitō shidō [A Study of the Rikken Dōshikai and the Early-Kenseikai: The Opposition Party during the Growth of Party Politics in Japan], included in *Rikkyo Hōgaku* [St. Paul's Review of Law and Politics], vol. 21 and vol. 25 (1983 and 1985).

"Washinton taisei to kokusai kyōchō no seishin: Jon Makumari Memorandamu" [The Washington Treaty System and the Spirit of "International Cooperation": John V.A. MacMurray's 1935 Memorandum], included in *Rikkyo Hōgaku* [St. Paul's Review of Law and Politics], vol. 23 (1983).

Refer to the references in the article by Kindai Nihon Kenkyūkai for studies by other researchers preceding the paper's publication in 1980. The author also wishes to introduce the following two papers not mentioned in that article, both of which take a unique viewpoint.

Maeda Yasuhiro, "Gotō Shinpei," included in *Gendai nihon shisō taikei no. 10 kenryoku no shisō* [Modern Japanese Thought no. 10 Ideology of Power], compiled by Kamishima Jirō (Tokyo: Chikuma Shobō, 1965).

Mizobe Hideaki, "Gotō Shinpei ron: Tōsōteki sekaikan to risei no dokusai" [Critique on Gotō Shinpei: His Aggressive View of the World and "Autocracy of Reason"], included in *Hōgakuronsō* [Kyoto Law Review], vol. 100, no. 2 and vol. 101, no. 2 (November 1967, November 1977).

Studies related to Gotō published after the Kindai Nihon Kenkyūkai article are as follows:

Kobayashi Michihiko, "Gotō Shinpei to shokuminchi keiei: Nihon Shokuminchi seisaku no keisei to kokunai seiji" [Gotō Shinpei and Colonial Management: Formation of the Japanese Colonial Policy and Domestic Politics], included in *Shirin*, vol. 68, no. 5 (September 1985).

Koshizawa Akira, "Dairen no toshi keikakushi" [History of Urban Planning in Dalian], included in the *J+C Economic Journal* issued by the Japan-China Economic Association, no. 134–136 (October–December 1984), "Chōshun no toshi keikakushi" [History of Urban Planning in Changchun], ibid., no. 165–169 and no. 173 (May–September 1987 and January 1988).

Liu Mingxiu, *Taiwan tōchi to ahen mondai* [Governance of Taiwan and the Opium Issue] (Tokyo: Yamakawa Shuppansha, 1983).

Mochida Nobuki, "Gotō Shinpei to shinsai fukkō jigyō: Mansei fukyōka no toshi supendingu" [Fiscal Outlays for Urban Reconstruction during the "Chronic Depression" of the 1920s: Gotō Shinpei and the Rebuilding of Tokyo], included in *Shakaikagaku kenkyū* [Journal of Social Science], vol. 35, no. 2 (March 1983).

Sakai Tetsuya, "Nihongaikō ni okeru sorenkan no hensen (1923–37): Nihon gaikōshi no wakugumi no saikentō" [Changes in the View of the USSR in Japanese Diplomacy (1923–37): A Review of the Framework of Japanese Diplomatic History], included in the Journal of the Association of Political and Social Science, vol. 97, no. 3 and no. 4 (April 1985).

Sakurai Ryōju, "Meiji makki ni okeru dentōgyō seisaku no seijiteki haikei: Tokyo shinai dentōgyō o daizai toshite" [Political Background of the Electric Lighting Business Policy at the End of Meiji: A Study of Electric Lighting Business in Tokyo], included in *Nihonshi kenkyū* [The Journal of the Japanese Society for Historical Studies], no. 282 (February 1986), "Tōkyō shigai densha no shiyūka o meguru seijikatei: Keien jidai no ichisokumen" [Political Process of Municipalizing Streetcars in Tokyo: One Aspect of the Katsura-Saionji Era], included in *Shigaku-zasshi* [The Monthly Organ of the Historical Society of Japan], book 95, no. 7 (July 1986).

Saitō Seiji, "Amoy jiken saikō" [A Re-examination of the Amoy Incident], included in *Nihonshi kenkyū* [The Journal of the Japanese Society for Historical Studies], no. 305 (January 1988).

Suetake Yoshiya, "Taishō-ki ni okeru Gotō Shinpei o meguru seijijōkyō" [Political Situation of Gotō Shinpei in the Taishō Era], included in *Shigaku-zasshi* (The Monthly Organ of the Historical Society of Japan], book 96, no. 6 (June 1987).

Yoshimura Michio, "1920 nendai ni okeru nisso kyōchō no mosaku: Gotō Shinpei no enkaishū shokumin kōsō o chūshin ni" [Quest for Japan-Soviet Cooperation in the 1920s: Centering on Gotō Shinpei's Ideas for Colonizing Primorsky Krai], included in *Taiheiyō ajia-ken no kokusaikeizai funsōshi* [History of International Economic Disputes in the Asia-Pacific Region], compiled by Hosoya Chihiro (Tokyo: Tōkyō Daigaku Shuppankai, 1983).

About the Author

Kitaoka Shinichi was born in 1948 and studied at the University of Tokyo, specializing in modern Japanese politics and diplomacy (B.A. in 1971, and Ph.D. in 1976). He taught at Rikkyo University (1976–1997) and his alma mater (1997–2004, 2006–2012), while serving as ambassador extraordinary and plenipotentiary to the United Nations (2004–2006). He later became a professor at the National Graduate Institute for Policy Studies (GRIPS, 2012–2015), president of the International University of Japan (IUJ, 2012–2015), and is currently president of the Japan International Cooperation Agency (JICA, 2015–). He is emeritus professor of the University of Tokyo and Rikkyo University. He has written numerous books and articles in Japanese. Three of his other books are available in English: *Self-Respect and Independence of Mind: The Challenge of Fukuzawa Yukichi* (2017), *The Political History of Modern Japan: Foreign Relations and Domestic Politics* (2018), and *From Party Politics to Militarism in Japan, 1924–1941* (2020). He has received many honors and awards including the Medal with Purple Ribbon in 2011 for his academic achievements from the government of Japan.

（英文版）後藤新平　外交とヴィジョン
Gotō Shinpei, Statesman of Vision: Research, Public Health, and Development

2021年3月27日　第1刷発行

著　者　　北岡伸一
訳　者　　イアン・アーシー
発行所　　一般財団法人出版文化産業振興財団
　　　　　〒101-0051 東京都千代田区神田神保町2-2-30
　　　　　電話　03-5211-7283
　　　　　ホームページ　https://www.jpic.or.jp/

印刷・製本所　　大日本印刷株式会社